Comparative Social Policy

Comparative Social Policy:

Concepts, Theories and Methods

Edited by

Jochen Clasen

BLACKWELL
Publishers

First published 1999

Blackwell Publishers Ltd
108 Cowley Road
Oxford OX4 1JF
UK

Blackwell Publishers Inc.
350 Main Street
Malden, Massachusetts 02148
USA

British Library Cataloguing in Publication Data

A CIP catalogue record for this book is available from the British Library.

Library of Congress Cataloging-in-Publication Data

Applied for.

ISBN 0631207732 (hbk) 0631207740 (pbk)

Commissioning Editor: Jill Landeryou
Desk Editor: Paula Jacobs

Typeset in $10^{1}/_{2}$ on 12 pt Times New Roman
by Best-set Typesetter Ltd., Hong Kong
Printed in Great Britain by MPG Books Ltd, Bodmin, Comwall

This book is printed on acid-free paper

Contents

List of Tables   vii

List of Contributors   ix

I   Introduction   I
Jochen Clasen

Part I   Welfare States and Comparative Social Policy   13

2   Trends and Developments in Welfare States   15

Catherine Jones Finer

3   Theories and Methods in Comparative Social Policy   34
Deborah Mabbett and Helen Bolderson

Part II   Comparative Analyses in Selected Policy Fields   57

4   Comparative Housing Policy   59
John Doling

5   Institutions, States and Cultures: Health Policy and
Politics in Europe   80
Richard Freeman

6   Comparing Family Policies in Europe   95
Linda Hantrais

7   Full Circle: a Second Coming for Social Assistance?   114
John Ditch

8   Comparative Approaches to Long-term Care
     for Adults   136
     Susan Tester

9   Unemployment Compensation and Other
     Labour-Market Policies   159
     Jochen Clasen

Part III Themes and Topics in Comparative Social Policy   179

10   The 'Problem' of Lone Motherhood in Comparative
     Perspective   181
     Jane Lewis

11   Inside Out: Migrants' Disentitlement to Social
     Security Benefits in the EU   200
     Simon Roberts and Helen Bolderson

12   Accumulated Disadvantage? Welfare State
     Provision and the Incomes of Older Women and
     Men in Britain, France and Germany   220
     Katherine Rake

     Bibliography   247
     Index   277

List of Tables

Table 2.1	Hallmarks of welfare statism	17
Table 2.2	An Esping-Andersen/Leibfried/Deacon typology of welfare states	24
Table 2.3	A worldwide typology in the making?	25
Table 3.1	The redistribution paradigm	39
Table 4.1	Approaches to comparative housing policy	63
Table 4.2	Housing variables for selected countries, East and West	71
Table 7.1	Cash assistance as a proportion of GDP 1980–1992	123
Table 7.2	Social assistance: percentage difference from the mean – all cases after housing costs (1992)	129
Table 10.1	Lone-parent families as a percentage of all families (most recent national sources)	183
Table 10.2	Divorce rates per 1,000 population	184
Table 10.3	Extra-marital birth rates, 1960–1990	184
Table 10.4	Registration of births outside marriage, England and Wales, 1969–1994	185
Table 10.5	Live births to teenagers in selected countries, 1971, 1980, 1990. Births per 1,000 women aged 15–19	185
Table 10.6	Percentage of lone mothers employed full time and part time, most recent national data	189
Table 12.1	Average monthly pension income (FF) of the over-65s by source, France, 1993	226
Table 12.2	Retired women's and men's average (mean) net weekly income by source – Great Britain, 1988–1989	228

Table 12.3   Career breaks in Britain, France and Germany   230
Table 12.4   Women's and men's average lifetime
             participation in the labour market, Britain,
             France and Germany   232
Table 12.5   Women and men in the National Insurance
             scheme, Great Britain   235
Table 12.6   Low pay in Britain, France and Germany   237

List of Contributors

Helen Bolderson
is Associate Reader in the Department of Government at Brunel University. Since 1990 she has conducted, together with colleagues, several comparative studies of social security policies and delivery systems in European and OECD countries and an evaluation for the UK Government of a European Action Programme for Disabled People. Publications include: *Social Security, Disability and Rehabilitation: Conflicts in the Development of Social Policy* (Jessica Kingsley, 1991); (with F. Gains) *Crossing National Frontiers: An Examination of the Arrangements for Exporting Social Security Benefits in Twelve Countries* (HMSO, 1993) and (with D. Mabbett) *Delivering Social Security: A Cross-National Study* (The Stationery Office, 1997).

Jochen Clasen
is Professor of Comparative Social Research in the Department of Applied Social Science at Stirling University. His main research interests are comparative social policy, social security and unemployment policies. Recent publications include *Social Insurance in Europe* (edited volume, Policy Press, 1997); (with Arthur Gould and Jill Vincent) *Voices Within and Without. Responses to long-term unemployment in Germany, Sweden and Britain* (Policy Press, 1998) and (with Richard Freeman) *Social Policy in Germany* (edited volume, Harvester Wheatsheaf, 1994).

John Ditch
is Professor and Head of Social Policy at the University of York. His research has included comparative studies of child support and social

assistance, the impact of changes in circumstances on benefit administration and the needs of first-time applicants for benefits. He is Co-
ordinator of the European Observatory on National Family Policies.
He is the author, joint-author or editor of a number of studies which
examine the functioning of social security systems, the development
of social policy in the European Union and has a particular interest in
comparative family policy.

John Doling

is Professor of Housing Studies in the Department of Social Policy
and Social Work at the University of Birmingham. He has published
a number of papers on housing policy in Finland. He has also published *Comparative Housing Policy: Government and Housing in
Advanced Industrialized Countries* (Macmillan, 1997) and 'Housing
policies and the Little Tigers: how do they compare with Western
countries?' (*Housing Studies* 1998, forthcoming). Currently he is undertaking research into housing policy in the new industrialized countries of South and East Asia.

Richard Freeman

is Lecturer in European Policy and Politics in the Department of
Politics, University of Edinburgh. He has written on the role of
prevention in health policy and is editor, with Jochen Clasen,
of *Social Policy in Germany* (Harvester Wheatsheaf, 1994). He contributed a chapter on Germany to Ranade, W. (ed.) *Markets and
Health Care. A comparative analysis* (Longman, 1998) and is currently completing a book on health politics in Europe (Manchester
University Press, forthcoming). He is co-convenor of the ESRC Research Seminar on Welfare and Culture in Europe, and is developing
a cultural account of health policy regimes.

Catherine Jones Finer

is Reader in Comparative Social Policy at the University of Birmingham. Her current research interests include social action in Naples/
southern Italy. Recent publications include *Promoting Prosperity:
The Hong Kong Way of Social Policy* (Hong Kong: Chinese University Press, 1990); *New Perspectives on the Welfare State in Europe*
(edited volume, Routledge, 1993), to which she contributed a chapter
'The Pacific Challenge: Confucian Welfare States' and *Crime and
Social Exclusion* (co-edited volume with Mike Nellis, Blackwell,
1998), to which she contributed a chapter on 'The New Social Policy
in Britain'. She is editor of *Social Policy and Administration*.

Jane Lewis
is Professor of Social Policy at the University of Nottingham. She was Professor of Social Policy at the London School of Economics until 1996, when she became a Fellow of All Souls College, Oxford, and Director of the Wellcome Unit for the History of Medicine. Her research interests are mainly in gender and social policy and she is the author of *Women in Britain since 1945* (Blackwell, 1992); editor of *Women and Social Policies in Europe* (Edward Elgar, 1993) and author, with K. Kiernan and H. Land, of *Lone Mothers in Twentieth Century Britain* (Oxford University Press, 1998).

Deborah Mabbett
is Lecturer in the Department of Government at Brunel University. Her research interests centre on comparative political economy, with a particular focus on social security. Recent publications include *Trade, Employment and Welfare: A Comparative Study of Trade and Labour Market Policies in Sweden and New Zealand, 1880–1980* (Clarendon, 1995), 'Reforming social security in economies in transition: problems and policies in the former Soviet Republic of Moldova', *International Social Security Review* no. 50 and several publications co-authored with Helen Bolderson, most recently *Delivering Social Security: A Cross-National Study* (The Stationery Office, 1997).

Katherine Rake
is Lecturer in Social Policy in the Department of Social Policy and Administration at the London School of Economics. Her research is currently focused on comparative analysis of income inequality and welfare state provision for the older population, looking particularly at the structure and source of differences between women and men. She was recently involved in an EU-funded project looking at pension reform in East and West Europe.

Simon Roberts
is Research Fellow at Brunel University where he works at the Centre for the Evaluation of Public Policy and Practice and with the Health Economics Research Group. His research interests are European social security systems and international and EU arrangements for co-ordinating them. Publications include 'The implementation of Dutch public management reforms 1980–1996', in Pollitt, C. et al. (eds) (1997) *Public Management Reform: Five Country Studies.* Helsinki: Ministry of Finance; and (with S. Cox, D. Seddon,

H. Mountfield and E. Guild) *Migration and Social Security Hand-book: A Rights Guide for People Entering and Leaving the UK* (second edition, CPAG, 1997).

Susan Tester
is Senior Lecturer in Social Policy in the Department of Applied Social Science at Stirling University, where she specializes in commu-nity care, aging, and comparative social policy. She has an extensive background in social research and was formerly based in London at the Centre for Policy on Ageing, the Policy Studies Institute, and the London School of Economics. Her publications include *Community Care for Older People: a Comparative Perspective* (Macmillan, 1996); *Common Knowledge: a coordinated approach to information giving* (Centre for Policy on Ageing, 1992) and *Caring by Day: a study of day care services for older people* (Centre for Policy on Ageing, 1989).

1

Introduction

Jochen Clasen

It has been argued that methodological and conceptual problems
involved in cross-national research are, basically, no different from
social research generally and that there is therefore no need for
a textbook on comparative social research (Przeworski, 1987;
Esping-Andersen, 1993). However, recent texts on comparative
methodology for the study of either social policies or welfare states
(Janoski and Hicks, 1994) or social research generally (Øyen, 1990;
Hantrais and Mangen, 1996b) have demonstrated the degree to
which methodological and conceptual problems are compounded
once research crosses national borders. This volume is not a textbook on comparative methodology, although methodological issues
are addressed. Instead, taking as its starting-point the growing
interest in comparative social policy analysis the book aims to convey
both the fascinating and challenging issues involved in conducting
research of this kind. It reflects on theoretical, conceptual and
methodological aspects involved in comparative social policy
analysis generally – and in a number of social policy fields and
themes in particular. Aimed at readers who already have some
knowledge of social policy, this volume combines general with specific overviews, critically reviewing theoretical approaches, discussing
prevailing concepts, reflecting on methodological difficulties and illustrating, with examples from across a wide range of social policy
analysis, what can be gained by conducting comparative social policy
research. In short, it aims to stimulate interest in the field and to
provide an instructive starting-point for cross-national social policy
research.

Of course, there are various types of comparisons (across time, within countries, etc.) and some comparative studies might find greater diversity within rather than across countries (e.g. within India). What is more, the term 'nation' is not always synonymous with the political construct of a 'country'. However, in this volume 'comparative' and 'cross-national' have been used synonymously and exclusively applied to research which systematically investigates one or more phenomena in two or more countries or 'nations' as given contexts for actors and institutions. It should also be noted that the focus of the volume is not comparative research of welfare states but of social policy. In terms of academic interest and body of knowledge, there is a significant difference. On a broad level, comparative welfare state research now goes back some three decades (for an overview see van Kersbergen, 1995, ch. 2). Its primary aim has been to determine the causes of welfare state development. However, much of it has not really been about what might be regarded as the heart of comparative social policy analysis, namely 'the complex task of examining the welfare order in different countries' (May, 1998, p. 22). Instead it focuses largely on changes in one single parameter: the level and variation of national social spending as a 'proxy of welfare stateness' (Esping-Andersen, 1993). Few studies (e.g. Flora and Heidenheimer, 1981) have included additional indicators (the year when key social policy legislation was implemented or the degree of coverage of certain social programmes). Although providing some more information, these data say little about the roles of, principles within and distributional impacts of different welfare arrangements across countries. Nevertheless, for a long time these parameters served as key variables in welfare state studies which tried to explain their variation across countries and over time in relation to 'independent' variables such as degree of industrialization, urbanization, economic prosperity or working-class strength.

Studies of this kind are based on correlational approaches and have been used to advance 'grand theorizing' about welfare state development (Amenta, 1993). They have become increasingly sophisticated over the years – yet their heyday probably belongs to the past, overtaken by research which is less reliant on highly aggregated data and with a greater historical awareness and sensitivity towards subtle cross-national similarities and differences in social policy arrangements. Rather than including all OECD, or even more, countries such an approach made it necessary to focus the analysis on a smaller number of countries (Baldwin, 1990; van Kersbergen, 1995). What is more, instead of finding explanatory causes for welfare state development *per se*, there has been a shift towards investigating the causes of policy change within particular social policy components or programmes, such as health care, pensions or social care arrangements (e.g. Pierson, 1994). This is not the place to comment on the relative decline of the large-scale correlational approach – nor to praise the growing interest in case studies. As outlined in chapter 3 of this volume, each of those approaches has distinct advantages as well as methodological and conceptual difficulties and there remains a need for both large-scale comparative studies, identifying broad similarities and differences, as well as contextually rich case studies (Alber et al., 1987; Heidenheimer et al., 1990). Indeed, some kind of combination of both approaches seems most beneficial in terms of theory advancement (Allardt, 1990; Esping-Andersen, 1993).

However, for the moment the shift in research interest from the general to the more specific, from the correlational to the case study approach, can be understood as a process of catching up. The number of cross-national studies of particular social policy fields is still relatively small and this particular approach is still in its infancy – notwithstanding some notable pioneers such as Kaim-Caudle (1973) and Heclo (1974) for analysing income maintenance policies, Donnison (1967) for housing policy, Rodgers (1979) for social services and Kamerman and Kahn (1978) for family policy. The wider interest in social policy formation and delivery across countries began to accelerate only in the 1980s (Higgins, 1981; Jones, 1985; Bolderson, 1988) and mushroomed towards the end of that decade and in the early 1990s. Simultaneously, the debate about social policy programmes (previously largely confined to British and American academics plus some individual Scandinavian contributors) became much more international, with more scholars contributing to the debate in the English language (see Jones Finer in this volume). This process of internationalization in turn produced greater awareness of the diverse nature of particular fields of social policy, stimulating new questions of research and leading to theoretical advances and new conceptual insights (see Mabbett and Bolderson in this volume). Gradually, it seems, comparative social policy analysis is becoming an established sub-discipline, catching up with developments in other branches of social science, such as political science, where international and comparative aspects have had a strong profile within the research agenda for some time (see Eckstein and Apter, 1963; Blondel, 1969; Daalder, 1997).

A number of factors have contributed to the growing interest in comparative social policy. They include contextual changes in political and macro-economic frameworks (EU integration, globalization) and others such as profound changes in labour markets, household and family forms, demographic structures and shifts in inequality which have been, or will be, commonly experienced by most developed countries. Together, these developments have exerted similar pressures on traditional social policy arrangements and influenced national debates about policy reform. Growing interdependence between and similar challenges across countries, but not necessarily policy responses, have put into question social policy research which remains locked into analysing developments within one country.

The growth of cross-national research groups and discussion networks, bringing together those with particular interests in social policy areas such as housing, family policy, health, social security, pension reform, etc. is another sign of the internationalization of social policy analysis. New and faster ways of communicating globally, in addition to new journals keen to publish comparative contributions, have certainly facilitated this process of internationalization of knowledge and its dissemination – with an additional impetus coming from international bodies interested in making use of applied research in order to inform policy debate. The EU and the setting up of various European Observatories are a good example of this.

This much increased international exchange of concepts and ideas regarding particular social policy fields is testament to a quest for greater knowledge about national welfare arrangements, their impact and their interaction with other policies. Indeed, one of the achievements of Esping-Andersen's (1990) seminal work on 'three worlds of welfare capitalism' was to demonstrate that both 'welfare effort', as the key variable in structural–functionalist theories, and the 'strength of the labour movement', as the equivalent in the 'power resource model', were too broad for a proper understanding of the development, and the societal impact, of national welfare systems. Another achievement was to trigger off a debate on welfare typologies, methods and concepts (Taylor-Gooby, 1991; Lewis, 1992; Baldwin, 1996) which, in turn, pointed to the need for a better understanding of common features and crucial differences between not only individual welfare states but particular policy programmes in order to unravel why and how which welfare needs, or demands, are being transformed into social policies. Taking stock of what has been going on in the field by critically reviewing key concepts, competing theoretical approaches and a variety of methodological tools across a range of policy fields and key themes, this volume hopes to give readers an idea of what comparative social policy is about and why it has become a crucial aspect of modern social policy analysis.

The Structure of the Book

Written by academics with considerable experience in both teaching and research in comparative social policy, all chapters provide systematic overviews. All reflect on relevant conceptual, theoretical and methodological approaches as applied to a particular policy field or relevant to a particular theme, and each chapter ends with a brief guide to further reading. However, the book is divided in three parts and each of those parts has a particular purpose.

Part I

The opening two chapters have a more general role than those in subsequent parts. Together they provide a broad overview of the academic interest in comparative welfare state research and a discussion of major theoretical and methodological aspects relevant to comparative social policy generally. Recently there has been a realization of the need for more cross-national research taking account of non-statutory benefits in kind and cash or alternative means of distributive policies such as the tax system (Greve, 1994; Kvist and Sinfield, 1996). However, as implied earlier, welfare states *per se* have long remained the predominant focus of implicit and explicit comparative social policy research. Thus Catherine Jones Finer in this volume provides a broad reflection on the historical background and prospects of welfare states. She argues for a broad and 'inclusive' definition of the welfare state as a topic for research at the expense of a more 'exclusive' one which has long been centred on principles and practices of European corporatist forms of welfare provision. Illustrating the academic interest in the topic she puts the development of the British welfare state after the Second World War in a comparative perspective and explores the changing nature of welfare statism over time. Such a broad and sweeping perspective allows her to illustrate the very different context within which the contemporary welfare state and the future of welfare statism is being debated compared with earlier decades. She also addresses the European Union's belated interest in social policy within its main project of political and social integration and the difficulties in overcoming the reluctance to increase involvement in the area. She questions the broad and global description of the shift from corporatism to 'individualistic liberalism', which is widely assumed to be constituting the future of welfare states. Instead, the focus on individual countries with different principles and forms of social policy provision should allow for a more fruitful discussion on, and assessment of, trends, especially if the 'newly emerging welfare states' with new types and patterns of welfare provision 'in the making' were given more consideration in comparative social policy research.

Potentially cross-national comparison can render important theoretical insights through theory development and testing. However, Deborah Mabbett and Helen Bolderson illustrate that there are major methodological and conceptual problems involved in cross-national social research generally and comparative social policy analysis in particular. Reflecting on major theoretical approaches and methodological tools, the authors illustrate that 'comparative social policy research' is a rather broad term. It applies to studies which test hypotheses based on large-scale regression analysis of macro-economic and social indicators with the aim of advancing 'grand theorizing' of welfare state development. At the other end of the scale are 'micro' case studies of particular policies in sometimes two or three welfare states which are more sensitive to 'specific institutional, historical and political features' of social policies – but have perhaps limited power of generalization. The 'regime theory' can be regarded as capturing the middle ground between those two types by identifying salient policy configurations and interactions in a few supposedly distinct types of welfare states. With reference to major examples in the field, Mabbett and Bolderson discuss the respective theoretical and conceptual strengths and weaknesses of each of those approaches and conclude with a deliberation of how a combination of different methods might be able to overcome common problems of conceptualization and measurement in cross-national research in social policy.

Part II

This part includes six chapters, all of which aim to give readers an idea of the body of knowledge, prevailing approaches, important concepts and theories, as well as methodological difficulties within comparative research in particular policy fields. In addition to the selected fields others could (some readers might think should) have been incorporated such as educational policy, youth policy or fiscal welfare policy. However, the book does not claim to provide an exhaustive overview of comparative work in all conceivable fields of social policy, something which might in any case be impossible when one considers the vast range of policies which might legitimately be regarded as social policy (see Alcock et al., 1998). What is more, there is no clear boundary between what is seen as genuine 'social' policy and other types of public intervention even within a single country.

However, it is hoped that readers interested in a particular policy field which is not the main topic of one of the six chapters might nevertheless find the book of interest for two reasons. First, some of those policies are nevertheless discussed in one or more chapters. This is particularly the case for social security. While there is no single chapter devoted to this policy field, aspects of comparative social security research are covered by Ditch's chapter on social assistance, by Mabbett and Bolderson who illustrate many methodological and theoretical issues with reference to examples within social security, by Rake who reflects on pensions as the most important income source for older men and women, and also by Clasen and Roberts and Bolderson who focus on social security arrangements (or the lack of them) for certain social groups such as the unemployed and migrants respectively. Second, readers with a special interest in a particular social policy field not covered here might still find the chapters in part I and part III of interest since those cut across particular policy areas, providing general overviews, examples, illustrations and case studies which are of relevance to comparative social policy analysis generally. Of course, the hope is that the book as a whole appeals to readers, given that there are, inevitably, similarities of concepts, theories and methodologies across social policy fields.

In the first contribution to part II, John Doling points out that what is sometimes referred to as comparative social policy is actually more of an introduction into, and detailed description of, particular policies in a number of countries. While these can be of high quality, and providing important information, they are largely, as the author underlines, 'comparisons by juxtaposition' since they rarely explore or even explain cross-national similarities and differences in a systematic way. But what, exactly, are the features which make an analysis comparative? This is the question which Doling addresses in the first part of his chapter on housing policies. In latter parts he illustrates the relevance of, and problems involved in, acquiring and collecting different and comparable types of information for cross-national analysis. These are issues and questions which are not confined to housing but relevant to comparisons of any field of social policy. Thus, these sections can be read as reflections on aspects of cross-national policy research generally and their more extensive and explicit discussion in this chapter as paradigmatic for subsequent chapters.

More exclusively relevant to housing policy are Doling's reflections on the historical development of research interest in comparative studies in the field. He demonstrates early attempts at categorizing national patterns of housing policy and provision with the aim of developing typologies as an element of theory building. He also illustrates the parallels between competing theoretical concepts within studies on welfare state development generally (see chapter 3) with those applied in housing policy. A major research interest in the field, the focus on national patterns and characteristics of tenure, lends itself to an illustration of a number of theoretical and methodological problems involved in comparative investigations in this policy field.

Richard Freeman discusses comparative research in health policy and politics in Europe. In line with recent research in this field, he argues that a precondition for an understanding of health care policies across countries is an acute awareness of the importance of institutional differences in, for example, the finance and organization of health care. Although much depends on definitions, institutions 'create interests as well as being created by them' and thus offer collective actors opportunities to control and shape policies. This goes some way to explaining national patterns of health care spending or the ability to implement or block reforms. However, institutions need to be conceptualized and operationalized for empirical comparative research and this is where problems occur, as Freeman demonstrates with reference to the notion of national 'health systems' and by discussing the different versions of institutionalisms which have been adopted by researchers. He concludes the chapter with a call for 'reframing' the notion of institutions by taking account of their 'cultural specificities' as a way forward in comparative research in health policy and politics.

Family policy is perhaps the area which has gained most in terms of both political attention and research interest, particularly within comparative perspectives. To some extent this might reflect the recognition within social policy research generally of the family as a source of welfare provision which has long been neglected, but also the significant changes in family and household structure and patterns of labour market participation in many countries. Most notable is the rise of female employment which has put pressure on the development of adequate responses to demands of reconciling unpaid care work with paid employment. Cross-national research in this field has been hampered because of the lack of a clearly defined administrative arena of, and political responsibility for, family policy in many countries. One of the major requirements of comparative research therefore, as Linda Hantrais demonstrates, has been the attempt to identify and locate precisely the conceptions of 'family' as applied differently by statistical agencies, administrative organizations and policy makers within and across countries. Reviewing the by now large body of material, the main studies undertaken and the conceptual issues involved, the author shows that findings are, to some degree, influenced by the selection of countries and that a combination of different methodological approaches might be best suited for cross-national research in the field.

John Ditch discusses key research concentrating on the development of social assistance programmes, which are the 'last safety net' in most welfare states. Despite the growing importance of means-tested benefits there have been suprisingly few international or systematically comparative studies of their structure and effectiveness. Ditch illustrates the considerable variation of national social assistance programmes regarding their respective character and scope, policy objectives, operating principles, eligibility criteria, the role of local administration, the value of benefits and rules of conditionality. Such complexity makes a simple 'ranking' between national programmes difficult, although it is not impossible to identify a set of broad types of schemes.

Political interest in long-term care has been prompted by financial concerns over the costs of caring for an ageing population. The same concerns have also contributed to the recent research interest in the issue which, long neglected, is now hugely topical in most advanced countries. Different socio-economic and demographic factors and political ideologies clearly underpin long-term care policies in different countries which, as Susan Tester demonstrates, makes this a complex area of study and a prime example of investigating the importance of the discourse on principles of care and of the implications of the shift in emphasis in social policy towards non-statutory forms of welfare provision. Tester reviews selected studies of the topic and reflects on key concepts and the ways in which they have been operationalized. She illustrates how researchers have managed to combine different methodological approaches, enabling them to reduce the limitations of existing data, and points out that the welfare regime approach needs some adaptation in order to be useful as an analytical frame capable not only of investigating income maintenance but also social care policies.

In the final chapter of part II Jochen Clasen reviews comparative research in labour market policy which is also a somewhat neglected field within social policy analysis. Labour market programmes have come to be conventionally regarded as consisting of 'active' (training, work experience, etc.) and 'passive' (i.e. benefit) programmes. However, such a division is not necessarily helpful for comparative analyses. Instead, the chapter takes an inclusive perspective and discusses theoretical approaches and analytical interests across a range of studies which can broadly be distinguished as primarily interested in policy description, policy explanation or policy evaluation. Cross-national analyses in all of these areas are confronted with a number of methodological problems regarding the operationalization of central concepts such as 'unemployment' or 'benefit level', the equivalence between national policy programmes and the search for meaningful parameters, such as 'wage replacement ratios', as the adequate basis for policy typologies.

Part III

Common to all three chapters in the third part of the volume is that they are not devoted to a particular policy field. Instead, by cutting across fields their purpose is to illustrate, with reference to a particular theme or topic of research, the need to explore carefully issues in order to gain an awareness of sometimes subtle cross-national differences and thus to avoid producing spurious or even misleading results. As such, from different angles, they highlight essential components of comparative social policy research such as mapping, contextualization and taking account of policy interaction, all of which facilitate a more informed and valid conceptualization which is crucial within comparative social policy research.

Building on a discussion of national differences in structural patterns of lone motherhood, types of dependency (on state benefits, markets or partners) and the different ways and degrees in which lone motherhood is publicly debated as a 'problem', Jane Lewis illustrates the need for proper contextualization particularly for those types of comparative analyses which aim to investigate causes for cross-national variation and similarity. This can be a difficult task since it requires that attention be paid to a number of cultural, political, economic and social variables across countries. Yet contextualization is a necessary part of good comparative work. Through it, a better understanding can be gained of, for example, the wider role of national policy logics and of prevailing political ideologies towards particular social groups. Those help to explain differences in the roles ascribed to, and policies directed at, lone mothers in different welfare regimes.

A similar case for contextualization as the basis for proper conceptualization is made by Simon Roberts and Helen Bolderson. They illustrate that 'mapping' of a particular territory of investigation is an essential element of comparative social policy analysis, especially if that territory has been less well researched. The exclusion from, or restriction of, the receipt of social security benefits by legal rules as experienced by different groups of migrants within member states of the European Union is such a territory. A careful assessment of different forms of disentitlement provides the basis for the conceptualization of the roles different types of restrictions play and the identification of patterns between countries. Only such a procedure allows researchers to move on to more analytical and general questions regarding, for example, the origins of and causes for change in disentitlement regulations. The authors demonstrate how a careful empirical 'mapping' can feed into, and contribute to, more abstract discussions about central concepts in social policy, such as 'non-discrimination', 'need', 'citizenship' or 'social rights'.

In the final chapter, Katherine Rake demonstrates that in order to understand the impact of particular policies, it is not sufficient to know about differences in national entitlement rules and forms of policy delivery, but to investigate the interaction between those policies and other forms of public intervention. This is demonstrated with reference to a number of policies and the ways in which they influence the income position of older men and women in Britain, Germany and France. Rake's central question is how, in different welfare states, national policies translate into different outcomes, and points to a major problem in comparative analysis: that there is not only variation in the level of the independent variable (here the distribution of income for a particular social group) but also in the dependent variable (policies and their contexts). This rules out simple tests of hypotheses and presents a number of difficulties regarding methodological and conceptual aspects, which compared to single-country studies are compounded in cross-national research. Rake illustrates how those problems can be tackled and through this shows both the complexity involved in and the fascination of social policy analysis which goes beyond borders. This, indeed, is what this book as a whole hopes to portray.

Further reading

Each of the following chapters concludes with a brief guide to further reading in particular areas. For those readers who would like a more general overview or starting-point there are a few texts which might be worth considering. While cross-national social policy analysis has only recently become a more established element of the study of social policy, it is sometimes instructive to go back to some early examples of the interest in the broad range of 'social policies abroad'

(Kaim-Caudle, 1973; Rodgers, 1979) or the comparative development of particular policy areas (Heclo, 1974). For those interested in current issues it would be difficult to ignore Esping-Andersen (1990; see also 1996) for its impact on the debate on the understanding of variation and similarities of national welfare 'regimes' since the early 1990s.

Both Hantrais and Mangen (1996b) and Janoski and Hicks (1994), the latter with an emphasis on quantitative and combined quantitative and qualitative approaches, provide good resource books on methods of cross-national research (see also Øyen, 1990). Broad characteristics of national social policy patterns and policies are discussed in Clasen and Freeman (1994), Gould (1993), and Cochrane and Clarke (1993) and George and Taylor-Gooby (1996). The concept and role of 'social insurance' in ten European countries is discussed in Clasen (1997b). Ginsburg (1992) compares welfare arrangements and their distributional effects in four countries, focusing on social divisions. Sainsbury (1996) and Lewis (1992) provide accounts of national welfare state policies in relation to gender issues. Baldwin (1990) demonstrates the importance of an historical perspective in explaining policy change. Important comparative articles can be found in the *Journal of European Social Policy* but also other national and international journals which are referred to at the end of specific chapters of this book.

Acknowledgement

I would like to thank Bent Greve and the Department of Social Science at Roskilde University for providing a congenial environment in which this volume was prepared.

Part I

Welfare States and Comparative Social Policy

2

Trends and Developments in Welfare States

Catherine Jones Finer

Introduction

This is a challenging brief to respond to. It calls for an exercise in comparative analysis at a level of generality only to be achieved by drawing extensively on the researches and observations of others. Up to a point, the same is true of most ventures into cross-national analysis, as the following chapters will confirm. Nevertheless the comparison of whole systems over a period of time – and within the space of one chapter – constitutes more of an essay-writing than a research-reviewing proposition.

As such, this chapter will be illustrative of a form of comparative social policy discourse distinct in itself: the would-be interpretative, integrative review. This is not a 'specialism' in the conventional sense of the term, since most scholars would be ill-advised to devote themselves entirely to such a level of activity, at the expense of developing a more particular knowledge and skills base of their own. Yet it can be an activity conducive to enhanced specialist activity, to the extent that the broader reflection adds a useful perspective to more particular forms of understanding. The present essay is intended to serve as an example of the genre for critical purposes.

Hallmarks of Welfare Statism

The implication behind the title is that welfare statism is still what the study of social policy is mainly about. Yet not every commentator would agree with this even as a starting proposition since, for some, 'the welfare state' already amounts to a Western idea whose time has been and gone. In short, despite the familiarity of the term, there exists no starting agreement as to what precisely is to be accounted a welfare state. Hence it is for the author to decide in the light, not least, of the range of 'trends and developments' she wishes the essay to encompass.

For pragmatists of the 'welfare state is a state possessed of social services' variety, the welfare state is still with us and likely to remain so for so long as there are states around, possessed of some form(s) of state-backed social services available on some terms to some people. Welfare statism reduced to such a minimalist stipulation is little more than a mark of 'development'. Whereas for maximalist champions of the ideal-type citizenship-based, institutional-redistributive, in their eyes 'true' welfare state – never very widely aspired to by governments even within the developed world – the rational perception must now be of an endangered species, if not one on the verge of extinction.

Neither definitional extreme makes much sense for the purposes of this chapter. To be useful, a review of recent trends and developments calls for something more than a celebration of the past; of what might have been or 'ought' to be (see Baldwin, 1996, pp. 36–7). By an equivalent token, it also calls for something less than a review of the entirety of the developed and developing world's social policy and social services' performances to date. The practical requirement is for a working definition of welfare statism located somewhere in between: one which can encompass the variety of states which have conventionally been classed as 'welfare states'; and which might also in principle serve as a benchmark for establishing when a welfare state has ceased to be, and/or for the admission of others to this status.

Naturally this is more easily said than done. There was never an agreed view about the nature of welfare statism *per se* – nor seemingly much appetite for one.

> A remarkable attribute of the entire [welfare state] literature is its lack of much genuine interest in the welfare state as such. Welfare state studies have been motivated by theoretical concerns with other phenomena, such as power, industrialization, or capitalist contradictions; the welfare state itself has generally received scant conceptual attention. If welfare states differ, how do they differ? And when, indeed, is a state a welfare state? (Esping-Andersen, 1990, p. 18)

Welfare statism evolved amongst Western countries in the wake of the Second World War in the absence of 'club rules'; not least

Table 2.1   *Hallmarks of welfare statism*

Ingredient	Indicators
Rich capitalist free market	OECD ratings
Civil rights	Freedom from arbitrary constraints; rights of redress versus public authorities; freedom of speech and of conscience; rights of peaceful protest
Political rights	Freedom to vote 'in private'; freedom to stand for election; freedom to campaign peacefully for change
Social rights	Entitlements to social protection by virtue of: citizenship and/or occupation; and/or contribution record; and/or proof of need according to non-arbitrary criteria
Approved social obligations	Civic, civil, third-sector social activity

because its self-declared pioneer (Britain) was neither interested in nor capable of monitoring how others were getting on with their own versions of this big idea, after the 1940s. None the less there were common underlying characteristics linking the post-war soon-to-be-dubbed welfare states. They were all predominantly capitalist/free market in their economics, professedly liberal–democratic in their politics – and equipped with governments keen to convince their respective voting publics that they could offer them a better life by way of a better society than anything experienced before. Welfare statism was thus not just about governmental responsibility for popular well-being *per se*, but about the well-being of people equipped with civil and political rights (e.g. Marshall, 1950), coupled with notionally solidaristic sentiments in an atmosphere of post-war positivism, in the context of an otherwise free market system. The balance of the mix was never the same from one set-up to the next, but the principal ingredients were consistent (see table 2.1).

None of the criteria shown in table 2.1 could be described as fixed, hard-and-fast, yes-or-no; which is why welfare statism could be such an amorphous idea from its beginnings. By the same token, it remains difficult to establish in empirical terms when or if any particular welfare state might have ceased to be – save by reference to internal standards viewed in retrospect, which can be a misleading exercise in itself. Furthermore, for all the varieties of acknowledged welfare state capable of being identified (see below), it remains difficult to establish in empirical terms when an additional state or states should be considered eligible for admission to this, in effect, club. Or else, how far must welfare statism, bound by ties of supposed cultural affinity, remain confined to a 'fixed membership', Western, European-led company of states?

The core concern of this chapter will be with the fortunes of the original agglomeration of Western welfare states. There are two main, in a sense rival, groupings to bear in mind, based on geography and cultural affiliation: the anglophone world of the British 'old commonwealth' of nations (which can include the USA in this context), versus the Western-Continental-European world of French and especially German acculturation. In addition there are two 'peripheral' groupings of contrasting import: the supermodel welfare states of Scandinavia (the 'Scandinavian rim') versus their so-called rudimentary counterparts of Southern Europe, 'the Latin rim' (Leibfried, 1993). Interest in the idea of there being such different types of welfare state developed from the 1970s, in the context of a widespread debate about the efficacy of welfare states and welfare statism in general. This was a debate destined to impact both on the efforts of the European Community (*sic*) to develop a 'human face' and on the prospects for other forms of welfare statism to attain ascendancy around the world.

It may be argued that Britain, by virtue of her anglophone credentials in relation to Europe, has been of pivotal significance within this evolutionary pattern. But no such claims are being advanced here. Patterns, after all, are in the eye of the beholder. It is enough for present purposes to acknowledge that, since the author is British, the following account will be from a British perspective, though not one particularly in support or defence of the British welfare state.

Early Days and Heydays of the Welfare States

The British welfare state was a first response to its own and others' warfare states. This is not merely to echo the Archbishop of Canterbury's dictum (Temple, 1941) with regard to the qualities of Britain as a welfare state in the making, by contrast with the ethos of Nazi Germany. To the extent the British hit upon the notion of a welfare state and to the extent this was identified via the Beveridge Report 'with the war aims of a nation fighting for its life' (Marshall, 1985, p. 79), the idea could scarcely fail to be a winner, especially among those who subsequently turned out to have been on the 'winning' side.

Just so could William Beveridge – author of the 1942 *Report on Social Insurance and Allied Services* – emerge for a time as one of the most acclaimed social reformers of his generation: touring Europe and North America, by invitation, in support of his plan for universal, minimalist, flat-rate social insurance, to be backed by commitments to full employment, universal education and a universal health service. Copies of the Report were even parachuted into wartime Germany – to be officially recorded as 'an especially obvious proof that our enemies are taking over national socialistic ideas'! (Harris, 1977, p. 420). Elsewhere, the identification of the Report with a 'brave beleaguered Britain' rendered it near irresistible in its day.

> Now, when the war is abolishing landmarks of every kind, is the opportunity for using experience in a clear field. A revolutionary moment in the world's history is a time for revolutions, not for patching.
>
> ... [The] organisation of social insurance should be treated as one part only of a comprehensive policy of social progress. Social insurance fully developed may provide income security; it is an attack upon Want. But Want is one only of five giants on the road of reconstruction and in some ways the easiest to attack. The others are Disease, Ignorance, Squalor and Idleness. (Beveridge, 1942, p. 6)

It was stirring stuff; the sort of thing few politicians of the emergent postwar 'free world' could afford not to be associated with. Fortunately enough for them, however, this was no detailed blueprint for a welfare state so much as an exhortation and exultation in aid of the *idea* of a welfare state. No one, not even in Britain, took Beveridge's plan on board in its entirety (though Britain naturally enough came closest to doing so). None the less, nearly everyone took something of the spirit of his rhetoric on board. It was tailor made, after all, for putting heart back into the people.

Precise ideas about how best to put heart back into the people were conditioned by local circumstance, experience and expectation. Witness, outstandingly, the contrast between the British and (West) German approaches to post-war reconstruction. Britain embarks on an instant legislative programme of minimalist but universalist social insurance to be backed up by seemingly maximalist, universalist health and education undertakings, the whole to be underscored by a Keynesian-type governmental commitment to the maintenance of full employment; all ostensibly by way of a reward to the people of Britain for sacrifices deemed already to have been made. The people of Britain had earned – and expected – their welfare state without delay. For them the future was bright, even if it was unknown. Compare this with the needs-be resort of (West) Germany to a programme of fundamental economic reconstruction, backed by Marshall Aid but based on 'traditional Bismarckian' principles of long-term, corporatist, social partnership via requisite short-term collective self-denial. By the time (West) Germany's economic performance was such as seemingly to permit a path-breaking move into dynamic pay-as-you-go pensions reform (1957), the British were searching for ways in which to keep their own 'static-funded' National Insurance system afloat, swamped as this had been by the claims of too many citizen pensioners too soon – and crippled as it had been by limitations of fund-raising on a flat-rate basis in conditions of rising, but increasingly disparate, standards of living.

The British resort to instant post-war universalism had in other words been a leap in the dark: a case not so much of forward planning at last (after all the years of typically reacting to social problems) as of a heady, politically needs-be, blind faith in the future. No other sets of politicians variously emergent from the Second World War felt inclined or driven to take such risks – and certainly not in imitation of the Beveridge Report. France's newly instituted *Régime Générale* of social insurance (1945) was never, for all its superficially Beveridgean overtones, expected to be capable of imposing a single standard system right across all the regional and occupational divisions of France, least of all on the basis of a flat-rate contributions and benefits philosophy! Even the loyal Dominion of Canada contrived merely to echo rather than replicate the Beveridge Report for itself (Marsh, 1943); whilst the USA (still coming to terms with the New Deal) did nothing whatsoever about the famous Report, apart from welcoming Beveridge on tour.

It is interesting that the country and government conspicuously receptive to Beveridge's ideas – and to those of British economist J.M. Keynes before him – should have been one of the few European countries *not* to have been formally involved in the Second World War. Universalism without the trappings of a war halo: it was a message successive Swedish governments of a social democratic disposition were to find no difficulty in putting across to successive generations of voters. In other words British experience did contribute to the development elsewhere of a brand of 'maximalist universalist' welfare statism destined to be increasingly removed from the makeshift creeping incrementalism of Britain's own welfare state, and one which was to prove much more influential – or at any rate much more written and talked about – in Europe.

Britain itself was conspicuous rather for lack of influence and exchange with welfare-state Europe after the 1940s. In part this stemmed from lack of interest – a fact soon compounded by Britain's relatively poor showing economically by comparison with the 'miracle' rates of growth soon achieved not merely by West Germany (from its near-zero starting-point) but the rest of North-western Europe and Scandinavia. It takes success to spawn admirers and would-be imitators.

More fundamentally, however, there was that about the British welfare state *per se* which was in a sense self-limiting. The concepts of welfare statism emanating not merely from the Beveridge Report, but from the legislative programme of 1945–49, were essentially static. The Beveridgean image of wiping out giants, once and for all, on the road of social reconstruction was a powerful one for its day. Yet it offered little scope and hence no preparation for the possibility of having to adjust definitions of want, disease, ignorance, squalor and idleness in the future, to accord with future perceptions of what might minimally (let alone maximally) be required. Beveridge himself, for all his personal experience of 'rising standards of poverty' from the 1900s to the 1940s, seems to have seen the welfare state as essentially a one-off job. Even the National Health Service was expected to save money within a fairly short timespan, thanks to the reductions to be expected in working days lost from sickness.

This helps explain why proportionate expenditure on the British welfare state was – by European welfare state standards – relatively slow to grow. The culture of flat-rate national insurance (alongside a burgeoning private occupational pensions industry) amounted to a built-in drag on growth in government social security expenditure, which the spreading panoply of means-tested benefits (so unantici-pated by Beveridge) and even the eventual, grudging, temporary cross-party agreement on state earnings-related pensions (SERPS) (1975) for the 'non-occupationally covered', was never anywhere near sufficient to counterbalance. Meanwhile the National Health Service (NHS), the in-kind flagship of the British welfare state, was unique among all the government-backed health care systems of non-communist Europe in that its annual budget was set by central government. Whatever the rhetoric of optimality, therefore, the NHS had a built-in capability for being kept or cut down to size as a considerably less than open-ended service.

This was a far cry in spending terms from the predominantly pluralistic social insurance-driven – and thence dynamic – pensions and health care undertakings of the likes of (West) Germany and France. Yet at the same time it was hardly less of a far cry – albeit in an opposite sense – from the experience of that other collection of countries to which Britain was supposed to belong: the anglophone/Anglo-Saxon community of the British ex-imperial 'old commonwealth' of nations, the USA included. None of the latter, no matter how impressive their rates of economic growth by comparison with Britain, went in for governmental social spending to as much as even the British extent.

Why was this? In the simplistic language of the dominant welfare state literature of the 1960s, the answer was obvious: the low spenders were inadequate, incomplete welfare states; i.e. *reluctant, residual, laggard* welfare states. Japan and Switzerland were placed in the same category: rich countries which could and should afford to be doing much more in aid of popular well-being than they had been persuaded to do so far. Looking back, the fatuousness of this blanket categorization-by-default may seem apparent; but it was not so at the time, even to the predominantly British and American authors then exchanging views in English on the nature of the welfare state. Significantly, the rest of the anglophone world seemed to have contributed little to this discussion and few continental Europeans had been contributing to it in English. So the ascendancy of the high-spending European welfare state model, in the eyes of many 1960s British and American welfare academics, was in part a product of distance learning. It was to take time, better communications and above all a shift of motivation to break away from this mind-set.

1970s on: the Re-birth of Ideology and Scepticism

The welfare states had seemed the answer to many if not all of the big questions hitherto unresolved about the role and responsibilities of the state in society. They had even seemed to signal 'the end of ideology' in Bell's (1962) famous phrase. Henceforth there would be only 'ways and means' to discuss; annual budgets to agree upon; additional needs or perhaps fresh problems to respond to. So it was for 20 years of relatively painless growth, until the experiences of the oil-crisis-led 1970s changed the world of and for the welfare states.

Patently this was not just economic trouble – for all that economists from the Marxist left to the marketeer right were for once agreed in their diagnosis that the welfare state was a formula set to fail at last (e.g. Gough, 1979; Friedman and Friedman 1980). The precise relationship(s) between welfare statism and economic performance had hitherto been presumed (i.e. presumed positive) rather than subjected to rigorous open-ended analysis, at least by conventional 'informed opinion' (see for instance Titmuss, 1987a). Once this vital relationship had been seriously called into question, however, the floodgates were open to grievances of all sorts.

Interestingly enough, the scale of grievance expressed tended to be in inverse order to the scale of the ongoing welfare state commitment. For instance it was Americans in general and Californians in particular who protested loudest and longest about runaway taxes, big government and bureaucratic excess (e.g. Jones, 1981). Where was the Swedish backlash? Why should the French have voted in a socialist president Mitterand two years after the British had voted in 1979 for Mrs Thatcher to commence 'rolling back' their own welfare state? Evidently, the bigger the welfare state, the stronger and more entrenched was likely to be its political following: which is what right-wing cynics had been predicting all along.

All the same, the welfare states were open to question as never before, as a result of which they commenced attracting a wider spread of academic attention than ever before. Thus the 1980s were the years not merely of 'crisis' conferences on the welfare state (most notably the OECD conference of 1981), but the beginnings of a major multi-national literature, at last, on the welfare states and comparative social policy. These by now 'mature' welfare states were revealed as being not merely quantitatively but qualitatively distinct from one another (some, as it were, more than others); in pursuit of social policies not necessarily directed to the same ends, let alone via the same sorts of means or to the same demonstrable effect.

In the event, the big question of the relationship between types of welfare state and types or levels of economic performance was never (or so it still seems) to be convincingly resolved. Apparently – and hardly surprisingly – there was no incontrovertible, demonstrable relationship, or pattern of relationships, to be discerned between identifiable characteristics of welfare spending (etc.) and measurable yardsticks of economic performance (e.g. Pfaller, et al., 1991, for a late brave effort). Which is not to say that such relationships did not – and do not – exist; merely that the business of identifying them has thus far proved too complicated and conceivably non cost-effective.

Meanwhile, however, the study of differences had spawned a dialogue and thence the beginnings of a literature on contrasting putative types of welfare state. Not surprisingly, this started off as a Euro-centred debate. However, it is interesting that one of its acknowledged forerunners should – *post mortem* – have been Britain's Richard Titmuss, whose implied intent in identifying his own three types of welfare state had been to show not merely his contempt for the 'residual' United States, but his distaste for 'achievement–reward' continental Europe (Germany), by comparison with his approval of 'institutional–redistributive' Sweden and even (potentially)

Table 2.2 *An Esping-Andersen/Leibfried/Deacon typology of welfare states*

Type	Example
Liberal	UK (Esping-Andersen)
Conservative Corporatist	W. Germany (Esping-Andersen)
Social Democratic Corporatist	Sweden (Esping-Andersen)
Post-Communist Corporatist	Poland (Deacon)
Rudimentary Latin rim	Portugal (Leibfried)

Britain (Titmuss, 1974). Nevertheless Gøsta Esping-Andersen declared himself intrigued by Titmuss's observations, prior to coming up (1990) with his own since-famous three-way classification of the welfare states: into Liberal (potentially the entire democratic world of rich but relatively low social spenders, potentially including Britain), Conservative Corporatist (Germany/continental West Europe) and Social Democratic Corporatist (Sweden/Scandinavia). Stephan Leibfried (e.g. 1993) subsequently added a 'Latin rim' of 'rudimentary' southern European welfare states (hardly a 'proper category' this – see M. Rhodes, 1997), whilst Deacon (1993 and subsequently) has being working out where and how some of the ex-communist states of Eastern Europe might fit in (table 2.2).

The Euro-centredness of the debate thus far was obvious, especially to non-Europeans. Francis Castles was among those to protest that, just as there could be more than one type of corporatist state, so also was there more than one type of liberal state. Specifically, he objected to the bracketing of the United States with (in his case) Australia, whose own brand of 'egalitarian means-tested liberalism' was, he insisted, quite distinct from the stigmatizing welfare residualisms of the US (e.g. Castles and Mitchell, 1993). Comparable claims could be made for the welfare-minded liberalisms of New Zealand and Canada, not to mention for the 'minimalist liberal universalism' of British Beveridgean tradition. Nor were US commentators content to remain on the defensive. America was not a reluctant welfare state but a different kind of welfare state: the product of a different popular perception as to what the good society should be about (notably Marmor et al., 1990). Furthermore it hardly made sense to dub the American model 'exceptional', when it corre-

Table 2.3 *A worldwide typology in the making?*

Governing intent *Social ethos*	Conservative *Preserving society*	Egalitarian *Improving society*
Corporatist *Groupism*	Near example: Christian Democrat Germany	Near example: Social Democrat Sweden
Liberal *Individualism*	Near example: 'free-for-all' USA?	Near example: Liberal–egalitarian Australia?

sponded more closely than any European model to the systems within which most people of the developed democratic world actually lived (e.g. Rose, 1991). So it seemed there was another typology in the making: one with less space in it for Europe (table 2.3).

Yet this was still only a typology in the making, to the extent that it made no necessary allowance for yet other, further parts of the world (notably Asia Pacific – see below) of potential relevance to the debate.

Meanwhile, however, this concern over types of welfare state was not the purely academic exercise it might appear. Just as earlier modes of teaching and writing about social policy had been both product of and contributant to the regimes to which they belonged (witness the relationship between the development of social administration and the development of the welfare state in Britain), so was this latter cross-national debate related to an ongoing source of tension in cross-national relations. How far was a continental (corporatist) European model of the welfare state to be consolidated and safeguarded against the forces of 'liberalism' (not least as championed by Britain) in a post-modern world dominated by a global economy? It makes sense to review the European project first, before attempting to pronounce on what it seems to be up against.

1970s–1990s: Welfare Statism in and of Europe

The original common market as set up under the Treaty of Rome (1957) had been just that: a set of arrangements designed to ensure common conditions of and access to economic activity throughout all the member states. Considerations of social policy – save those actually pertaining to the free movement of labour along with goods and services – were conspicuously not part of this agenda. With the qualified exception of Italy, the original signatories were already established welfare states in each their own right, with no wish and no perceived need to see this area of national customs and practices interfered with. Indeed, the 'great age of the welfare states' by then under way was, in its inherent international jealousies, antithetical to the very idea of there being a supranational social policy community in the making (notwithstanding Richard Titmuss's hopes for such in respect of the first and third worlds acting in redistributive cohesion – Titmuss, 1987b). Subsequent additions to the membership of the EEC/EC only added to its heterogeneity in social policy terms, to the extent that practically every typology of welfare states subsequently produced (admittedly most of them by and for Europeans – see above) had ended up with members of the European 'Community' distributed right across its range of categories (see Baldwin, 1996, pp. 38–9).

Unfortunately for organized Europe, however, this trend towards increasing social policy diversity took place over a period when it was increasingly being felt, in pro-European circles, that the Community was in need of a human face in the sense of an own social policy identity. It was no longer enough, from the 1970s, to presume that Europe could simply be about market regulation, with popular well-being (and contentment) left to the ministrations of the welfare states. The welfare states were themselves discredited (albeit to varying degrees); rising unemployment was no advertisement for a mere market-led Europe; Brussels could seem the epitome of distant, self-serving big government. In short, organized Europe was in need of a user-friendly face-lift.

But how was this to be achieved? The mainstream social policy territory of the welfare states was still sacrosanct to them as sovereign (welfare) states. Since members of the European Commission were hardly in a position to claim superior democratic credentials as a basis for mainstream social policy innovation, the best they could contrive was to initiate programmes and build up responsibilities in areas additional to the established concerns and activities of the welfare states; and to do this also without facing member governments with 'excessive' calls for money. Witness therefore the poverty in so many respects of the EC's poverty programmes from 1975, so scrupulously designed in both their application and evaluation as not to offend against national or local sensibilities, and thence so unremarkable in their effects (e.g. Room, 1986). Witness also the use of European regional funds to redistribute resources and opportunities – again on a needs-be modest scale – not directly between citizens of the Community but via the offices of intermediate governing bodies and organizations already in being. Just so was it possible, in the words of one commentator, for 'The regionalization of social policy . . . to preempt the Europeanization of social policy' on a true citizenship basis (Anderson, 1995, p. 158).

Nevertheless, there were those who saw or wished to see in the Delors era (1985–95) a sign of more positive things to come.

> The renewal of European integration after 1985 quickly captured the imagination of many scholars. Their enthusiasm sometimes obscured deeper dynamics, however, particularly in social policy. Some foresaw the contagion of integration leading to the construction of a federal European welfare state . . . That such criteria were unrealistic should have been more evident. The EC was constitutionally barred from most welfare state areas, and it was not a nation state, let alone an instrument for the social democratic rebalancing of the international economy. (Ross 1995, pp. 357–8)

By the time of President Delors's departure from office (1995), the talk was rather of the extent to which the pressures of the single market compounded by the approach of EMU could be prevented from forcing 'downward competition' on the welfare states, as they vied with one another to attract outside investment and struggled to approximate to Maastricht-style qualifications for monetary union (Leibfried and Pierson, 1995; Beck et al., 1997). Paradoxically in the latter respect, the one bold measure intended to ensure an ever-closer union between the member states of the EU was turning out, in advance, to be one of the biggest single causes of tension and disunity, especially in its hard-hitting consequences for public social expenditure.

Even so, deep-rooted aspirations continue to die hard. *The Social Quality of Europe* (Beck et al., 1997) was being marketed at the time of writing as part of an urgent attempt to mobilize concerned social scientists of Europe in support of that

> social quality of Europe [which] revolves around such concepts as optimal social participation, integration, solidarity, a sense of belonging and a sense of purpose to one's existence. Fundamental to these concepts are employment, security of income, adequate housing and good health. (Beck et al., p. i)

It is the latter, end-results (as against procedural) specifications which remain the most troublingly controversial. (Hence their exclusion from the intendedly non-controversial specifications offered at the start of this chapter – see table 2.1.) Traditional liberalism, no matter how 'fair-minded', had never gone in for promises of this order. The Keynes–Beveridge undertakings of late 'new liberalism' (alias welfare-state labourism) in Britain had been definitionally abandoned under Margaret Thatcher; whereas leading continental European governments, as powerfully represented within the EU, have never reneged on a conviction that the safeguarding of employment (especially) is central to the business of government. Hence the difficulties arising from their failures to deliver on this front; and the bitter irony of seeing their problems compounded by the requirements of European monetary union. Hence the near-wistful tone of the collection *The Social Quality of Europe*, most of whose contents, in their quality of analysis, serve only to undermine the message the editors of the volume wish to put across.

> Europe will be a Europe for everyone, for all its citizens, or it will be nothing. It will not tackle the challenges now facing it – competitiveness, the demographic situation, enlargement and globalization – if it does not strengthen its social dimension and demonstrate its ability to ensure that fundamental social rights are respected and applied. (Comité des Sages, 1996, p. 23)

Maybe so. But the righteousness of the observation does not in itself render it a realistic proposition, let alone 'quality social science'.

Post-modern Welfare Statism

This is not to be a discourse on the theoretical niceties of post-modernism as variously interpreted and disputed in relation to social policy (see for instance Hillyard and Watson, 1996; Fitzpatrick, 1996; Wilson, 1997; Carter, 1998). Post-modern in the present context refers simply to after the era of the modern (post-war) welfare states, in the cumulative wake of such shocks to confidence and complacency as the economic downturns of the 1970–80s, the ascendancy of Margaret Thatcher, the collapse of East Europe, the costs of unification in Germany, the machinations of Maastricht and the spreading talk of globalization.

Thus post-modern, in this would-be pragmatic sense, refers to

> the fading of various historical and other utopian visions of development in terms of which the post-World War II welfare state has often been understood ... Paradoxically the welfare state, based on the pragmatics of a society that combines a market economy and a democratic polity, remains in place with a measure of stability and

autonomy, even while the grand narratives [of Marxism and Neo-conservatism] lose credibility as guides to the course of history and to the future of the welfare states. (Mishra, 1993, p. 19)

According to Mishra, the above adds up to a swing away from European optimistic, positivist traditions of welfare statism to something more closely resembling North American practice: more modest in aspiration, less idealistic in its pursuit of 'the good society', less corporatist, more individualist, more particularist and above all less publicly expensive in its approaches to decision making. As a professor of social policy in Canada, of previous British-based experience, Mishra has been well placed to observe the trends, at least between Britain and North America, to which he draws attention. Meanwhile, by way of confirmation from an Eastern European perspective, Zsuzsa Ferge has offered a more schematic account of seemingly the same phenomenon, in 'The changed welfare paradigm: the individualisation of the social' (Ferge, 1997a). In the terms of the discussion advanced earlier in this chapter, both are referring to a shift away from forms of corporatism to forms of individualistic liberalism as constituting the future for the welfare state.

But to which states is this supposed to apply? Is the post-modern welfare state to be understood as a type (albeit a dominant type) of state for the future, or as a universal destination? The more closely one approaches actual trends and developments in actual states, the more obvious does the scope for disagreement – not to say distasteful withdrawal from discussion – become.

Certainly the idea of a universal destination implies that some welfare states will have – or have had – further to travel than others. Mishra acknowledges as much in his depiction of the post-modern as being more closely related to norms of American than European tradition. It is in just such a context that one may look on recent British experience as having been of pivotal potential. No matter how dramatic it might have seemed to observers (not to mention end-users) on the spot, the shift from Beveridge-style liberal universalism to post Thatcher-style liberal stakeholdership was arguably not that great. It was the excesses of 'dependency-inducing' welfare statism that had accumulated in between these two which were ostensibly to be got rid of; not the idea of a welfare state *per se*. To be sure, the old forms of even flat-rate minimalist national insurance were destined for removal since, like socialism, the welfare state had to be 'liberated from our history and not chained by it' if it was to prosper in the new world order (Blair, 1996, pp. 13–14). The end was indubitably more important than the means. The end this time was success, for each and every active participant – and thereby for the enterprise which was Britain.

At the time of writing this does not look to be a form of 'destination' either accepted or acceptable in the heartlands of Europe, whose governments are still of necessity struggling to find ways of reducing unemployment without undermining social security. Such can be the weight of institutionalized tradition and expectation in conditions of democracy. By the same token, however, something of the post-modern vision might find needs-be acceptance among the so-called still unfinished, rudimentary welfare states of southern Europe (see for instance Petmesidou, 1996, on the case of Greece) and, even more so, among hard-up governments and politicians in Eastern Europe – however much their voters might complain (e.g. Ferge, 1997b).

No less intriguing, from a quite different perspective, is the possibility that yet other states, hitherto not accounted members of the world of the welfare states at all, might effect a short cut to the status of post-modern welfare state without ever having experienced its modern precursor even by North American standards. This is precisely what has lately been remarked of Argentina and Chile, latterday success stories of Latin America (e.g. Barrientos, 1997; Hiscock and Hojman, 1997; Lo Vuolo, 1997), no matter how short lived and insecure their claims to some of the prerequisites of welfare statism (table 2.1) might appear to be.

Much the same has also been remarked and implied in respect of the tiger economies of Asia Pacific, but in this case with much less justification. It is true that Japan, especially, has long been bracketed with the likes of the US in cross-national league tables, as being a low spending welfare state. Yet the Japanese protest, with reason, against the glib categorization, on the grounds that theirs is not a 'liberal' regime by the standards of the US or for that matter the anglophone world in general. Indeed, by the standards of table 2.3, Japan is best categorized as a conservative corporatist welfare state, to be distinguished from the likes of Germany principally by the fact of its relatively low social spending record. Nor should Japan be presumed to be alone in this, by Western standards, novel combination of characteristics.

The literature on the developing, democratizing 'Confucian' polities of Asia Pacific is as yet in its infancy for the purposes of comparative social policy. This is in part a comment on the hitherto range of interests and imagination of Western comparativists, accustomed as these have been to travel more often from west to east than –

figuratively as it were – from east to west. More fundamental, however, in the light of past experience with regard to places elsewhere, has been the dearth of indigenous contributions to prevailing cross-national (predominantly English language) debates.

However, to the extent that Western interest has been aroused, there now looks to be at least another category of welfare statism in the making: that of the conservative corporatist low social spender. An alternative title, possibly less confusing, might be Confucian 'corporationist' welfare state, on the account of the negligible voice traditionally allowed to labour in these societies, all of which proclaim themselves as being run in the style of a corporation (e.g. Jones, 1990a, 1990b, 1993). Yet even this much would be an imposition from outside. There is no reason to suppose, once an indigenous comparative social policy literature begins to materialize, that one such category will necessarily be enough – or, for that matter, that this might be seen as relating to Western patterns and categories along the lines here suggested (e.g. Ku, 1995, for early critical commentary to this effect). An Asia-Pacific based categorization of welfare states would be a welcome stimulus to east–west thinking in both directions.

Conclusion

This has been an essay as much about comparative social policy as about trends and developments in welfare states. Necessarily so: since in such an interdisciplinary, international field it is pre-eminently writers and what they choose – or have the opportunity – to write and publish about which determines the content of what is likely to be studied and the perspectives from which it is likely to be studied.

I have argued here for an inclusive rather than exclusive working definition of welfare statism on the grounds that, if we are interested in studying the developed, democratic world in comparative perspective, it makes sense not to rule out too much of it by mere accidents (or contrivances) of definition. To be sure, a logical alternative to this approach would be to narrow down the definition of welfare statism more than ever before, with a view to distinguishing European patterns of experience from developments (to be suitably renamed) elsewhere. Yet this, in itself, would be to run counter to the original open-ended characteristics of Western welfare statism, not to mention the vagaries and rivalries of European welfare statism, as a would-be subject for specialist treatment in itself.

The reputed prospects for welfare statism, as here reviewed, could be summed up as a 'choice' between two rival versions of convergence. From a traditional European – and especially EU – perspective, convergence has been about harmonization (either up- wards or downwards, but preferably upwards) between the social policy regimes of organized Europe, in the interests of community building on a continental scale. Whereas for the prophets of the globalized post-modern world order, there can be only one direction for convergence: downwards, on world scale. Yet neat as this paired summing up may seem, neither forecast has to be correct nor, in my view, seems likely to be correct for the foreseeable future. Rich people, even relatively rich people, can afford to carry on as they are – or in this case to have their elected governments attempting to satisfy what voters continue to prefer – for probably longer than outside observers may care to appreciate. This does not tell us why rich people express collective preferences and tolerance levels so seemingly diverse, merely that divergent trajectories, once estab- lished, are not easily brought back together again. Such at least has been an underlying theme of this chapter.

Inevitably, this has been one person's selective interpretation of trends and developments. There has been no pretence of trying to offer the impossibility of an unbiased, objective review, but neither has there been an attempt to play down or disguise the element of 'own judgement' directing the line of argument. The object of the exercise has been to stimulate ideas and provoke discussion, rather than to supply information *per se*. In particular, in the light of the chapter's opening remarks, it is to be hoped that the level of general- ity invoked may stimulate or provoke fresh thinking in respect of more particular fields of specialism – and home ground.

Further reading

For obvious reasons, there tend not to be many single-authored works giving an overview of the field, beyond the level of the intro- ductory text. However, the following recent publications are in their different ways all eminently worthwhile.

Deacon (with Hulse and Stubbs) (1997) does not quite live up to its title, but contains interesting material especially in relation to Eastern Europe. Esping-Andersen (1996) is quite the best collection from the point of view of the present chapter, not least for its section on 'emerging new welfare states' (Latin America, Asia Pacific and East Europe). Midgley's (1997) title, again, turns out to be somewhat grander than the book, yet the author offers a wealth of useful infor- mation, unpretentiously presented, especially in respect of social work and international social welfare. Pinch (1997) is an interesting overview, unusual by comparative social policy standards, in its emphasis on geographical perspectives.

Of particular regional interest, Abel and Lewis (1993) is a distinguished collection on a region too long ignored by comparative social policy. Beck et al. (1997) is, on the whole, an excellent collection of papers dealing with social policy prospects in Europe, for all that the book as a whole fails to put its message across convincingly. Castles (1993) is a very useful collection for broadening perspectives on comparative social policy. Greve (1996) is a useful collection for presenting a Scandinavian perspective. Leibfried and Pierson (1995) is another excellent collection on Europe, especially interesting for what the editors have to say about Europe as constituting a multi-tiered policy-making system. Takahashi (1997) is a valuable 'insider' introduction to Japan.

The journal *Social Policy & Administration* produces a special regional issue per annum Vol. 29 No. 3 (1995) on Asia Pacific; Vol. 30 No. 4 (1996) on Europe; Vol. 31 No. 4 (1997) on Latin America.

3
Theories and Methods in Comparative Social Policy

Deborah Mabbett and Helen Bolderson

Introduction

In one sense a discussion about theories and methods in comparative social policy is 'about everything'. As Joan Higgins has put it 'acts of comparing are part of our daily lives'. For example, parents compare their babies 'to see whether they are unusually fat or thin, or small or large' (Higgins, 1981, p. 7) and the photographer places a figure in the foreground of a mountain.

In another sense, it may be said to be 'about nothing'. Many of the issues surrounding the theories and methods in comparative work are not exclusive to cross-national studies, or to social policy. There is no distinct social science 'cross-national method' although such research highlights some of the issues in making scientific, as opposed to impressionistic, comparisons. For example, while access to a wide and more varied range of data than is provided by single country material is one of the main advantages of cross-national work, the non-equivalence of the data can be a major issue. Cross-national research also underlines the problems involved generally in developing research methodologies and in conducting research which has explanatory power or moves off in new directions.

We may begin by trying to understand some of the issues by reference to the natural sciences. A 'comparative method' is used in the natural sciences where, for example, two different substances are injected into the same constant tissue to compare their effects. In the social sciences similar experiments are attempted when the results of a social intervention (e.g. social work) are evaluated by comparing the condition of two groups, where one has been subject to the intervention and the other, an identical control group, has not.

Although there may well be problems in the natural science of how to measure the results of the experiment, it is clear that the social science experiment is less rigorous. The effect of the intervention cannot be isolated from other factors which may have affected the clients, the controls can rarely be matched exactly, and, indeed it may be difficult to know how many, and which, variants they need to be matched for. None the less, there is a well-developed evaluative tradition in comparative social policy (see Bolderson, 1988). We discuss some examples in the next section, 'Evaluative Studies'.

There are also other ways in which comparison in the social sciences is used as a substitute for experimentation in the natural sciences. Scientists use experiments to advance the development of a theory. For example, a physicist may write down a model, in the form of equations, to explain a set of observations, and then conduct experiments to test whether the implications of the model are valid. This methodology has an affinity to the way in which nineteenth- and early twentieth-century sociologists used the comparative method. They tested theories about the development of societies (e.g. Comte, Spencer); formulated universal social laws (as in Durkheim's work on the causes of suicide); created typologies and models of society (e.g. Hobhouse); explained particular configurations (as in Weber's account of the rise of Western capitalism) (see Fletcher, 1972). The descendants of this tradition in comparative social policy include Wilensky (1975), who was explicitly concerned with examining the industrialization theory of welfare development, and Esping-Andersen (1990) who correlated three models of the political economy of capitalist countries with different welfare configurations. Their work is discussed in the third, fourth and fifth sections.

Other distinguished contributors to comparative social policy have moved away from comparison as a 'controlled experiment'. Historians in particular are prone to argue that it is not possible to standardize or control sufficiently to test models across countries. Furthermore, an emphasis on 'testing' imposes competition on theories which can be made to be complementary. Baldwin (1990) deals with the battle between socio-economic and political explanations of the welfare state in a single sentence: '[s]ocial issues play an important role here, but only as filtered through the parliamentary membrane' (p. 54). Clearly unimpressed by 'legions of empirical studies identifying a link between the labor movement and the expansion of the welfare state' (p. 42), Baldwin opts instead to examine several national cases over a long span of time. In historical case studies, theory is the servant rather than the master, generating explanations and guiding the search for data.

A feature of this work is its willingness to grapple with the historical and institutional specifics of the countries under study. This is characteristic of the classic studies of the policy process in a comparative perspective. Heclo (1974) used inductive and interpretative methods to understand the interaction of party politics, interest groups, bureaucrats and socio-economic factors in the formation of social policy. Notwithstanding its attention to detail, Heclo's study draws out theoretical implications and illuminates patterns of development in public policy making. Historical case studies often also aim for commonalities in their explanations, while acknowledging idiosyncratic features. For example, Baldwin ranges over time and country to develop the thesis that welfare is the product of the interests which different social groups have in arrangements which share risks to their advantage.

One methodological issue presented by the use of case studies is that it is hard to identify a single method or system in the gathering and organization of data. The most distinguished contributions in the field seem to suggest that years of immersion are needed to write a good case study. In the section headed 'Uniqueness and Generalization in Case Studies' we turn to examine the methodology adopted by researchers who have not had the luxury of immersion, but who also wish to avoid imposing a particular theoretical approach. We give some examples of designs of cross-national research projects which do not use the standardizing methodology which is characteristic of the classic comparative method.

The material which follows is, by necessity, highly selective. Many distinguished contributions to comparative social policy are not mentioned, and some do not fit in any of the methodological groupings which we have identified. Furthermore, our selection of examples is biased towards comparative studies in social security. This is partly because social security is our own area of specialism, but it also reflects the early development of standardizing methodologies for analysing social security. Comparative studies of other areas of social policy, such as health care systems, have developed apace in recent years (see, e.g., Wall, 1996), and this has highlighted new issues in comparison and contributed to the development of new methodological approaches.

Evaluative Studies

We begin by reviewing some studies which can strictly be said to be comparing social policies, as opposed to comparing welfare systems or comparing whole social configurations. This means that they focus on a narrowly defined set of interventions, such as cash benefits for various contingencies. A grounding in social policy is reflected in the care taken to describe the allocation system (conditions of eligibility and entitlement), and in an evaluative underpinning concerned with the effectiveness of the government in achieving an allocation of resources which meets needs. This means that researchers are usually interested in, for example, the adequacy of provision, the coverage of the population, and the equity or otherwise of treatment of different groups in the population.

For example, in their comparative study of child support in 15 countries, Bradshaw et al. (1993b) set themselves two objectives: 'to quantify the value of the total [child support] package and assess its contribution to meeting the needs of a variety of family types at different income levels' (p. 256). In addressing the first objective, the researchers emphasized the importance of developing a comprehensive and consistent measure of the child support package, including cash benefits, tax allowances, housing benefits and the provision of health care, schooling and pre-school facilities. As we discuss further in the next section, many researchers have used aggregate statistical data on government social expenditure to measure social policy activity or 'welfare effort'. Statistical services, such as Eurostat, even provide breakdowns of welfare expenditure by function which would seem to allow researchers to study welfare effort in particular social policy areas. However, Bradshaw et al. rejected the possibility of using aggregate data on expenditure on family policy to compare child support across countries. Not only do the available data have some obvious omissions (e.g. the value of tax allowances is not included), but also the high level of aggregation means that it is not possible to compare outputs across different households or to detect differences between countries in the composition of interventions within each functional area.

Aggregate expenditure data were, therefore, inadequate for Bradshaw et al.'s evaluative task, which required information on social policy measures as they affected a variety of family types in different economic circumstances. The researchers therefore opted for the 'profile' or 'model families' method, whereby they calculated entitlements to the child support package for a range of different households. This enabled them to draw comparisons which would shed light on issues of concern in UK social policy, such as the extent of targeting towards low income families, the treatment of lone parents, and the implicit equivalence scales in the assistance offered to families of different compositions.

To some extent, the data on the child support package for different family profiles enabled policies to be evaluated against certain axiomatic concerns or values (effect on incentives, uniformity of treatment, responsiveness to different needs). However, Castles and Mitchell (1992) (see also Mitchell, 1991) have argued strongly and influentially that evaluation should focus on the effectiveness of social policy in achieving the ends of reducing poverty and redistributing income. Castles and Mitchell also showed that there was no simple linear relationship between welfare expenditure and redistributive impact. By the same token, Bradshaw et al. (1993b) could not assume that those countries with the most generous child support packages would also have the lowest prevalence of child poverty. Instead, they had to turn to another data source for information on child poverty, and then examine the correlation between 'package size' and poverty outcomes.

Both Castles and Mitchell (1992) and Bradshaw et al. (1993a and b) used the Luxembourg Income Study (LIS) to provide comparative data about poverty and redistribution. LIS is a databank where household income and expenditure surveys from different countries are held and developed to facilitate comparative analysis of the distribution of income (Smeeding et al., 1990). The difficulties of comparing income distributions cross-nationally, and the contribution made by LIS, are discussed by Atkinson et al. (1994, 1995b). Among the issues to emerge, it is shown that a number of countries have crossing Lorenz curves, which means that they cannot be ranked as having more or less inequality without taking a view about the relative importance of inequality at different points on the income scale. Focusing on the position of the poorest groups leads to the use of inequality-based measures of poverty (e.g. per cent of population below half average income). While this focus reduces the complexity of comparison, rankings of poverty rates are also sensitive to the exact line chosen, the equivalence scales used, and other details.

The development of LIS gave a major boost to research in what Uusitalo (1985) has called the 'redistribution paradigm'. This approach to the analysis of social policy is based on a conceptualization of household income formation where the market provides the foundation ('primary' income distribution) and different instruments of state social policy modify the primary distribution en route to generating a final income distribution (table 3.1).

LIS provides data on each stage in this welfare-generating process up to row 4, and some data on row 5. This means that it is possible to calculate income-based poverty rates for different countries and to compare the role of the primary income distribution, cash benefits

Table 3.1 *The redistribution paradigm*

Wages and salaries, income from self-employment, rents and interest	= Factor/primary income
+ cash benefits	= Gross income
− direct taxes and social security contributions	= Disposable income
− indirect taxes + benefits in kind (health, education, housing services, etc.)	= Final income

Source: Adapted from Uusitalo, 1985, figure 1

and income taxes in generating (and ameliorating) poverty. Mitchell (1991) used LIS to evaluate the 'targeting efficiency' and 'poverty reduction efficiency' of ten countries' social security systems. She established that the Australian social security system had a significantly higher level of poverty reduction efficiency than the other nine countries, reflecting the high use of income-testing in the Australian system and the setting of benefits at a level which took families up to the poverty line but not significantly above it. Other findings were more unexpected. It was notable that social insurance-based systems showed high targeting efficiency (most money went to the pre-transfer poor). This was linked to a general pattern whereby countries with low post-transfer poverty rates tended to have high pretransfer poverty rates. This pattern is not as paradoxical as it sounds. It may reflect second-order effects of the transfer system on the primary income distribution. For example, where there is a generous state pension, people rely on it and would be in poverty without it (pre-transfer), whereas where the state pension is minimal, there is more private provision, which lowers pre-transfer poverty.

What insights can the analysis of income and expenditure datasets give to comparative social policy? Two limitations are widely acknowledged. First, the datasets do not provide any account or explanation of policy. As O'Higgins et al. (1990) note: '[LIS] creates a demand for additional historical, institutional and legal knowledge about the countries being studied' (p. 159). They speculate that this demand might be met, at least in part, by building into the database descriptions of the different countries' social programmes (p. 169). A related suggestion from Atkinson (1990) was that LIS needed a complementary policy database, which would allow the income-generating process to be modelled explicitly (p. xxiii). While research along these lines has proceeded, it is evident that significant areas of social policy cannot be parameterized. For example, benefit entitlement depends not only on income, family circumstances and age (variables routinely captured in household surveys) but also on administrative judgements about disability, other special needs or unemployment.

This problem is related to another acknowledged limitation of the redistribution paradigm: its very strong cash income orientation. O'Higgins et al. (1990) note that data on non-cash income, especially the value of public services (row 5 in table 3.1), can significantly alter the cash income picture of inequality and poverty (p. 165). However, it is not clear how data on access to services should be interpreted. Where the data have been assembled, they have tended to suggest that services do not have a strong redistributive impact between income classes (Le Grand, 1982). However, Ringen (1987) has argued that the essential goal of service provision is not income redistribution, but the promotion of equal access in relation to needs. Success in achieving the latter aim cannot be verified from household income and expenditure statistics: the arrangement of services to meet needs is closely connected with, and indeed often dependent on, the assessment of needs by expert professionals.

Looking at how the use of LIS datasets has developed in the 1980s and 1990s, we would suggest that the contribution to policy analysis has been less than commentators expected at its foundation. This is partly because of the limited development of complementary policy information, and partly because the 'redistribution paradigm' does not capture all the aims of social policy (we return to the multiple aims and objectives of social policy in the section 'Regime Theory and the Multiple Objectives of Social Policy'). Instead, LIS has proved to be a rich source for developing a research agenda around the idea of a 'welfare society', which goes beyond public sector welfare measures to examine the interactions of market, family and state in the generation of welfare (Higgins, 1981; Rein and Rainwater, 1981, 1986; Shalev, 1996).

Comparative evaluative work in social policy has contributed greatly to our understanding of welfare effort, both in showing how welfare effort can be made up of a range of interventions and in drawing attention to the complex relationship between effort and outcomes. In the discussion of regime theory in the next section, we show how these insights have informed 'grand theorizing' about the welfare state. First, however, we take a step back in the chronological development of comparative analysis. There is an important body of work which assumed that welfare effort was unproblematic to measure and unidimensional in nature, and which sought to explain varying levels of welfare effort across countries by reference to macro-social, economic and political factors, and to it we now turn.

Common Factors, Explanations and Models

The studies discussed in this section are concerned with developing and testing hypotheses about the development of the welfare state. By contrast with the research discussed in the previous section, these studies tend to treat the welfare system as a whole rather than examining particular areas of social policy. Furthermore, they are not evaluative in intention, in that they are not attempting to examine how effectively needs are met by particular policy designs. One consequence is that the research is often careless of the distinction between inputs, outputs and outcomes, tending to view all three as aspects of the welfare configuration.

This section discusses how theories of welfare effort have been developed and tested using regression analysis, and the following section turns to regime theory, which is not susceptible to a linear regression approach, instead requiring the researcher to identify and analyse the interactions within clusters. A leading exponent in the first area of research was Wilensky; in the second Esping-Andersen is a key figure.

Both Wilensky and Esping-Andersen draw on 'grand' theories of political and economic development to derive hypotheses about the welfare state. In Wilensky's case, key ideas came from theorists of 'the logic of industrialism', 'the end of ideology' and 'convergence' (e.g. Kerr et al., 1962; Bell, 1962). All these theories stressed increasing similarities between societies as a result of industrialization, and underplayed the significance of political differences. Part of Wilensky's achievement was to link these theories to a separate empirical tradition which had tested the role of economic development in determining social security benefit levels (see the discussion of studies by Aaron, 1967, Cutright, 1965 and Pryor, 1968, in Wilensky, 1975, pp. 16–18).

As noted above, the use of regression analysis is one of the main methodological features of this area of research. Regression analysis imposes a strong methodological structure on the research. First, the researchers must choose a 'dependent variable' which is what they are seeking to explain. The theories under discussion here are about 'welfare effort', but this is an abstract concept which has to be 'operationalized', or measured, if the theory is to be tested empirically. Finding 'empirical referents' to correspond to theoretical concepts is an important process which can reveal limitations in the theories. Two measures of welfare effort have been widely used: transfer payments alone, and government expenditure on welfare service provision plus transfer payments. Only relatively recently have these differences in measurement been bestowed with a theoretical interpretation of how different factors might explain the development of a 'transfer state' and a 'service state' (Huber et al., 1993).

The next step is to undertake a theoretically informed search for 'independent variables' which might explain the level of the dependent variable across countries and through time. Theory provides some clues about where to look for explanations, but, again, empirical referents have to be found to correspond to theoretical concepts. A good example is the detailed discussion of how to operationalize 'degree of state centralization' in Huber et al. (1993). They note that most measures of this concept 'appear to have been dictated by data availability, and the fit between available measures and the concepts proposed in the comparative historical and theoretical literatures is not very good' (p. 720). These problems partly reflect the nature of the data requirements imposed by regression analysis. For each independent variable, consistent observations must be obtained for all the countries and time periods to be included in the regression.

Once the dependent and independent variables have been chosen, regression techniques generate three main statistical findings:

1 coefficients which measure the relationship of the independent variables to the dependent variable;
2 measures of significance, indicating how important each of the independent variables are in explaining the dependent variable;
3 measures of fit, indicating how much of the variance in the dependent variable is explained by the independent variables.

Note that a single coefficient (and measure of significance) is generated for all the observations of each variable included (thus the terminology 'common factors explanations'). This means that the analysis requires that the independent variable has the same effect on the dependent variable across countries (in cross-section analysis), through time (in time-series analysis) or both (in the analysis of pooled data). It is possible to include 'interaction effects' in regression analysis, whereby variable A is expected to work one way in the presence of variable B and another way in the absence of B, but only a limited number of interactions can be allowed before the analysis runs into statistical problems such as inadequate degrees of freedom (too many explanatory variables relative to the number of observations to be explained).

In principle, regression analyses can adjudicate between different theoretical accounts of the same phenomenon. Wilensky (1975) sought to explain differences in welfare effort across countries and through time using indicators of economic development. Other researchers have stressed the importance of political factors (Castles and McKinley, 1979; Castles, 1982; Alber, 1981; Korpi, 1980). A thriving research programme has developed as these alternative accounts have been tested and new explanations added, e.g. the role of religion (Wilensky et al., 1985; Castles, 1994), and the structure of the state (Huber et al., 1993). Wilensky himself has developed a further model which combines the influence of industrialization (convergence) and politics (divergence) and includes the role of democratic corporatism and the power of mass-based Catholic and 'left' political parties (Wilensky, 1990).

However, it has to be admitted that, on the whole, findings from large-scale regression analysis have failed to resolve theoretical debates. There is no agreed view on the role of social democracy, the effect of policy maturity, economic growth or population aging on the level of welfare effort. Partly this is because of a shortage of good empirical referents for some of the theoretical concepts; this contributes to a situation where 'too many theoretical propositions are being represented by too few measures' (Amenta, 1993, p. 757). Partly the problem is that country-specific factors ensure that no regression of common factors can achieve a good fit. Finally, there are problems with taking a uni-dimensional view of welfare effort, instead of looking at the whole configuration of social policy.

What, in the end, has been the contribution of the comparative study of the determinants of welfare effort to our understanding of the welfare state? Underpinning the debate between different researchers over the choice of explanatory variables was a fundamental issue about convergence. Wilensky (1975) put forward the hypothesis that 'economic growth makes countries with contrasting cultural and political traditions more alike in their strategy for constructing the floor below which no-one sinks' (p. 27). Economic development was given a central place; political choices and preferences were relegated to the sidelines.

While many researchers who disputed the convergence theory tackled Wilensky on his own ground by refining the regression analysis of welfare effort, it is also evident that some of the issues presented by convergence theory were methodological. One problem concerned the countries included in the data set. Convergence theory was most strongly supported when the data were drawn from countries across a wide range of levels of economic development. Differences among the developed countries were not explained. Regression analysis was less suited to analysing a developed country sub-sample because of the smaller number of cases. Regression analysis also needs a well-defined dependent variable, but differences among developed countries concerned the nature as well as the quantity of welfare effort. The multi-dimensional analysis of welfare states required different methodological approaches.

Regime Theory and the Multiple Objectives of Social Policy

Regime theory extends and enhances common factor analysis in two main directions. First, the idea that there are different types of welfare state replaces the emphasis on ranking welfare effort. Second, regime theory looks at whole configurations of policies, emphasizing the conjunctions and interactions between social policy and 'its reciprocal political and economic institutions . . . [R]egimes are the specific institutional arrangements adopted by societies in the pursuit of work and welfare. A given organisation of state-economy relations is associated with a particular social policy logic' (Esping-Andersen, 1987, pp. 6–7). Whereas regression analysis requires that the relationship between variables obeys a common structure across countries, regime theory allows for different patterns of relationships.

To understand how Esping-Andersen's (1990) *Three Worlds of Welfare Capitalism* has come to be one of the most-cited books in comparative social policy, it is useful to distinguish between these two aspects of the work: the multi-dimensional characterization of welfare effort and the interaction between politics, economic conditions and social policy. The discussion of Esping-Andersen in the social policy literature has centred on the multi-dimensional characterization of welfare effort. The data for this work are multi-country information on the detail of social policy interventions (e.g. eligibility and entitlement conditions for benefits, etc.). Using such data, countries are grouped according to certain generic similarities in their social policies.

The data for the analysis of interactions between political systems, economic structures and social policies are of a different order. We would argue that the analysis of regimes in this sense has proceeded most fruitfully through case studies. That this is not how regime theory is usually understood in social policy reflects the particular methodology employed in *Three Worlds*, but this methodology is not representative of the 'reciprocal' analysis of the political, economic and social policy dimensions of regimes generally. We leave the discussion of 'reciprocal' regime theory to the next section, and concentrate here on the multi-dimensional characterization of welfare states.

Esping-Andersen focuses on two key dimensions:

1 decommodification: the degree to which social policy makes individuals independent of the market;
2 stratification: the degree to which the welfare state differentiates between different groups (e.g. according to occupational status). The opposite of stratification is solidarity, whereby the welfare state offers the same benefits and services to the whole population.

These concepts originate in political theory. Decommodification is a social democratic political strategy which, Esping-Andersen hypothesized, would be reflected in the design of social policy interventions. Stratification is a conservative strategy which one might find signs of in both state-corporatist and liberal regimes, although a liberal regime might leave stratification to the market.

As discussed above, an important step in developing an analysis like this is to find empirical referents for the concepts. For stratification Esping-Andersen (1990) produced a range of indicators (table 3.1) and refrained from combining them into a single index. For decommodification, however, Esping-Andersen constructed a composite indicator which combined average and minimum benefit levels (positive for decommodification), contribution periods, waiting days, individual pension finance share (negative) and coverage (positive). While coverage can be measured by comparing the size of the apparently eligible group with the number receiving benefits, this measure was not used where benefits were means tested, and instead an arbitrary weight was assigned. An *ad hoc* adjustment was also made to the contribution period variable in the case of means-tested programmes.

The decommodification index combines two things: the generosity of benefits and the conditionality attached to their award. While one aspect of conditionality – that created by requiring prior insurance contributions – can be measured readily, other aspects of conditionality to do with intrusive and rigorous administration are harder to measure. Esping-Andersen (1990) sees means-tested benefits as 'highly conditional in terms of offering rights' (p. 54), but this is assumed, not revealed by the data. The example of the decommodification index shows how difficult is the search for measures and indicators which can be applied across countries in a uniform fashion. Coverage worked as an indicator of conditionality for some systems, but the coverage figures for Australia and New Zealand were too high to support what Esping-Andersen wanted to argue about the relationship between means-testing and decommodification, necessitating an *ad hoc* adjustment to those countries' decommodification scores.

Other comparative researchers in the modelling tradition have suggested that it is possible to construct a multi-dimensional picture of the welfare state without recourse to such elaborate statistical manipulation. Castles and Mitchell (1992) show how four 'worlds' can be located with a simple two-dimensional structure obtained by cross-tabulating welfare expenditure and benefit equality (difference between minimum and average benefits). More recently, Bonoli (1997) has offered a two-dimensional classification with welfare expenditure and contribution financing as the key variables. In both these examples, the old measure of welfare effort has reappeared, albeit as just one dimension within the analysis. One can recognize a familiar basic point in both these classifications: aggregate expenditure is not linearly related to redistributive impact because of the presence of insurance-based benefits. Castles and Mitchell detect the presence of insurance through benefit (in)equality; Bonoli through the share of contribution financing.

Titmuss (1974) made an early contribution to the multi-dimensional analysis of welfare effort by identifying three conceptions of the role of social policy and linking each conception to principles of entitlement to benefits and services. Titmuss argued that earnings-related contributory systems reflected an 'industrial achievement–performance' conception, universalism an institutional conception and means-testing a residual conception of social policy. The purpose of Titmuss's classification is to explain the logic of advocating a particular basis for entitlement (means-testing, etc.) by connecting it to a wider view of the role of social policy. While Titmuss noted that some countries (or, more precisely, some national traditions) appeared to give more weight to one principle than another, he did not attempt to explain each conception with a theory about there being different types of welfare state. Indeed, because policies are introduced under particular sets of conditions at different historical moments for a wide variety of target groups, elements of all three bases for entitlement are likely to coexist in a country's social policy.

In Bolderson and Mabbett (1995), we suggested that different rationales for social security payments could be analysed systematically to enable different countries' social security systems to be located within a common framework. We argued that 'broad-brush' characterizations of systems did not survive confrontation with the complex detail of actual arrangements. For example, adherence to insurance principles varies widely across different contributory systems. We found that '[r]ules governing benefits in insurance systems can be very complex, and inside the web of rules lie important differences between systems in the extent to which strict relationships between contributions and benefits or earnings and benefits are maintained' (p. 124).

We presented an analytical framework from which we generated a set of questions which could be used to locate different countries' social security systems along different axes or dimensions. Developing the questions revealed how some widely used social policy concepts had system-specific meanings which made it difficult to apply them to comparative analysis. For example, 'residualism' is associated with close matching of assistance to the gap between needs and means, and means testing is often taken as the central indicator of residualism. However, this ignores the needs testing side of the allocative system. Furthermore, adjustment of assistance to needs and means can be done by a variety of administrative procedures ranging from close enquiries into personal circumstances to use of a few easily verified indicators. While the former approach to administration harks back to the Poor Law, the latter more resembles a modern taxation system.

There are similar problems with 'universalism' and the closely related concept of social citizenship. Looking at social security, we find that benefits often described as universal, such as child benefit, are more accurately categorical (payable to those in the category 'caring for children'). Universality is often defined by what it is not: not means tested and not contributory. Yet this can encompass a multitude of benefits using categories which entail widely varying levels of selectivity. The universality of child benefits or old age pensions reflects their straightforward eligibility conditions (age, and little else). There are benefits payable to reflect additional needs arising from disability which are neither means tested nor contributory, but they are not always envisaged as universal because proving eligibility (membership of the category 'disabled') is often an onerous process.

In the end, we would have to say that the comprehensive multi-dimensional classification of social policy interventions in Bolderson and Mabbett (1995) ended up being too complex to be useful. The problem with deconstructing broad-brush characterizations is that the results militate against clear and all-encompassing cross-country contrasts. The study was more revealing about the range of objectives, rationales and instruments which characterize social policy than it was about the differences between countries.

Comparison and Convergence

In the discussion at the start of the previous section, we noted that regime theory was not just about the multi-dimensionality of welfare effort. Regimes can be characterized in terms of the reciprocal relations between political institutions, economic structure and social policy. Esping-Andersen (1990) analyses these relations by 'chang[ing] gears, methodologically speaking' (Part II, pp. 142–3). Instead of developing comparative indicators for a number of countries, Esping-Andersen confines his discussion to three countries, selected as 'exemplars' of the different regime types. He argues that the three regime types exhibit distinct configurations of macro-economic policy, wage bargaining institutions, labour force participation, welfare sector employment and transfer payments.

One important implication of regime theory is that different types of welfare state can coexist in the global economy. Each regime type is affected by, and responds to, international competitive pressure in a distinctive way. This idea is captured in the subtitle of Esping-Andersen (1996a): 'National Adaptations in Global Economies'. The 1996 study is part of a burgeoning comparative welfare state literature which consists of country case studies organized around the theme of globalization, often more or less explicitly addressing the question, 'Can the welfare state compete?' (see, e.g. Pfaller et al., 1991; Cochrane and Clarke, 1993).

Wilensky's argument that welfare states would 'converge' in the course of economic development and industrialization provoked a vigorous response from researchers who argued that 'politics mattered' (e.g. Stephens, 1979; Korpi, 1983). One can see similar divisions between convergence theorists and those who attach importance to 'national adaptations' in the debate over the impact of globalization. The new convergence theory is that all market economies are subject to competitive constraints on state welfare activity. Extensive welfare states cannot compete with those which make minimal, residual provision in an increasingly integrated global economy. Competitive pressure on the ability of the state to supply welfare is accompanied by intensified demand, arising from the aging of the population. This convergence theory is accompanied by convergent policy advice, with international organizations advocating a common set of solutions to these global pressures, involving improved efficiency in public-sector provision, curtailment and 'targeting' of cash transfers, and privatization.

A methodological gulf can be observed between proponents of the view that globalization will enforce (downward) convergence on welfare states, and those who argue that distinctive national solutions remain possible. The argument for convergence rests on logical deduction rather than observation. The central argument is that high welfare expenditure leads to higher labour costs which result in lower profitability. Since mobile capital will migrate to high-profit areas, it follows that capital will migrate away from redistributive welfare states, eventually causing an economic crisis unless there is reform. While it is possible to find illustrations which seem to support this argument (such as the recent economic crisis in Sweden), the theory does not rely on instantiation for its validity. There has not been a uniform process of welfare state retrenchment, but adherants of the globalization argument can claim that this is because of (ultimately doomed) 'holding operations' rather than reflecting a capacity to adapt. The logical–deductive structure of globalization theory also means that it is inherently 'universal' (applicable in any setting) rather than 'comparative' in the sense of gaining insights by highlighting differences between countries.

By contrast, the national adaptation arguments are based primarily on 'instances' (country studies) but are relatively weak on theoretical insights. Arguably, this is because they are not really comparative enough (Pierson, 1995, p. 202). The theory that responses to international competitive pressure vary by regime type seems to have some validity (Rhodes, 1996), but the difficulties of classifying countries into regimes and the variety of reform paths taken by different countries mean that this theory works only at the most general level.

Uniqueness and Generalization in Case Studies

In the context of comparative social policy, the characteristic feature of a case study approach is that the research examines the specific institutional, historical and political features of each country covered, instead of imposing a standardizing framework whereby only pre-selected items of data are accepted for incorporation into the analysis. Furthermore, case studies allow an open view to be taken about causal linkages, with historical analysis often used to examine how events unfolded.

An early and deliberate step away from standardizing methodologies and mono-causal frameworks and explanations was taken by

Heclo (1974) in his seminal study of the policy processes involved in the development of income maintenance provisions in Sweden and the UK. In 'tracking the intractable' (p. 10) he rejected 'the analysis of general correlations among aggregate variables' in favour of 'inductively building up generalisations from detailed if somewhat less tidy accounts' (p. 12). The data for his case study were documentary and conversational, drawing on some original material, but also that from other scholars.

As we noted in the Introduction to this chapter, the relationship between theory and observation is more interactive in this type of study than in those that use a standardizing methodology and attempt to test hypotheses. Heclo related his data to existing theories about the influence of political parties, interest groups and bureaucracies, drawing out the important part played by the 'middle men at the inter-faces of various groups [who had] transcendable group commitments, in but not always of their host body' (p. 308). In developing this theme, Heclo was generalizing from observation, i.e. developing theory inductively. However, he also sought to ensure that this theorizing was backed by a rationale or interpretation, stressing that 'the opposite of being definitive is not . . . to be arbitrary . . . While it is no doubt unrealistic to expect clear-cut proofs, it is nevertheless possible to produce reasons and adduce evidence for thinking that some relationships are more likely than others' (p. 16).

Heclo (1974) showed, among other things, that the administrative structure of the state can exert a pronounced influence on the development of social policy. The analysis of the role of political decision-making structures, government systems and bureaucracies is the domain of the flourishing 'institutionalist' school in comparative social policy. While researchers have tried to incorporate institutional variables in big comparative studies of the type discussed above (e.g. Huber et al., 1993), institutionalist arguments are ideally suited to the case-study technique because specifics of the organization of government are elevated to a central place in the analysis, and the argument is often historically contingent. Detailed policy studies can, none the less, yield generalizable theoretical insights. For example, Pierson (1994) uses studies of the USA and Britain as the basis for generalizations about the politics of welfare retrenchment, offering up not only a classification of retrenchment strategies but also some basic ground rules for the study of retrenchment.

Another permutation on the relationship between theoretical insight and the comparative use of case studies can be found in Baldwin (1990). Baldwin's analysis has a very strong analytical direction, whereby the welfare state is seen as a set of institutions for risk sharing, and the research question concerns the breadth of this sharing or, in other words, the extent of solidarity. Baldwin identifies 'limited, but crucial areas' of social policy and historical episodes and waves of reform to focus the selection of material (p. 53). Compared with Heclo (1974), Baldwin's study reads as if it was founded on a more developed set of theoretical preconceptions, although of course one cannot necessarily infer the path travelled by the researcher from the organization of the finished product.

If the research does not begin with a strong theoretical direction, and the researcher does not have the luxury of a long period of immersion to allow issues and themes to rise to the surface, then, we would argue, it is important to adopt a research methodology which is systematic yet open in its approach to gathering comparative material. In a study of the governance and delivery of social security in five countries (Bolderson and Mabbett, 1997), we focused on contingencies (incapacity, unemployment, lone parenthood, elderly with an insufficient insurance pension) rather than specified benefits, in order to capture country-unique provisions and institutions within a comparative framework. Respondents were asked for descriptions of the delivery processes, standardized by stages (entry, review, exit), taking in all eventualities of entitlement, disentitlement, return to work, availability of additional or substitute benefits, etc. The research provided an account of the problems of benefit delivery as perceived by respondents in the organizations involved in social security in each country. It became apparent that there were certain commonalities across countries in the nature of the problems faced. It proved to be possible to develop a theoretical account of structures for the devolution of decision-making power and their alignment with financial responsibility. However, this analysis provided only a partial structure for the information gathered in the research (while at the same time raising further questions which were not anticipated, and therefore not answered, in the data-gathering exercise). Other theoretical directions could also be taken; for example, it is possible to compare the evidentiary basis of benefit decision making (Mabbett and Bolderson, forthcoming).

However, as in all the studies which try to get closer to culture-specific factors, there are problems of applying the methodology. The sources for the data included on-site visits and face-to-face interviews, and these are especially resource intensive in the cross-national context. Moreover, the research was about processes which involve discretionary decisions which are vulnerable to local and idiosyncratic interpretations. Full-scale surveys, followed by in-depth interviews, are difficult to conduct across several countries (see Bolderson, 1988, describing Mitton et al., 1983) and the best has to be made of a research 'safari' (Hantrais and Mangen, 1996a, p. 4), complemented by information from other national sources.

Perhaps the greatest challenge in comparative work is to understand not only the idiosyncrasies of national conditions but also the conceptual frameworks of actors in each country. There are differences between countries in the way in which social policy interventions are interpreted and understood. Despite the internationalization of education and the efforts of international organizations to promote common analytical frameworks, distinctive national intellectual traditions survive. Therborn (1993) has suggested that nations belong to families, defined by at least four types of connection (lineage, separated siblings, affinity groups and partnerships). Affinity groups, connected by processes of diffusion and policy borrowing, have been analysed in social policy, while the importance of lineage is well established in the comparative law concept of 'legal families'. One issue of current importance is how 'contractual bonding' among states in the EU (a 'partnership' family connection) will be affected by the diverse cross-cutting family ties of member states.

In a trenchant analysis of the use of the concept of poverty in international comparative work, Atkinson (1995) argued that comparing poverty rates by using a supranational definition of poverty implicitly imposes a supranational set of policy objectives and priorities. If the purpose of the analysis is to assess the comparative effectiveness of anti-poverty policies, this should be done against national objectives, which means measuring poverty by using national rather than supranational definitions. Atkinson's discussion illustrates how standardization of data results in the loss of information about distinctive national social policy institutions and ways of thinking. It may be frustrating to find that categories, institutions or policies such as 'economic activity', 'heads of households', 'working hours', 'average wages' and 'family benefits' are differently defined and calculated in different countries, but it is also interesting (see Hantrais and Letablier, 1996). National statistics do not differ just for administrative or other practical reasons but because they reflect different ways of thinking about the institutions they describe (Desrosières, 1996). The problem is to find methodologies which can reflect these deeper issues without losing their way in a mire of detail.

Conceptual frameworks and cultural differences affect not only policy making but also practice in welfare institutions. An example of the fruits of recognizing structural and cultural diversity among welfare professionals is the recent work of Hetherington et al. (1997).

The research examined the social work role in child protection in England and other European countries, following an earlier work which described the legal and administrative functioning of the French child protection system (Cooper et al., 1995). The method involved groups of practitioners, in each of the countries, who were both the subjects of the research and the researchers. They completed questionnaires about a case study, video-recorded discussions about it, and commented on each other's videos. The method was developed further using English and French practitioners who were paired and followed each other's cases. The methodology recognized that 'no equivalence could be assumed' between the meanings of words or the roles and functions of practitioners (Cooper et al., 1992, p. 34). However, recognition that ethnocentric assumptions would have to be suspended did not mean that the comparisons ran into sand. The researchers considered that agreements could be forged about the meanings of analytical categories such as 'structure', 'function' and 'culture'. These were broad and presumably culturally neutral enough to act as comparators and to incorporate within them the embedded 'bits of systems' or 'ways of doing things' (p. 35) which by themselves could not be compared or transplanted.

In drawing up the case study for discussion by the practitioners, it was not possible to take a real case from either country without major adjustments for purposes of standardization which, however, made it unintelligible. A fictional case had to be invented jointly by the French and English practitioners/researchers 'which was neutral with respect to the systems of both countries, but recognisable' (Cooper, 1992, p. 5). We draw attention to this as it corresponds with the attempts made to trace the delivery processes of benefits in circumstances unencumbered by country-specific structures and provisions in the otherwise quite different study of the delivery of social security benefits (see above).

The approach was clearly useful as a learning exercise. It fulfilled the oft-cited purpose of comparative work as 'holding up a mirror to one's own society'. The practitioners from each country sought not only to understand the others' structures, values and practices, but also reflected on how they differed from their own and on how these might change in the light of new knowledge.

Where the purpose of comparative work is to learn lessons from other countries (often a hoped-for result when governments commission comparative work, but notoriously dangerous to attempt using more conventional methods), the interactive method used in this study clearly signals a big step forward. Beyond this, the methodology also enabled the researchers to develop a hypothesis about the effects on practitioners of the different relationships between social work and the law in the two countries.

Conclusion

Cross-national social policy-orientated studies describe, analyse and map different countries' welfare configurations, their specific policies, or their responses to common issues. They are used to test or develop theories or hypotheses, to construct models, to conduct evaluations, to show more clearly the contours of one country's arrangements, to promote 'peripatetic learning' (Goodman and Peng, 1996) or the borrowing of policies or practices.

This chapter has shown that a wide variety of methods are used in cross-national social policy oriented studies. This is not surprising, since the projects undertaken differ in their scale and focus and the researchers who conduct them come from diverse academic disciplines, and use different combinations of deductive and inductive thinking. Their selection of methodological tools is likely to depend on their expertise, inclination and funding arrangements as well as on the more scientific requirement of fitting the method to the objective of the research.

Despite the diversity of methods used, we can see that these different comparative studies face common problems. In the evaluative studies discussed above, the problem is to ensure that the research is comparing 'like with like'. In the child support example discussed, the researchers anticipated that a comparison of cash benefits for children would lead to an incomplete and biased comparison, and they developed the concept of a 'child support package' to ensure that what they were measuring across countries was equivalent. One of the limitations of early work comparing welfare states on a macro level (see above) was that the researchers assumed the cross-national equivalence of welfare effort as measured by the statistical branches of international organizations.

To make progress in explaining the development of the welfare state comparatively, it was necessary to acknowledge the national differences which lay behind aggregate measures of welfare state activity. However, recognition of difference would not in itself advance the progress of comparative research. Progress called for the development of equivalizing concepts which captured differences and allowed them to be explained systematically. We have discussed how some of these concepts have more theoretical coherence than others (e.g. the limitations of the trichotomy of insurance, universal and means-tested benefits) and some are so overburdened with theoretical significance that it is a struggle to operationalize them (notably decommodification).

Comparative analyses which use case studies approach the problem from a rather different direction. It is tempting to suggest that case studies do not utilize equivalizing concepts, but this would be an oversimplification. The case study approach allows the researcher to tell a country-specific story, and thereby escapes the problem of operationalizing concepts in a uniform way across countries (usually by attaching numbers to them). However, on another level, concepts are operationalized in case studies through exemplification, allowing complex theoretical ideas to be developed as the story unfolds. An attractive feature of the best examples of this genre is that they can be read on several levels. Baldwin (1990) can be raided for facts on the countries he includes, or used to provide ideas for application in the context of other countries.

It may be that there is a life cycle in the development of concepts and measurements in comparative social policy. 'Birth', or inspiration and discovery, require a certain methodological openness, which tends to dictate research techniques such as visits, use of archival sources, and other forms of 'immersion' which cannot be applied to more than a few countries at a time. As hypotheses are developed and explicated, it becomes possible to employ standardizing methodologies, construct equivalent measurements, and test hypotheses over large numbers of countries. It is only at this stage that theories lay claim to generality or universality. With this widening of view, one might expect some refutations of the small-sample conjectures, but the reality is that *ad hoc* modifications are made and the theories become more and more complex and less and less accessible to proof or disproof. The research discussed above shows some signs of this tendency.

Many comparative researchers would challenge the idea that there is some natural or desirable progression from case studies to universal propositions supported by standardized measurement of key concepts. Amenta (1993) argues that '[c]ase studies and close comparisons of countries have been and will remain the main means for understanding the development of public spending policies' (p. 760). He notes particularly the weakness of quantitative research relative to historical analysis in untangling issues of causality. Advocates of small studies also argue that attempts to develop general theories for countries with a wide range of socio-economic and political structures are misguided. While nothing is certain, we feel confident in concluding that comparative social policy will continue to be a terrain contested not only by different theoretical accounts but also by a wide range of methodological approaches.

Further reading

Each of the main areas of comparative social policy discussed in this chapter has yielded recent additions and extensions. European integration has provided an additional stimulus to comparative work with a policy focus, and recent studies such as Eardley et al. (1996a and b) and Millar and Warman (1996) exhibit wider scope and more flexible methodologies than those reported above under 'Evaluative Studies'. Janoski and Hicks (1994) report on the application of new techniques to statistical methods of comparison. Van Kersbergen (1995), a student of Esping-Andersen, brings both case study and standardizing methodologies to bear on a study of Christian democracy and the welfare state. Esping-Andersen's (1990) *Three Worlds of Welfare Capitalism* also helped to provoke a flurry of analyses of the gender dimension of welfare state comparisons (Lewis, 1992; Sainsbury, 1994). Following in Heclo's (1974) footsteps are the historical institutionalists, including Skocpol (1995), Pierson (1995, 1996) and Steinmo (1993), who has produced a unique study of the revenue-raising side of comparative social policy.

Part II

Comparative Analyses in Selected Policy Fields

4

Comparative Housing Policy

John Doling

This chapter draws on studies of comparative housing policy that have been based on industrialized countries. Many of the points made, the characteristics of comparative studies, their limitations and advantages, however, relate equally to studies involving non-industrialized countries.

The Development of the Comparative Study of Housing Policy

Until 1967 the vast majority of the English-language papers and books about housing policy each dealt with housing in a single country, mainly the USA or Britain. In that year David Donnison published a book that constituted a major development into the comparative field (Donnison, 1967). Using information gained from a research project for the United Nations requiring him to investigate housing policy in European countries, he stood back from the minutiae of policy objectives and instruments to develop a typology of policy regimes that, placing the European communist countries in one category, divided Western economies into a number of distinctive categories. The nature of these categories, and the processes that were identified as giving rise to them, will be considered later in this chapters. For now it will be noted that a significant aspect of Donnison's book was not simply that it was first, nor even that, being widely read – it being published by Penguin, and with a revised edition with Clare Ungerson appearing in 1982 (Donnison and Ungerson, 1982) – it could accurately be described as a seminal work, but that it was in a sense so far ahead of its time that it was some years before it produced offspring: a case of someone exposing a breach in the frontiers of knowledge through which few others were at first sufficiently advanced to be able to join him.

Thus over the next ten years only a small number of housing policy researchers took up a comparative interest and it was not until the end of the 1970s that there was a significant volume of comparative activity. For example, in the USA, Burns and Grebler (1977) produced their multi-country analysis of the statistical relationship between each country's stage of economic growth and both public and private investment in their housing sectors, whereas McGuire (1981) concentrated more on policy. In Britain, Headey (1978) published a comparative study of housing policy and housing consumption in Sweden, Britain and the USA, his findings showing far greater equality in consumption across all population groups in Sweden than was apparent in the other two countries.

The book that at this time had the most impact and significance in the sense of establishing an analysis that was fundamentally different from Donnison's appeared in 1981. Kemeny (1981), who had lived and studied housing in Britain, Sweden and Australia, published *The Myth of Home Ownership*. This was part of the slow, steady expansion of comparative research in the first half of the 1980s. Newson's (1986) international bibliography of housing policy listed just over 3,000 publications of which about 8 per cent were categorized as comparative, meaning that they dealt with two or more countries. From the mid 1980s, expansion was increasingly rapid. Key publications that stimulated researchers in many countries included a number by Harloe and his colleagues: a short, contentious journal article on comparative theory and method (Harloe and Martens, 1983); a book on the private rental sector in the USA, West Germany, France, The Netherlands, Britain and Denmark (Harloe, 1985); and another on all tenures in the same set of countries (Ball, Harloe and Martens, 1988). But arguably the main stimulus to interest from the mid 1980s was an initiative centred on the Swedish Building Research Institute to develop a European-wide network – the European Network for Housing Researchers (ENHR). Following an inaugural conference in Sweden, the network has rapidly expanded to a membership that in 1997 numbered around 800. Of these the largest national groups are from Sweden, the Netherlands and Britain. In most years since 1986 there has been one, sometimes two, ENHR-sponsored international conferences, whilst the quarterly newsletter keeps network members abreast of literature and the activities of research groups.

With this mushrooming of interest, there has been a growth in comparative publications that, among other things, has widened the number of countries whose housing policies and developments are now recorded in the English language. More and more journal editors are eager to publish comparative papers. All this has contributed to a far greater dissemination of knowledge than hitherto about housing systems in all industrialized countries, as well as some of the non-industrialized ones. If a second edition of the Newson bibliography were to be produced 12 or 13 years after the original it would doubtless run into several volumes. Those wishing to find out about housing in countries other than their own, therefore, will in most cases not face too onerous a task in tracking down relevant material. In turn, the content of university modules on housing policy, at both undergraduate and postgraduate levels, have increasingly come to incorporate comparative elements. Writing at the end of the millennium, therefore, this is an area of research and study that has firmly established itself in the fields of social and public policy, urban studies and geography.

What Does 'Comparative' Research in Housing Policy Mean?

Of the growing literature on housing policy, much of what passes for comparative study is not explicitly comparative at all. Thus there are a number of edited volumes, the chapters of which each provide an introduction to a different country (for example, Balchin, 1996; Wynn, 1983). In some cases, however, there is a lack of common structure with each chapter largely addressing different issues and providing different types of empirical information. This may happen because the editor has not imposed a sufficiently strong template or brief (e.g. Hallett, 1988), but can also occur where the editor has selected papers, conceived and written independently and given at a conference, and then convinced a publisher that they would make a good book (e.g. van Vliet and van Weesep, 1990; Lundquist, 1992). Many, if not all the chapters may, individually, be of high academic quality, but even though the editor may provide an introduction and conclusion, perhaps identifying a number of themes, this form of comparison is often little more than juxtaposition. In addition, many of the papers in journals and conference proceedings are single-country studies of housing policy that may be read by researchers from that same country or from another. So, overall, in many papers and edited volumes the task of comparing is not tackled by writers but rather left to readers to sort out for themselves should they wish.

It is not always the case that edited volumes constitute comparison by juxtaposition. Where the editor has imposed a strong template or added substantial introductory and concluding chapters (e.g. Pooley, 1992; van Vliet, 1990) the comparative dimension may take on a more overt and central focus. Equally it is not always the case that, where a book about a number of countries is written by a single author, the comparative dimension is necessarily strong. Emms's (1990) study of management of social housing contains a chapter about each of five countries – UK, France, West Germany, The Netherlands and the Soviet Union – that he studied. There is a good deal of descriptive information about each that provides the reader with detailed knowledge of the main features of their social housing systems. However, each chapter largely stands alone with little exploration within them of cross-country similarities and differences. Since together these chapters account for 291 of the book's 312 pages, with the residual concentrating on the British scene, there is little room for specifically comparative analysis.

Much of the last two paragraphs begs the question that, if placing information about a number of countries in series does not in itself constitute comparative analysis, then what does? One answer is that, at a minimum, it requires statements of comparison – country X is the same as or is different from country Y – to be made by the writer. This in turn requires that, at the very least, information about X and Y, and perhaps other countries, is placed in parallel. This could take the form of tabulations, perhaps with each column representing a different country, about which the writer comments on similarities and differences. Of course the information need not be confined to the statistical but can in other ways describe aspects such as the policy instruments used or the institutional framework of policy. The studies commissioned by the Swedish National Board of Housing (Hedman, 1994), in drawing together a wide range of information for OECD countries about the nature of housing policies and the characteristics of housing stock, provide an example of an approach that presents a range of types of comparative statement.

Where the focus is on the content of housing policy – objectives, instruments, institutions and so on – the purpose, as table 4.1 indicates, may be largely descriptive and it has to be noted that whereas such studies do make comparative statements they can be doing so in a form that constitutes empiricism. A response to the empiricist label is that this may not hold where the study moves from description to evaluation, from policy content to policy conclusion. Here the objective may be to gauge the effects of policies, as in Lundquist's (1986) study of the conversion of social housing to other tenure forms in the

Table 4.1 *Approaches to comparative housing policy*

Focus of study	*Questions*	*Primary purpose*
Context to content	Why and how policy came about	Theory testing and generation
Content	What are the policies?	Description and classification
Context to conclusion	What are the results of policies?	Evaluation and policy lesson learning

USA, Germany and the UK in order to reach conclusions about the equity effects. A similar objective, as in the studies of housing allowances by Kemp (1990) and Oxley (1987), may be to assess differences in specific policies, how from country to country the policy differs in detail as well as its aims and consequences. Similarly, Barlow and Duncan (1994) examine the efficiency of national structures for the provision of new housing. These approaches therefore focus analysis by asking specific, evaluative questions. Although it is not always the case, these questions may be motivated by a desire to draw policy lessons, asking which policies work best and which might be exported in full or in part.

A feature of all these approaches is that they are comparative in a restricted sense: they compare aspects of housing policy. A different view is that it should not be the policies themselves that are compared, but rather that the policies should be examined in a comparative setting or framework, thus enabling the focus not only on questions of how policies in different countries are the same or different, but why are they the same or different (Higgins, 1981; Doling, 1997). On this view, therefore, comparative housing policy studies should be, in the terms of table 4.1, about the context to content focus, about explanation rather than description and with the question 'why?' leading to both theory generation and theory testing. It is an approach that rests on a belief that using more than one country brings something to the analysis that provides greater theoretical insights. Thus, for example, if a researcher was convinced on the basis of the analysis of housing policy in one country that climate played a significant role in leading governments to enact the policies they do, comparative analysis based on countries with different climatic regimes would enable a test of the proposition, of the generalizability of relationships. So, comparative housing policy can be seen as a means of separating out the general from the specific: what applies to all countries and what to only one. It can in this way aid the search for either support or rejection of theories of policy formation. It can also, as Dickens et al. (1985) have argued, undercut beliefs about facts and relationships, formed on the basis of observation of the researchers' own country, that suggest they are natural and given constants.

Theory and Comparative Housing Policy

Those comparative studies that have sought to explain how and why policy systems differ between countries have drawn on a number of theoretical frameworks. An approach to presenting these is to recognize that one of the decisions facing the researcher is about the level of analysis: grand, high-level theories about the role of the state in advanced industrialized societies; low-level theories about the operation of political processes and policy formation; or, between these two, theories of the middle range. Examples of studies at each of the three levels are presented.

High level

Of the first group, by far the most common approach has been to start from the position that housing policy in industrialized countries is the outcome of macro-processes that lead to convergence (Barnett et al., 1985; Schmidt, 1989). In the main, these macro-processes are encapsulated in formulations referred to as logic of industrialism and logic of capitalism theories. Donnison (1967) was responsible for introducing the former to the study of housing policy when he combined the notion of housing policy regimes, these being generalized pictures of how countries organize their housing policies, with a view that countries moved from one regime type to another as they progressed economically.

The first of the regime types was characteristic of countries such as Spain, Greece and Portugal which were, when Donnison was writing, only just experiencing mass urbanization. Housing was seen as an area of consumption, rather than production, and therefore constituting investment which would be at the expense of economic growth. The pattern of government responsibility for housing in these countries, then, has been generally passive, with housing taking a subordinate position to the needs of economic development and the new urbanites being left to their own devices in the pursuit of adequate housing.

Donnison argued that a second pattern of responsibilities was to be found in those countries such as Switzerland, the United Kingdom, Canada, Australia and the USA which have what he called 'social' housing policies. Their salient feature is that the principal role of governments is to support only selected groups in the population by helping those who cannot secure housing for themselves in the open market. So, this response is not based on a view that governments bear responsibility for the housing of the whole population but only for selected groups such as residents of inner-city areas, lone parents, migrant workers and others who are distinguished by the difficulties they have in the labour market and hence in the 'normal' housing market.

The 'comprehensive' pattern – Donnison's third model – occurs where governments accept the responsibility for ensuring that the housing needs of all their population are met. In such countries as Sweden and West Germany, housing was not viewed as a burden on economic growth, but as itself making a contribution to economic development. Government intervention was thus thought of as a permanent rather than a temporary feature with the general commitment being towards long-term projection of needs and resources, and long term programmes of housing provision – though not necessarily through direct public provision.

Donnison's (1967) three models – the embryonic, the social and the comprehensive – appear to have been inspired by his reading of discussions of more general social policy regimes: but he added to them another idea, popular at the time, that what governments did by way of social policy in general was not primarily the result of political or ideological objectives but rather policies were the necessary outcomes of economic development. As countries advanced from one economic stage to another they experienced similar sets of problems, associated with the demographic and social correlates of economic growth, and they responded to those problems in similar ways, irrespective of their ideological predilections. Policies were thus not about politics but economic imperatives – hence the 'logic of industrialism' and 'politics doesn't matter' labels that were applied to the proposition – so that over time economic progress would force increasing similarity in their social policies. For Donnison this meant that his three models of housing policy type were actually stages. He argued that as countries advanced economically they would move, inexorably, from the embryonic to the social and, finally, to the comprehensive model.

Schmidt (1989) argues that some of those writing within a Marxist framework whilst, on the one hand, criticizing the logic of the industrialism approach have, on the other, sometimes replaced it with a logic of the capitalism approach. Harloe (1995), for example, has proposed that different countries have, at different times, pursued either residual – small-scale, and targeted on the poor – or mass – large-scale and open to all groups – forms of social housing provision. He relates these to epochs of capitalism when the structures of accumulation changed in fundamental ways, from liberal capitalism in the nineteenth century to Fordism in the twentieth, and post-Fordism after the 1970s, arguing that there has been a general tendency, as the epochs changed, to change the form of social housing provision. The mass model dominated in many countries during the Fordist period with a tendency towards the residual model in the post-Fordist.

In many other studies the processes of convergence are presented in less theoretically explicit terms as representing some common tendency to similarity. This has been particularly the case where researchers have reviewed developments across industrialized countries over the last two decades, when housing policy has been seen as conforming to a new period of economic restriction. In response to economic difficulties, governments have cut back on subsidies to social housing, sometimes shifting from production to consumption support with consequent impacts on the production of social housing (see Ambrose and Barlow, 1987; Tosics, 1987).

Middle level

Examples of studies based on middle-range theories are those conducted by Kemeny (1981) who, like Donnison, also attempted to categorize countries according to their housing policy regimes. He identified one group of countries – USA, Canada, Australia, New Zealand – which had enacted policies which favoured home ownership, e.g. subsidy systems which favoured the home buyer. He identified a second group of countries – Sweden, Switzerland, The Netherlands – in which governments had established large-scale, social-renting sectors – that is, forms of rental housing which were not driven primarily by profit objectives. So Kemeny argued that there were two distinct traditions: in the English-speaking countries there was a tradition of home ownership whereas the continental European tradition was of social, rental housing.

These two different outcomes were the product of what Kemeny (1981) called – and this is where the explanation differed fundamentally from Donnison's (1967) – political tenure strategies, by which he meant the *ad hoc* actions of national governments that established subsidy systems, institutions and legislation which modified the balance of advantage and disadvantage to be attached to different tenure forms. Thus in home-owning societies there had been established building societies or other financial institutions that were able to provide loans for middle-income house purchasers, subsidies and sets of legal rights that favoured home owners over renters. Given these different structures, the obvious question is: why have governments pursued the political tenure strategies they have? Kemeny, in his first and subsequent books (1981, 1992 and 1995), has built explanations around national ideology and culture, expressed crudely as the notion that in home-owning societies there is a strong orientation towards privatism and in cost-rental societies towards collectivism.

Also operating at the middle range are those researchers of comparative housing policy who, like those of other social policy areas, have adopted and modified the work of Esping-Andersen (1990). This does not stress the role of housing in the range of goods that were the focus of struggles between class interests to establish access to welfare goods so that housing was not, for example, included as a factor in his de-commodification indices (see chapter 3 of this volume). Barlow and Duncan (1994), however, deduce the housing policy characteristics of the three welfare state regimes. In liberal regimes, social housing will be limited in scale, aimed at low income groups and highly stigmatized. The underlying assumption of policy is that most people will seek to find market forms of housing with owner occupation in particular being favoured. In corporatist regimes, there will be overt use of subsidies but not in forms that will undermine existing social stratification. Social democratic regimes will have policy systems that aim to increase consumption and lower costs for all. Barlow and Duncan add a further regime type – the rudimentary welfare state – much like Donnison's (1967) 'embryonic' type, in which there is minimal state involvement in housing.

Low level

Research based on low-level explanations of housing policy concentrate on the processes of political decision making and the formulation of policy. Thus, in his study of post-war developments in housing policy in each of the main tenures – private renting, public housing and owner occupation – in post-war France and Britain, Duclaud-Williams (1978) focused on the micro processes by which decisions about policy were reached. Housing policy is placed in its political context, tracing developments, examining the relationship between politics and policies and focusing on decision making and the role of pressure groups. He concluded that the standard view of French politics, that stressed the instability of French governments' leading politicians to pass power to bureaucrats, did not stand up to the evidence of their adoption of housing legislation. In addition, he demonstrated that the strength of the local–central relationship evident in Britain was also a feature of the French political scene. Similarly, in terms of the level of theory, Heidenheimer et al. (1975) reflect on the influences shaping housing policies, arguing that there are significant differences between European countries and the US in the roles played by producer interest groups and political parties. In some European countries – they specifically identify Sweden – government has had direct control over financial institutions, enabling them to exert considerable influence over the construction industry. This has been important in the post-war period in creating a housing system with strong social dimensions. In contrast, in the US 'the house-building industry itself has played the largest single role in writing the policy' (p. 78). Here a coalition of financial institutions, construction and real estate interests not only succeeded in residualizing public housing to a welfare programme, but gained support for private building through subsidized housing loans.

The Focus on Tenure

In Britain and the USA, the origins of much of the writing about housing policy, there is a tradition of tenure ideology. Tenures are assumed to have characteristics that make them potent, independent forces influencing individual behaviour. Thus home ownership is often considered to provide independence and security; the property-owning democracy arising because it provides a stake in the future well-being of the nation. In contrast, social housing is deemed an inferior option creating dependency. (See Gray, 1982 for a discussion of the fetishism of tenure in Britain.)

Reflecting the importance of tenure at the ideological level much of the single (Anglo-Saxon) country studies of policy have themselves taken tenure as their principal focus. Hence, the large number of studies of home ownership, particularly related to class and wealth (see, for example, Saunders, 1990), and to council housing (see Forrest and Murie, 1988). This pre-occupation with tenure has carried over into comparative study. Much of the literature consists of examinations of a single tenure across a number of countries. This can be illustrated by Harloe's (1985) work on private renting or by Emms (1990) and Power (1993) on social housing. Other literature presents country-by-country discussions of housing policy largely based around the development of tenure patterns and characteristics (e.g. Balchin, 1996). Whatever the benefits of cutting the comparative cloth to reflect tenure divisions, and the cloth will always have to be cut in some way, there are limitations, both theoretical and methodological.

Consumption versus production

Tenure, of course, constitutes an aspect of the sphere of consumption determining some aspects of how housing is used over its lifetime, but its study may largely ignore the process whereby housing comes into being in the first place. Ambrose (1991) has sought to re-establish the sphere of production in comparative study through his presentation of the main stages in the housing provision process. This begins with an agent (or agents) that initiates development by assembling land and finance, as well as obtaining legal entitlement to develop. This leads into the construction phase during which the factors of production – land, labour and capital – are brought together in order to build dwellings. On completion of building, consumption may take place, though this stage may be periodically interrupted by re-production as the fabric and facilities of the building are repaired or improved. At each stage the agent and the ownership of land and dwelling may change. Also, at each stage there may be need for external financing.

For purposes of the present discussion, the main point about Ambrose's (1991) stages is that they indicate that there is much more to housing than its consumption. Indeed, policy in all industrialized countries reflects this with actions taken that can be related to some frequently experienced, external effects of housing provision. Thus unregulated production, that is, private production without constraints by the state, may result in patterns of consumption, typified by shanty-town developments, that encourage ill health, fire hazards, poor education and crime. Unregulated production and consumption may have other effects such as suburban sprawl that are deemed disadvantageous for society at large. In all industrialized countries there have been policies enacted that lay down requirements with respect to production matters such as standards of construction, materials to be used, densities, infrastructure and location. Another rationale for state involvement in housing production is tied to its location-specific character. If a government wishes to increase the consumption of many goods and services – food, computers, health care, education – it can often achieve increases simply by making more money available. If the country itself is not able to meet the increased demand, food, computers, doctors, medical supplies, teachers and textbooks may be imported. Importing houses may not be easily feasible and any state desiring greatly to enhance supply may require central co-ordination of the factors of production. Hence typically in periods of great shortage, such as in the aftermath of war, the governments of industrialized countries have involved themselves in, at least, the development stage.

The shifting meaning of tenure

The difficulty indicated here is that far from being a universal concept, stable over time and space, tenure is a social construct that, in Harloe and Martens' (1983) words, 'can be seen in each country to be the product of a specific interrelationship of political, economic and ideological factors' (p. 266). Thus home ownership in Germany, where buyers are frequently in their forties and fifties having high incomes, is typically associated with settling down and family living. Much of the housing has been purpose built for the owner who will be intending to remain in it for many years (Ball et al., 1988). In contrast to Germany where home owning is a minority activity pursued by just over 40 per cent of households, in Singapore it has reached a much higher proportion (see table 4.2). Here, home ownership has been pursued as a deliberate policy to promote nation building through the stake that home ownership is seen as giving to population groups that came together in the post-colonial state. It has also been a mechanism for generating high levels of household savings that the Government has been able to use to facilitate economic growth (Lee et al., 1993). The contrast in building forms could scarcely be greater: robust, single-family houses in Germany and multi-storey apartment blocks in Singapore. Examples of national differences in the meaning of home ownership are numerous and relate to all dimensions of tenure: social, economic, ideological, legal and political. Equally, what tenure means in any one country can change over time. In Britain in the 1970s home ownership was about rising prices and safe investment, a picture that changed markedly in the 1990s as prices slumped and then stagnated, as many buyers experienced financial difficulties, and home ownership came to be seen more as a means of consumption than investment.

Having recognized the temporal and spatial specificity of tenure, Ball et al. (1988) have argued that analysis should recognize and be built around the concept of structures of housing provision. This recognizes the social agents – developers, builders, financiers, land owners, households – that are linked together in the provision of housing through political, social and economic ties. Because these social relations are configured in different ways their identification reflects the diversity of meanings attached to tenure. This means, in turn, that tenure as a 'single universal housing shorthand', in the

Table 4.2 *Housing variables for selected countries, East and West*

Country	Population (M) 1995[1]	Largest city as % total population 1995[2]	Urbanization (%) 1995[3]	GNP per capita ($) 93–4[4]	Dwelling units (000s)[5]	Built since 1970 (%)[6]	Owned (%)[7]	Rented (%)[8]	Collective and other (%)[9]	With piped water (%)[10]	Persons per room[11]	GDP on residential construction (%)[12]
Hong Kong	6.2	95.0	95.0	17,060*	1,580	38.3	42.6	53.0	4.4	85.7	2.3	2.2
Japan	125.3	21.5	77.6	37,560	40,835	70.3	59.8	38.5	1.7	94.0	0.7	5.5
Malaysia	20.0	6.2	53.7	3,160	3,448	—	63.4	25.0	11.6	65.0	2.6	3.6
Singapore	3.0	100.0	100.0	19,310	513	—	55.0	39.6	5.4	91.8	1.1	4.1
S. Korea	44.8	25.9	81.3	7,670	11,301	67.5	38.2	53.6	8.2	74.1	1.5	6.8
Taiwan	21.3	—	—	11,629	4,237	71.4	78.5	12.8	8.7	79.4	1.2	—

Table 4.2 Continued.

Country	Population (M) 1995[1]	Largest city as % total population 1995[2]	Urbanization (%) 1995[3]	GNP per capita ($) 93-4[4]	Dwelling units (000s)[5]	Built since 1970 (%)[6]	Owned (%)[7]	Rented (%)[8]	Collective and other (%)[9]	With piped water (%)[10]	Persons per room[11]	GDP on residential construction (%)[12]
France	58.1	16.3	72.8	22,760	21,535	45.0	54.4	39.6	6.0	99.7	0.7	—
Germany	81.9	7.9	86.6	23,630	34,547	30.6	39.0	60.3	0.7	100	0.6	3.0
Netherlands	15.5	7.2	89.0	20,071	5,802	42.0	43.2	56.8	0	100	0.7	2.5
Portugal	9.9	19.0	35.6	7,890	4,187	29.2	56.7	38.8	4.6	99.1	0.8	5.8
Spain	39.2	10.3	76.5	14,230	11,824	18.9	67.5	14.9	17.6	90.7	—	—
Sweden	8.7	17.6	83.1	24,830	3,830	32.8	55.9	40.0	4.1	99.0	0.6	—
UK	55.5	12.6	89.5	17,920	21,897	16.4	66.4	33.6	0	—	0.5	—
USA	263.0	6.2	76.2	25,850	102,264	36.5	64.2	35.8	0	98.5	0.5	2.4

Sources: [1,4] *Encyclopaedia Britannica Yearbook* (1996)
[2,3] *UN Statistical Yearbook* (1993)
[5-12] *Encyclopaedia Britannica Housing and Construction Tables*
* = GDP

words of Barlow and Duncan (1988, p. 226), cannot be considered valid and should be abandoned as a basis for analysis.

On this view, then, home ownership, private renting and social housing not only can, but will, be different in each country and exploring similarities and differences between countries is a task with few fixed points to simplify the task of the analyst. An alternative view is that notwithstanding national uniqueness there are some aspects of tenure that are inherent, and therefore immutable. Reflecting this, Ruonavaara (1992) proposes a distinction between the type of tenure, whether it be owning or renting, and the form that each type takes in a specific country at a specific time. This distinction can also be seen as being between the mode of possession that can be expressed in terms of ideal types – owner occupying and renting – and all other aspects of tenure such as forms of promotion and finance. The adoption of this approach provides the benefit that statistics on the tenure make-up of national housing stocks can form a directly comparable part of the analysis.

Acquiring Information

Insofar as the process of undertaking any comparative study involves the bringing together, and the analysis, of empirical information, researchers need to make strategic decisions about what information is required and how it is to be collected. The 'what' decision will of course be related to the particular approach, as defined in table 4.1, that the researcher wishes to adopt, as well as considerations of the theoretical framework to be used. Thus theoretical frameworks at the high or macro level may rely on broad statistical measures such as developments in tenure and new construction, whereas low or micro level theories may more generally require interview, documentary and archival data. These requirements in turn begin to determine the 'how' decision, the outcome of which may impose difficulties such as the need to speak and read the native language of all countries included in the study, as well as the amount of time that will be involved in collecting the data. Here, we consider some of the general sources of information available to the researcher along with some of their limitations.

Statistical sources

The search for information is assisted because each of the industrialized countries collects and publishes statistical information about their national housing system, in most cases including, as a minimum, characteristics of the existing stock such as numbers of dwellings, tenure, proportion with specific amenities and of new construction such as numbers and building types. Generally published by a central statistical unit or by the ministry responsible for housing, English-language versions are often available. A number of organizations have made the researcher's task easier by bringing together data from groups of countries. The *United Nations Yearbook of Housing and Construction* is global in its coverage drawing on national censuses, as does the *Encyclopaedia Britannica*. Whereas both include the list of data specified above, a recent publication (Hedman, 1994) from BOVERKET, the Swedish National Board of Housing, presents a more extensive list of data, but for a more limited set of countries, those who are members of the OECD. Other sources include the Netherlands Ministry of Housing that has brought together statistics for the EU member countries.

An indication of the sort of statistical information available is provided by table 4.2. From this it is possible to appreciate some of the characteristics of different groups of countries. The European and North American countries can be seen as being characterized by high standards in terms of low persons per room and the proportion of the stock having piped water (though Spain's proportion is relatively low). Within this group there are significant tenure differences corresponding to the Donnison/Barlow/Duncan liberal regimes (USA, UK) and their embryonic regimes (Portugal, Spain) that both have high levels of home ownership in comparison with their social democratic and corporatist regimes (Germany, Netherlands, Sweden). There are particularly marked contrasts, however, between the Western and the Eastern groups of countries. In the main, the latter are characterized by high levels of urbanization and concentration of population in the very largest cities reflecting rapid migration over the post-war period matched by residential construction levels high in terms of both number of units and the proportion of GDP expended. Yet the indicators of quality show that the average amount of housing consumed is lower in the Eastern countries with many homes not having piped water and internal densities being high. Although there is no uniform pattern of tenure within this group, however, with the balance between owning and renting varying considerably as, for example, between Taiwan and South Korea, the overall picture is of housing systems that differ from those previously identified in the West.

Limitations of the statistics

Whereas such statistical information is now widely available and can provide the researcher with broad, national pictures, there are limits to its usefulness. With respect to measures of the housing stock in each country, what might be thought of as the outcomes of policies, they might appear easily identifiable. But, even when the concept identified seems quite unproblematic – say, the number of dwellings in the national housing stock or the number of rooms occupied by the average household – there are considerable, and often hidden, difficulties. Far from providing an unproblematic set of data that enable clear, precise and unequivocal comparative statements to be made the reality is very different. Take the number of dwellings. In most data sets, this variable is actually counted in at least three different ways: all dwellings including vacation homes; all dwellings excluding vacation homes; and only those dwellings inhabited on the day of the survey. The degree of variation is considerable with one indication being that national figures may be as much as 10 per cent over- or under-estimated (Hedman, 1994).

Willem van Vliet (1990, p. 10) provides indications of the extent of similar levels of variation in statistics recording rooms:

> In the Federal Republic of Germany and Norway, rooms with a floor space of less than 6 square meters are not counted as rooms, whereas the Swedes disregard rooms with a floor space of less than 7 square meters and not receiving daylight. In Japan, kitchens with a floor space of less than 5 square meters do not qualify as rooms; in Ireland the cut-off point for kitchens is 10 square meters, and in France it is 12; whereas in Canada only bedrooms are counted and kitchens as well as living rooms are excluded altogether.

These differences could mean that national figures for the average number of rooms per dwelling are subject to an error of at least plus or minus 15 per cent. In addition, as a measure of policy achievement, this variable is problematic because the level will reflect not only policy but will also depend to a large extent on factors such as the number of children per family, and on cultural conditions which encourage or discourage the living together of the extended family. Conclusions about the effectiveness of different housing policy regimes or even the extent of government involvement can be markedly misdirected by the inconsistencies of the existing data. The general problems here, then, are ones that derive from a situation in which each country decides for itself what, when and how to record information about housing, including even not to collect certain variables at all. Individual countries carry out censuses of their housing stock in different years. When they do undertake a census they frequently use different definitions to other countries, and from time to time they may change their definitions so that there may not be consistency over time even for one country.

The difficulties are even greater where the researcher's task is to measure, not the outcomes of policy, but policy itself. The task is not an easy one. Take the case of the researcher who wishes to find some measure of national commitment towards housing, that is the extent to which states intervene in market processes thus altering housing outcomes. With respect to many areas of social policy such as pensions, social security and education, an approach would be to use public expenditure, perhaps related to GDP, as a proxy measure. For example, the higher government spending on pensions the greater is the commitment to older people taken to be. As Wilensky (1975) has pointed out, however, in the case of housing the 'bewildering array of fiscal, monetary, and other policies that affect housing directly and indirectly – even remotely – have made the task of comparative analysis of spending in this area almost impossible' (p. 8). So, taking full account of changes in interest rates that impact on mortgages and new construction, in taxation policy, in infrastructural investment and in the many other state decisions that affect housing outcomes poses a considerable difficulty.

Measuring housing policy in other ways is also difficult. In part this is because housing policy may be pursued through different policy means including regulation, taxation, subsidy and provision. Each of these may apply differently – different policy means as well as different levels of those means – to different tenures as well as the different groups in the population, perhaps in relation to income. Where local governments play a role, which will frequently be the case because of the locationally specific nature of housing, there may be geographical differences. In addition to these differences, states may, as we noted earlier, intervene not only in consumption but also in development and production as well as the re-production stages. Together, all these add up to extremely complex pictures that are difficult to trace and arguably impossible to reduce to a small number of statistical measures.

The literature

Some of these difficulties may be reduced by the use of secondary sources in the form of existing papers and books that provide information about housing and housing policy in different countries. In the case of many Western industrialized countries – those of North America, Australasia and Northern and Western Europe – such sources are relatively plentiful so that researchers can generally locate useful background as well as detailed information, written in English. The literature on the countries of Southern Europe – Portugal, Spain, Italy, Greece and Turkey – is less plentiful with these counties being less often included in edited volumes as well as in full comparative studies. The same could be said of the countries of Eastern Europe and the former Soviet Union, although there is not a complete dearth (e.g. Sillince, 1990). Moreover, the ending of communist rule has opened them up to Western researchers and research influence so that the literature is expanding. Although much of this is addressing the economic, political and social problems of reforming the previously state dominated systems to incorporate market mechanisms, it is also beginning to engage with Western theoretical frameworks and concepts (e.g. Turner et al., 1992).

The position with respect to the industrialized countries of South and East Asia – Hong Kong, Japan, South Korea, Singapore and Taiwan – bears some similarities, with a growing literature on individual countries (e.g. Ha, 1987). Despite the fact that data such as those contained in table 4.2 appear to indicate significant differences between Western and Eastern housing systems, however, there has been no great development in the literature that begins to explore and explain similarities and differences. Moreover, in general, the classificatory systems and theories applied to the Western countries have not been extended or tested against the newly industrialized countries of South and East Asia. Thus, how would Harloe's (1995) residual and mass models of social housing as outcomes of the logic of capitalism stand up to a detailed examination of data from these countries? Likewise, to what extent are the Donnison (1967) and Esping-Andersen (1990) taxonomies relevant to their cases? In short, whereas there is information available about housing policies in these countries the literature does not generally address issues that are common to the literature about Western countries.

Multi-dimensional strategies

The difficulties involved in obtaining appropriate information sometimes make the creation of multi-researcher teams a necessity, and particularly favour the production of edited volumes. A recent attempt to make a bridge between East and West of the type indicated illustrates some of the difficulties involved for the lone researcher, as well as the adoption of multi-dimensional strategies (Doling, 1998). Operating from a foundation in the West, finding out about housing policy in the East, beyond the level of the statistical information in table 4.2, poses a number of challenges. Language barriers result in attempts to undertake studies based around low-level theories about micro-processes of policy making, involving as they often do inter-view and documentary sources, being impracticable. In practice such study was pushed towards high and middle-range theories to which secondary sources of information better fit. This was achieved by utilizing: comparative studies of economic and social policy to indi-cate a hypothesis about how housing policy might be structured differently than in the West; single-country literature about the de-velopment of housing policy in each country; and key informants from each country who were able to confirm the accuracy of the information and interpretations.

Concluding Remarks

The comparative housing policy literature has developed enormously over the last two decades to the point where those wanting to find out about the broad characteristics of housing policy in most, if not all, industrialized countries will have relatively little difficulty in doing so. This is, however, a fairly liberal understanding of what the compara-tive label means and, if a requirement that explicit statements of comparison allied to explanation and theory is deemed necessary, the literature is much smaller in size. Even on this view the scope for different types of study is large. The researchers' choices include that of deciding what type of question to ask, which in turn is related to the elements of the context–content–conclusion chain as well as of the development–construction–consumption chain on which the fo-cus is to be directed. All have implications for what type of informa-tion is needed and for the possible ways in which that information might be collected. Of course, coming to appropriate decisions about theory, methodology and methods is one task, deciding whether the comparative framework is worthwhile is quite another. Here we have the issue, general across all areas of social policy, of what compara-tive study can tell us that the single country study cannot.

Further reading

There are a number of edited volumes that contain chapters on individual countries, of which by far the most comprehensive, in terms of the range of countries and the amount of detail, is van Vliet (1990). Balchin (1996), McCrone and Stephens (1995) and Wynn (1983) provide less comprehensive alternatives, with Sillince (1990) and Turner et al. (1992) including countries of the former Soviet bloc only, and Ha (1987) countries in South and East Asia. All these provide readers with general introductions to the development of housing policies in each country covered, as well as contemporary (at the time of publication) issues.

There are a number of similarly structured volumes that cover some restricted aspects of housing policy. Pooley (1992), which includes chapters on a number of European countries, covers the period 1880 to 1930 only. Emms (1990) and Power (1993) limit their interest to policies in relation to social housing.

There are an increasing number of journals that publish papers about housing policy in countries other than those of their country of origin. These include: *Housing Studies*; *The Netherlands Journal of Housing and the Built Environment*; and *Scandinavian Housing and Planning Research*. An up-to-date record of papers in the latest editions of these journals as well as in other journals, books and reports is included in the *European Network for Housing Researchers Newsletter*, published quarterly.

In addition to the sources of information about individual countries, there are many publications, both papers and books, that are explicitly comparative. Donnison (1967) and Donnison and Ungerson (1982) are early examples of attempts to classify policy regime types. Burns and Grebler (1977) is an example of a statistical approach using multivariate analysis to derive relationships between economic progress and aspects of housing investment. Books by Kemeny (1981; 1992; 1995) develop explanations for different tenure patterns, focusing particularly on home owning and cost renting societies. Harloe has looked at private renting (Harloe, 1985) and social housing (Harloe, 1995) in a logic of capitalism framework. Doling (1997) examines different theoretical perspectives on explanations of similarities and differences on a range of housing policy areas.

5
Institutions, States and Cultures: Health Policy and Politics in Europe

Richard Freeman

Welfare provision in Europe is distinguished by the extent of public intervention and, by the same token, the provision of welfare is a defining characteristic of the state in Europe. The European state is a welfare state, and health care in Europe is a public affair. Though they do so in different ways, almost all European states guarantee almost all of the cost of using health services to almost all of their citizens. Health systems are dominated by public spending, and health spending is one of the largest components of public budgets. This chapter provides a general outline of health policy and provision in Western European countries, giving a sense of the variety of arrangements for the finance and delivery of health care as well as of the issues which policy makers face. In describing the components of the health care state its focus, almost inevitably, is on public institutions.

In keeping with the aim of the book as a whole, the chapter pays less attention to the substance of provision and the detail of change than to the way it is conceived or 'framed' by and for cross-national research. It suggests that the institutional approach is essential to comparative studies of health and welfare and that, used explicitly, institutionalism provides a powerful set of analytic tools for understanding the development of health policy and provision in European countries. But much depends on the definition of institutions. The historical version of institutionalism, which emphasizes the role of formal organizations in the structure and functioning of health policy, gains in the scope and depth of insight it generates by interaction with a more sociological version, which emphasizes their cultural correlates.

Comparative research in public policy grew quickly in the 1970s and 1980s. Its development was driven partly by intellectual developments internal to the disciplines, notably political science, on which it drew. Attention was shifting from the 'inputs' to the political process to its 'outputs', from the interests shaping state activity to the content and effects of public policy. The question 'Who governs?' became 'What do governments do?' At the same time, new research was a response to the more immediate, applied, real-world problems of public policy making in post-growth economic and political environments. What states did or were supposed to do was suddenly less obvious than it had been; different states did different things in different ways, some more successfully than others. Moreover, both the academic and political contexts in which this happened were increasingly international. In social policy in particular, European integration prompted a new awareness of and interest in parallel arrangements in neighbouring countries.

It is perhaps inevitable that initial descriptions of public policy (what states do) should focus on organizations and the more or less formal rules which link them. Answers to questions about what sort of health system they have in Andorra are inevitably couched in institutional terms: enquiry concentrates quite appropriately on functional mechanisms of finance, delivery and decision making. For many, if not most, purposes, institutions are the system. But the immediate problems facing health policy makers since the 1970s (if not before) have been institutional, too. Essentially, they are problems of efficiency: at the macro-level, controlling the total volume of public resources consumed by health services; at the micro-level, ensuring that limited resources are allocated appropriately. These practical concerns, in turn, were coincident with the emergence of a new institutionalism in political science. This drew both on group theory and on structural–functionalism (Hall and Taylor, 1996). New institutionalists accepted that politics was about distributional conflict, but gave new attention to the ways that conflict was shaped and processed in particular ways by different sets of institutional organizations, rules and assumptions. And what was important about conflict was that it was systematic or structured: outcomes might be explained by structures as well as by the functions particular decisions were meant to serve (Hall and Taylor, 1996). Some of the best analyses of health systems – how they work and how they change – have been those which have made the role of institutions explicit.

Health Systems

Because the essence of public intervention lies in removing the immediate need for individuals to pay for medical care on consultation,
financial arrangements are the basis of the most-used descriptions
and classifications of health systems. There is some consensus that
there are essentially two major types of health system in Europe:
national health services, funded by general taxation, and *social insurance systems*, funded by payroll contributions. National health services are further characterized by public delivery (public ownership
of health care facilities, a salaried medical profession) and universal
coverage, and social insurance systems by private delivery (private
ownership of facilities, entrepreneurial physicians paid according to
services provided) and segmented coverage by region, occupation or
workplace (Weber, 1990). In Western Europe, national health systems predominate in the north, south and west (Denmark, Sweden
and the United Kingdom, Spain and Portugal, Italy and Greece), and
social insurance systems in the centre (the Benelux countries, France,
Germany and Austria) (Weber, 1990). The different patterns loosely
correspond to more general descriptions of welfare states as 'social
democratic' and 'corporatist' respectively (Esping-Andersen, 1990).

That said, national health services were established much later in
southern Europe than in the UK and Scandinavia: in Italy in 1978, in
Portugal in 1979, in Greece in 1983 and in Spain in 1986. Here, it has
been argued that formally ambitious but under-resourced social
welfare programmes amount to little more than an 'institutionalised
promise' (Leibfried, 1993; Parry, 1995). In turn, recent studies of
health policy in these countries suggest that these systems represent
a qualitatively different welfare politics, and that a 'third way' in
southern Europe is becoming increasingly significant in comparative
terms (Ferrera, 1996).

Performance and Reform

Different kinds of system have different performance outputs or
effects. Social insurance systems tend to consume a relatively high
level of financial resources. In 1995, health spending in France and
Germany was 9.2 per cent and 8.5 per cent GDP respectively (OHE,
1995). Sweden spent less (8.2 per cent GDP), the UK much less (6.8
per cent). Tax-based systems make for a greater degree of financial
equity among users (Wagstaff, et al., 1992), though the degree of
choice of provider which social insurance systems allow to users,
coupled with fee-for-service payment systems which encourage pro-

viders to supply high levels of service of high quality, makes for higher levels of user satisfaction (OECD, 1992). In turn, differential performance is reflected in different sets of reform strategies.

> Waiting lists, inefficient management of health services (especially hospitals), and limitations in the choice of provider are the most common problems reported by countries with NHS systems. On the other hand, oversupply and overconsumption are the main problems reported by those with social security systems, and the financing and insurance functions of social security systems raise some concerns about their equity. (Elola, 1996, pp. 244–5)

Attempts to resolve these problems have led to some convergence between systems, from different directions, on what has been identified as the 'public contract' model of health provision (OECD, 1992). In essence, this means that health care is financed from public sources, either through taxation or through compulsory insurance contributions; that health finance is administered by public agencies who are not also health care providers, and that providers, if not independent or even private bodies, are invested with the organizational and managerial autonomy to compete for contracts with purchasers. What is important about the model is that it seems suited to both macro-economic and micro-economic efficiency (OECD, 1992). Italy, Sweden and the UK have all sought to improve the micro-economic efficiency of their health systems by increasing elements of management and competition, albeit to different degrees and in different ways. France and Germany have sought to increase macro-economic control over costs with more assertive central regulation, while also enhancing the element of selectivity in agreements formed between purchasers and providers (Ranade, 1998).

In the 1980s and early 1990s, comparative health policy research addressed two key problems. First, what works? – why do some systems appear to be more efficient (less expensive and more productive) than others? Second, if different systems are subject to common economic and demographic pressures, why is reform more successful in some countries than others? Why do institutional differences remain? How significant are they?

Understanding Health Spending

Throughout the 1980s, debates in health economics took place against the backdrop of more fundamental ideological argument. Public choice theorists argued that it was the increased element of public spending in health finance which had unleashed demand for health care. Guaranteed access to publicly funded health care meant that consumption was unconstrained by cost. The principal test of this hypothesis was the extent to which problems of cost were greater in health systems in which a higher proportion of finance was derived from public sources.

Yet in practice, the country most dependent on private finance for health, the United States, is also the one in which health spending is proportionately greatest. 'Countries with a preponderance of private funding generally do not have lower expenditures than countries which rely more on public funds' (Pfaff, 1990, p. 20). The opposite also holds: 'Countries with a larger share of public financing do not generally seem to be characterized by higher health care expenditure . . . When the share of public health care expenditure increases by 10%, health care expenditure is predicted to fall by about 5%' (Gerdtham et al., 1992, p. 79). And within the group of systems dominated by public finance, there are some significant differences between those financed by taxation and those financed by compulsory insurance contributions (Pfaff, 1990). In the period 1960–1970, the growth of health spending had outstripped total domestic spending furthest in Italy and Sweden and least in the UK, with France and Germany showing a comparable rate in between. By 1980–90, however, health spending appeared most controlled in Sweden, with that of Italy falling to the levels of France and Germany. It is arguable that this reflects the consolidation of public health services in Sweden through major reform in 1970 and 1983, and the introduction of the *Servizio Sanitario Nazionale* (National Health Service, SSN) in Italy in 1978. Meanwhile the elasticity of health spending in the UK has remained consistently lower than that of France and Germany.

Against the views of the public choice theorists, the empirical evidence suggests that public funding makes for public control. In practice, 'cost-rationality' is considerably weakened almost everywhere by the third-party finance of health care – even in private systems, health care costs are borne predominantly by insurance companies. In turn, 'privately funded health care systems are apt to offer less countervailing power to the providers' ability to create demand for their services and thus to expand health expenditures than publicly funded systems' (Pfaff, 1990, pp. 21–2, cf Culyer, 1990). Conversely, where the public sector is large, it is better able to act as a 'consumers' cooperative' (Evans, 1987, quoted in Pfaff, 1990) in its bargaining with professional and other private providers. Since its foundation, for example, NHS spending has been determined by government decision. In social insurance systems, however, the number of actors in the health care arena makes for decision-making processes of inordinate or unusual complexity. In comparison with national health services, these systems are complicated by the addition of an essential new actor, the insurance funds. Though they are the institutional lynch-pins of the system, the funds have an uncertain legal and political status. They are semi-public, required by government to carry out certain functions but organizationally separate from it. And though regulated by government, they must satisfy their members, whose interests may lie to some extent in containing the growth of contributions, but they certainly also consist in maintaining health care entitlements. Meanwhile, the funds are not a single body but a set of organizations divided by territory and occupation, fragmented as much as segmented, competing as much as complementary. In Germany in particular, at least until recent reform, this has left them relatively weak *vis-à-vis* a more tightly organized medical profession, with which they must negotiate prices. That is to say that different health systems are not more or less expensive in themselves; different ways of financing health care provide governments with greater or lesser prospect of controlling health spending. Health spending is unleashed and controlled by different institutional arrangements.

Understanding Health Reform

The universalization of the health care state in the post-war period represented something of a compromise between states and medical professions. Expanding access to health care was promoted by Left parties in government in the UK in the mid-late 1940s, in Sweden and Germany in the early 1970s, and in Italy in the late 1970s. In general, however, doctors are resistant to the increased opportunities for regulation that expansion entails; consequently, it tends to take place on terms with which the profession is ready to concur. Contemporary studies read this as the outcome of pressure group politics (Eckstein, 1960).

More recent comparative work has emphasized the defining importance of institutions in shaping the outcomes of pressure group activity (Immergut, 1990, 1992; Moran and Wood, 1993). Different political systems provide groups like medical professions with different opportunities to shape public policy: it is this which explains much of the cross-national variation in ways of paying the doctor. Immergut (1992) poses the question in the following way: 'Given that medical associations throughout Western Europe possess a legal monopoly of medical practice and are regarded as highly influential politically, how then can one explain the significant variation in West European health policy?' (p. 392). The answer is that some political processes are more open than others: 'In Sweden, the executive could enact legislation without fearing vetoes from the parliamentary or electoral arenas ... In France, unstable parliamentary majorities shifted decision-making to the parliamentary arena. In Switzerland, decision-making was moved to the electoral arena. The result was three distinct patterns of political behavior and policy results' (Immergut, 1992, p. 398). Rather than the medical profession acting as a veto group on public policy, what is important is that it faces veto points in the decision-making process (Immergut, 1992). Similarly, though more broadly, Moran and Wood (1993) conclude their study of medical regulation in Germany, the US and the UK with the observation that: 'Much of the scientific heritage of modern medicine is common to all advanced industrial societies ... (and) many of the economic pressures on doctors, especially in recent years, have been similar in different countries. These common influences and pressures are, however, mediated through distinctive national institutions – and thus of necessity have different impacts on the medical professions of different nations' (p. 138).

Different institutional settlements for health care may be in part the result of pluralist, competitive politics, but they also structure subsequent competition: institutions create interests, as well as being created by them. Increasing access to health care meant establishing new and specific policy competences for national governments, for example, as well as organizational interests such as sickness funds and health authorities, on whom the administration of policy depends. Decision making is shaped by institutions and interests which have themselves been shaped by previous decisions: later decisions are constrained by earlier ones. In this sense, normal patterns of policy making may be described as 'path dependent' (Wilsford, 1994). Ordinarily, institutions and interests may be described as 'locked in' to the systems of which they form a part. Change, where it takes place, tends to be incremental.

Policy change is unusual, big change even more so. In comparative context, what is interesting about recent health reform in Europe is that some governments were able to instigate bigger change than others. The 1989–91 period in the UK is described as 'Big Bang' reform (Klein, 1995); in Italy, legislative stasis was punctuated by reorganization in 1992–93, while in Sweden, actual change at national level has been much less than at one time conceived by the Bildt government. In Germany, the Government's reform plans failed in 1989 but succeeded in 1993; in France, government *Plans* are regularly required to rescue the social insurance system but until recently have had little prospect of reforming it. What accounts for deviations from established paths of policy making? Why do they occur in some systems rather than others, at some times rather than others?

Change is a product of context and opportunity, or structure and conjuncture. As Wilsford puts it: 'structures are the institutions and processes that form the infrastructural framework for policy (decisions) within which dynamic events unfold over time. This may be thought of as an endogenous universe, which then may be subject to exogenous shocks, that is, conjunctures' (Wilsford, 1994, pp. 257–8). For example, the complexity of the German health political arena noted earlier usually militates against radical change. Competition and conflict occur not just between but also within key structural interests. The interests of regional governments differ between rich and poor states, and rarely are they the same as those of the federal government. Within the major parties, social policy interests clash with economic interests. Doctors in hospitals do not have the same concerns as those in local practice. Different kinds of sickness fund reflect the interests of different categories of member. At the end of the 1980s, with the responsible minister (Blüm at Labour and Social Affairs) outmanoeuvred again by the health political lobby, it was difficult not to see the post-1975 period as one of reform blockade (Rosewitz and Webber, 1990; Webber, 1988, 1989). But by 1993 the dynamic, experienced Seehofer, who had formerly been deputy to Blüm, had used his position in a government with a powerful majority to negotiate cross-party agreement on structural reform. His position had been strengthened by the background economic pressure imposed by a combination of world recession, high German wage costs and the deepening effects of unification (Wilsford, 1994). Structure and conjuncture had worked together to facilitate change.

In 1987 in the UK, the Conservative Government entered its third term with a dominant prime minister personally committed to a specific set of market-oriented policy goals. Conjunctural factors appear less strong here than in Germany, but structural ones are more so. Previous health policy decisions, such as the introduction of management in 1984–86, had created new organizational interests (managers themselves) who in many cases supported reform of the health sector. But more significantly, central government in the UK has greater institutional authority over health policy than its counterparts in France, Germany, Italy or Sweden. 'The lesson of the British case ... is that strong, centralized state structures in a policy domain can sometimes lead, paradoxically, to greater departures from the established policy path. That is, wholly new trajectories are made more easily possible by strong structures' (Wilsford, 1994, p. 265).

Understanding the Role of Institutions

The analytic strength of institutionalist approaches to health policy making lies in recognizing that institutions are created and reformed in a world already replete with institutions, and that those institutions distribute power unevenly among actors and interests (Pierson, 1994; Hall and Taylor, 1996). They explain why the outcome of conflict between groups differs between countries, and why institutional and organizational differences are as likely to be sustained as they are to erode. In doing so, they provide an important counterweight both to pluralist approaches and to the 'soft technological determinism' (Field, 1989) of convergence theory. But institutionalist analyses (like all analyses) are perhaps most interesting and most revealing at the point at which they break down.

If we are trying to understand reform, for example, when does the strength of interests matter more than the structure of institutions? And what is the effective difference between structure and conjuncture? Are institutional 'paths' truly separable from the economic and political landscapes they cross? If we are trying to understand health spending, what is the real impact of institutions on the 'fiscal imperative' (Wilsford, 1995) of cost containment? Across countries in Europe, for example, increases in health spending had slowed by the end of the 1980s. The elasticity of health spending in relation to GDP was much less after 1975 than before (Schieber and Poullier, 1990). Simply, and predictably, health spending grew more quickly in the period of the long boom from the mid 1950s to the early 1970s than in the period of economic austerity which followed.

In turn, if we are trying to describe differences between systems, which variables should we choose? Different countries seem to pursue common health policy objectives – adequacy and equity in access, income protection, efficiency at both macro and micro levels, freedom of choice for consumers and autonomy for providers (OECD, 1992) – which may imply that differences between countries in the organization and financing of health provision simply do not matter very much (Fry, 1991). Different systems exhibit a high degree of functional commonality, against which their specific organizational features are merely effects of the different political, economic and social structures of respective individual countries.

Whether or not they matter, organizational differences are much less categorical than is often assumed. Public health care is usually funded from a mixture of sources, including taxation, national or social insurance, private insurance and patient charges. Even the most strongly tax-based systems – Sweden is a good example – have a significant insurance component. And where health care is financed through social insurance, mandated premia are normally levied as a payroll tax on employers and employees. The implication here is that there is little real distinction to be made between the two principal methods of financing health care. While different systems can sometimes be treated as though they represented different health care regimes they can also, at another level, be seen to constitute little more than different forms of taxation.

The idea of a 'system' is implicit in most accounts of health care institutions. But health systems are not actually very systematic. It may be better to think of the health system of any given country as a number of systems – public and private, for example – superimposed one on the other, sometimes complementary (OECD, 1992), sometimes coexisting and sometimes competing. The parts do not necessarily cohere into a rational whole and it is important to be wary of introducing an artefactual rationalization in the process of modelling. We look for order where there may be none, or at least less than we would like. What we refer to as 'systems' are really no more than packages or clusters of typical characteristics. Actual systems, of course, are only approximations to ideal types: no pure form exists, and all contemporary health systems are mixed. Furthermore, any simple description can only be a snapshot, while health systems have been in a considerable state of flux during the 1970s, 1980s and 1990s. Health systems are dynamic systems, continually adapting and readapting to the wider political, economic and social systems of which they are a part. This means that what appears most basic and concrete (what states do and the way they do it) is in fact extraordinarily difficult to define, at least in categories which hold across countries.

In turn, the labile nature of health care institutions suggests that what is significant about a system may be less its internal structure (the identity of parts and the ways they connect in performing functions) than its interaction with its environment. Health systems, for example, are composed of functional subsystems of finance, delivery and regulation. Separately and in combination, these are embedded in (and are key elements of) the economic and political systems of advanced capitalist countries. The connection is well captured by the idea that the health care state, in Western Europe at least, has three 'faces': the health care state is not only a welfare state, but also a capitalist industrial state and a pluralist democratic state (Moran, 1995).

Research after Reform

The challenges facing health policy makers in Europe in the post-reform era are also those facing comparative and public policy research. Resource problems have not been solved, but have been made more visible: a central, incipient problem for health policy is now the management of explicit rationing within a framework of universal rights. This raises traditional questions of professional power as well as of ministerial authority and action; it also raises questions about the interests and activity of new actors such as health service managers and contracted providers of treatment and care. And underlying these are questions about participation, which means addressing different conceptions of the user of health care as citizen and consumer. Often in conflict, each presents its own internal contradictions. How is the tension between the citizen as tax-payer and contributor and as patient with rights to health care to be resolved? How far is the sovereignty of the consumer of health care compromised by continued dependence on agents such as doctors and third-party payers? Reform itself has been predicated on increasing concentrations of state authority, which has been used in turn to shift relationships away from hierarchies and towards markets and networks. As public agencies are repositioned in this way, how is their accountability – and ultimately their legitimacy – to be maintained? What forms does solidarity take, and how is it articulated?

For both intrinsic (disciplinary) and extrinsic (topical) reasons, the key problems addressed by comparative studies of the health sector tend to have been framed as institutional ones. But this work also tends to express a particular kind of understanding of institutions, both in terms of what is described and how it is analysed. It is a reading which, with a body of work in comparative public policy, can be categorized as 'historical institutionalism' (Steinmo et al., 1992, Hall and Taylor, 1996). Meanwhile, a 'sociological' or cultural version of institutionalism is emerging through studies of organization. '(T)he sociological institutionalists tend to define institutions much more broadly than political scientists do to include, not just formal rules, procedures or norms, but the symbol systems, cognitive scripts, and moral templates that provide the "frames of meaning" guiding human action' (Hall and Taylor, 1996, p. 947). In doing so, they emphasize the cultural embeddedness of institutions, ultimately challenging the distinction between 'institutions' and 'culture'. For the moment, there has been little interchange between the two schools (Hall and Taylor, 1996).

Health, Policy and Culture

Comparative research is now beginning to reframe institutions in terms which take account of their cultural specificity. As well as being sets of institutional arrangements, health systems are clusters of assumptions, values, traditions, norms and practices. Institutions – organizations, rules, routines, procedures and assumptions – are themselves cultural products; in turn, they shape cultures. Health systems are cultural systems.

Health policy and politics in Europe have been studied mostly without reference to their cultural contexts, perhaps because of an underlying assumption that 'culture' is a constant among advanced industrial countries. To confine the scope of health policy analysis to Europe and North America is assumed to hold key variables such as economic development, social structure and medical practice more or less constant. In medical sociology, the concept of culture is often a surrogate for difference within rather than between countries, usually based on social divisions of class, gender and ethnicity. In anthropology, it is a way of understanding differences between the practice of biomedicine in advanced industrial countries and cultures of healing in non-Western societies. Much of this is the product of different disciplinary traditions; its effect is that intra-European, cross-cultural comparison and contrast in studies of health care remain underdeveloped.

Interestingly, however, the concept of culture is now being used with increasing frequency in comparative social and public policy. It is as though culture and its relationship to policy have been newly revealed or made visible. There are two main reasons for this, though they are supported by the cultural or linguistic turn in social science more broadly. The first is the intensity of change which the public sectors of all developed economies have undergone since the end to growth in 1970s and which have made their cultural grounding or embeddedness seem less secure. The values and practices which were taken to be self-evident have come to be looked at more critically. There is a new awareness among both policy makers and analysts of the extent to which policy-making processes and outcomes are shaped by cultures, as well as of the way in which policy must itself address questions of culture, whether directly or indirectly.

The second reason is that a new interest in the cross-national, comparative study of social policy in particular has made established conceptions of culture and its relationship to welfare problematic. In part, comparison was prompted by crisis – a standard response to failure is to look for lessons or examples elsewhere. And, in trying to understand other ways of thinking and acting, researchers have begun to understand their own systems as culturally determined. There is a growing realization that to ignore culture is to misunderstand the nature of welfare states, or to understand them only in a limited way. The cultural dimension is crucial simply to distinguishing and describing welfare states, as well as to explaining differences between them.

But how can culture be described or 'captured' for research? How can it be operationalized? How, in reality, is it articulated? Garland warns against reification: 'a culture is not a monolithic kind of thing which can feature as a simple variable in an explanatory formula. It is, instead, a rich composite of densely interwoven meanings which loses all its content wherever it is discussed in generic terms. Cultures are bric-à-brac ensembles of specifics, local details and peculiarities' (Garland, 1991, p. 200). Yet culture is not merely fragmented; it is also ambivalent. It is conflicts and contradictions within cultures which may be important in precipitating social change: 'cultural contradictions within and between belief systems make just as important a contribution to social change as anything going on in the structural domain' (Archer, 1990, p. 117). And by the same token, it is the points at which culture and policy diverge which are likely to produce new insights into the relationship between the two.

For many, if not most, governments, for example, increased managerial capacity has been a key object of recent health sector reform. But that is not to say that policy intentions are everywhere the same, or that they are realized in similar ways. Elite perceptions of the necessity and appropriateness of reform, for example, vary between countries (Taylor-Gooby, 1996). This variation in part reflects organizational factors, such as different patterns of health finance and delivery, though it also testifies to broader and more fundamental differences in elite values and assumptions (Lockhart, 1981). Management itself, meanwhile, is a cultural practice, reflecting different assumptions about hierarchy, rationality and efficiency (Harrison et al., 1992). On both counts, we should expect the managerialization of the health sector to differ widely between countries. The development of new public management, for example, seems to be associated with 'state tradition' or culture; it has advanced furthest in the US and the UK and least in Germany (Ridley, 1996; Loughlin and Peters,

1997). Meanwhile, in the 1980s and 1990s, management has been concerned with operating on culture at the level of the organization (Peters and Waterman, 1982; Hughes, 1996). Institutional change, that is to say, is intimately connected to cultural change.

Public opinion surveys point to different levels of satisfaction with their health services on the part of different European populations (Blendon et al., 1990, Ferrera, 1993). And both within and between systems, there are significant differences in patterns of behaviour among the users of health care in Europe (Freeman, 1996). Lüschen et al., (1987, 1989) have explored differences in health behaviour between Germany and the US, relating them to systemic differences in the degree of self-responsibility required of patients. Few connections have otherwise been made between health systems, public opinion and health behaviour, though they would inform some of the more pressing problems facing health policy makers in Europe. For example, Hinrichs (1995) has argued that Germany's health insurance system rests on a specific 'moral infrastructure'. The continuing legitimacy of specific institutional arrangements in health and welfare is dependent on their capacity to reproduce the cultural norms on which they depend. Reform in Germany has risked undermining the 'culture of solidarity' by which the health insurance system is sustained (Hinrichs, 1995). In different kinds of system, such as the national health services of Italy, Sweden and the UK, the growth of private health insurance tends to reduce the commitment of influential sections of the population to universalist arrangements (Holliday, 1992; Ferrera, 1995; Garpenby, 1995). All of this is to reaffirm that health systems are embedded in particular normative frameworks which structure their development. Culture is an intrinsic, not residual feature of health care states: health systems can only be fully understood as cultural systems, as well as systems of finance, delivery and regulation.

The incipient dialogue between the different versions of institutionalism explored here raises the inevitable question of what is meant by the state, as embodied in the habitual concepts 'welfare state' and 'health care state'. Where the first, historical version 'brings the state back in' (Evans et al., 1985), the second reminds us that, as Dyson (1980) put it, the state represents 'not only a particular manner of arranging political and administrative affairs and regulating relationships of authority but also a cultural phenomenon which binds people together in terms of a common mode of interpreting the world' (p. 19, quoted in Wilsford, 1989, p. 136). Exploring this 'cultural phenomenon' means moving from the formal to the informal, from macro to micro, not for their own sakes – though that may be reason enough – but in order to provide better accounts of how the macro and formal work.

Further reading

For an introductory exploration of institutionalism see Rhodes, R.A.W. (1997), and for an influential application in welfare politics Pierson (1994). Döhler (1991) complements institutionalism with a policy network approach in comparing health care reform in Britain, Germany and the US.

For descriptive accounts of the health care systems of different European countries, see OECD (1992, 1994a); for introductory analytic comparison see Moran (1992) and Gray (1993). Abel-Smith et al. (1995) are more evaluative and prescriptive. Patterns of health care reform are assessed in OECD (1992), Abel-Smith and Mossialos (1994) and in European Communition (1995c), and analysed further in Altenstetter and Haywood (1991), Moran (1994) and Ranade (1998). The European Clearing House on Health Systems Reforms operates a literature database accessible via the Internet at: <http://www.leeds.ac.uk/nuffield/infoservices/ECHHSR/home.html>

Perhaps the most widely used source of comparative statistics in the field is the OECD's Health Data, of which the latest series was published in 1997. The OHE's regular compendia of UK health statistics include some useful European comparisons (see OHE, 1995). Useful journals include *Health Policy*, the *International Journal of Health Planning and Management*, the *International Journal of Health Services*, the *Journal of Health Politics, Policy and Law* and the *Milbank Quarterly*.

Acknowledgements

I am grateful to Mary Buckley, Viola Burau Mike Dent, Fiona Mackay and Charles Raab for reading and commenting on an earlier draft of this chapter, and for Oxford University Press for permission to reproduce material from the paper 'Competition in context: the politics of health care reform in Europe,' *International Journal for Quality in Health Care* 10(5), 1998.

6

Comparing Family Policies in Europe

Linda Hantrais

Family policy is an area of social policy which has attracted considerable interest as a focus for international studies. In the 1970s and early 1980s, the impetus came from path-breaking work by researchers such as Sheila Kamerman and Alfred Kahn, firstly in an analysis of government and families in fourteen countries (Kamerman and Kahn, 1978), and then in a study of income transfers in eight countries (Kamerman and Kahn, 1982). The choice of family policy in 1989 as the area to be monitored by one of the European observatories led to the production of annual consolidated reports on developments in national family policies in the 12 European Community member states. In the 1990s, research teams in Germany (Neubauer et al., 1993), France (Hantrais and Letablier, 1996; Lefaucheur and Martin, 1995), the United Kingdom (Bradshaw et al., 1993a; Millar and Warman, 1996) and the Netherlands (Willemsen et al., 1995) were funded to undertake studies of family policies within the European Community and in other OECD countries. The decision of the United Nations to nominate 1994 as the International Year of the Family served as further confirmation of the importance attributed to the family in the international arena and resulted in a spate of international events and studies of family policies (Arve-Parès, 1995; Commaille and de Singly, 1997; Dumon, 1994; European Commission, 1994b). The interest of the topic at European level was endorsed by the decision to attribute one of the seven thematic network awards made in 1995 under the European Union's programme for Training and Mobility of Researchers (within Framework Programme IV for Research and Technological Development) to the study of family change and the welfare state in Europe and beyond, co-ordinated by Peter Flora at the University of Mannheim. One of the aims of the network was to produce a series of publications on the relationship between family policy and national socio-economic and political characteristics. The first volume appeared in 1997 (Kamerman and Kahn, 1997).

Paradoxically, and despite the heavy commitment of resources to family policy studies, not all governments in the European Union would claim to have a family policy. Nor is it easy to find an agreed definition, across either nations or disciplines, about what is understood by a 'family'. Quantitative and qualitative comparative studies may fail to achieve their objectives because they do not take sufficient account of the need for a common understanding of the concepts involved and for detailed knowledge of the contexts within which policy measures are formulated and developed. The problem is, perhaps, particularly acute at the European level when attempts are being made to promote the convergence of policy objectives. Proposals for new legislation are often premised on the oversimplified assumption that national differences are disappearing and that economic integration will automatically result in the harmonization of social policies.

Multinational studies of family policy thus provide an appropriate body of material with which to illustrate not only the problems encountered by researchers undertaking comparative social policy analysis but also some of the solutions adopted in attempting to overcome them. In this chapter, attention is devoted, first, to a brief survey of the main studies undertaken in this area and to the approaches they have adopted, before going on to examine the conceptual issues involved in defining the family and family policies and in analysing the family policy process from a cross-national perspective. In conclusion, an assessment is made of the value of the comparative approach to the study of family policy.

International Comparative Studies of Family Policy

If it is assumed that, for a study to be comparative, the authors should set out to analyse systematically phenomena or groups of phenomena in one or more societies and cultures with regard to their similarities and differences, the aim being to establish typologies or systems of classification and/or to test hypotheses concerning the causal relationship between the observed phenomena and possible explanatory factors, many of the multinational family policy studies undertaken are not, strictly speaking, comparative. This does not mean that their contribution to the body of knowledge on social policy is without value, since they can bring important insights to the understanding of the ways in which the policy process operates within different national contexts.

Interest in family policy at European level, which is the main focus of the chapter, has largely developed as a result of concern about socio-demographic trends and was one of the main reasons for the establishment of a family policy observatory. European Commission documents, such as the first report of the Commission on *Social Protection in Europe* (European Commission, 1993), and the first report on *The Demographic Situation in the European Union* (European Commission, 1995b), which was a requirement of the Maastricht Treaty on European Union, have interpreted socio-demographic trends as indicating that all member states, like other advanced post-industrial societies, are facing social problems associated with population aging, changing family situations and labour market conditions, and the spread of poverty and social exclusion. Demographic trends – and in particular family and household change – are said to be driving policy, with the European Union providing a context for policy formulation. The 1994 White Paper on *European Social Policy* explicitly recognized that 'demography . . . will impact on and interrelate with social and economic policy' (European Commission, 1994a, p. 47), making it necessary to develop common policy responses. The problem areas identified in the early 1990s by the European Commission included the threatened breakdown of the stability of marriage and family unity, associated with a growing imbalance between the generations, social exclusion, exacerbated by unemployment, and the conflict between paid work and family life (European Commission, 1993).

In line with this approach, the European Observatory on National Family Policies was set up to monitor and analyse demographic, socio-economic and political changes which impact on families, to advise the European Commission and inform public and academic debate about family policies. Since 1989, national experts have been collecting data about the situation in their countries on an annual basis, reporting on key themes and issues and using a common questionnaire, covering topics such as changes in policies concerning cohabitation, developments in social protection and family incomes, and tax-benefit policies. The co-ordinator then processes the data and prepares a volume of country reports as well as a synthesis report analysing and commenting on the trends recorded (Ditch et al., 1995, 1996).

The annual reporting requirement for observatories and networks has proved problematic for both the national experts concerned and for researchers and policy analysts wanting to exploit the data, due not only to time pressures on observatory members but also to the absence of strictly comparable statistical data and policy developments (policy decisions at national level are not synchronized) for the year in question, and the lack of perspective on recent events. These problems were addressed to some extent in the Observatory report produced to celebrate the International Year of the Family: a broader time frame was adopted enabling the country chapters to provide more comparable material (Dumon, 1994).

Some large-scale multinational quantitative studies have tried to avoid the problems of secondary analysis by conducting new surveys of family life as a means of collecting data based on a common questionnaire. In a longitudinal survey carried out by Eurobarometer of the relationship between family and employment in the 12 European Community member states in 1990, Kempeneers and Lelièvre (1991) were looking for a causal relationship between labour market behaviour and patterns of family formation. They applied factorial analysis to draw out a contrastive typology which characterized policy environments in different groupings of countries.

The Social Policy Research Unit in York has developed a method, previously applied by Kamerman and Kahn (1982), based on 'model families', defined according to structure, size and income, to assess the impact of various packages of benefits on different types of families in European Union and OECD countries (Bradshaw et al., 1993a; Bradshaw et al; 1996; Ditch et al., 1995, 1996; Eardley, 1996). The advantage of this approach is that it enables researchers to compare like with like. In combination with detailed descriptive data on national systems, any number of countries and family types can be analysed to demonstrate the importance of a particular benefit and the relationship between different categories of benefits. A major drawback of the method is that it describes the system as it should work rather than as it does in reality, discounting some of the complexities of eligibility criteria and regional differences or factors such as the non take-up of benefits (Math, 1996). The method also presents the situation at a single point in time rather than over time, and it selects families that exemplify a range of experience rather than being representative of the main family types in a given society (Eardley, 1996).

Like the observatory, the model family studies and a number of other European-wide projects have drawn on a network of national informants who are experts in the field of study, thereby ensuring that data can be collected, checked and validated with relative ease. From their base in the Netherlands, Willemsen et al. (1995) constituted a

network of researchers and policy makers to analyse the role of
national policies in shaping the relationship between paid work and
the division of labour within households in 13 EU member states.
Rather than collecting quantitative data, informants were asked to
focus on examples of good or poor practice in their own countries.
Hantrais and Letablier (1996) drew together a network of European
researchers who had experience of conducting comparative studies of
families, the family–employment relationship and family policies in
the European Union to analyse and contrast the findings of quantitative and qualitative studies (*Cross-National Research Papers*, 1994–
96). Millar and Warman (1996) called on the knowledge and
expertise of researchers from the 15 EU member states and Norway
to examine the meanings and applications of the concept of family
obligations. They experimented with the vignette technique to
supplement data gathered by more conventional methods (Soydan,
1996). The 12-nation study carried out by Neubauer et al. (1993) at
the Gesellschaft für Familienforschung (Gefam) in Bonn involved
large-scale data collection by the German team across a wider range
of socio-demographic and economic variables. They worked in cooperation with national experts who served as native informants to
access and validate the data.

Much looser networks of researchers have been constituted to
produce edited collections of papers on topics that fall within the area
of family policy, such as the work on the gendering of welfare by
Sainsbury (1994), on intergenerational solidarity by Lesemann and
Martin (1993) and Attias-Donfut (1995), or on reconstituted families
by Meulders-Klein and Théry (1993). The methods exploited by the
contributors to these volumes range from secondary analysis of large-
scale databases to the interpretation of legal documents and qualitative in-depth interviewing, but in most case the authors confine their
material to their own countries, and the editors provide a more comparative, though rarely systematic, overview.

In her comparative analysis of the state and the family in industrialized countries, Gauthier (1996b) single-handedly spanned 22 countries from the turn of the century to the early 1990s, comparing the
development, nature, objectives and scope of family policies as well
as the socio-political contexts in which they were introduced, in an
attempt to draw a typology of models of family policy based on inter-
country differences. To this end, the author used secondary analysis
of large-scale quantitative data in conjunction with documentary
materials and information provided by national authorities.

The problem with many of the studies that seek to be all-
encompassing in their coverage, either of countries or the different

dimensions of policy, is that they tend to suffer from information overload, but without being able to guarantee the comparability of the data assembled. At the other extreme, a number of demographers and economists have used quantitative methods to isolate and analyse specific policy factors and their possible influence on demographic behaviour, but often with inconclusive or conflicting results due to the narrowness of the focus. Ekert-Jaffé (1986) used statistical analysis to examine the possible impact on birth rates of public provision of family allowances in European countries between the early 1970s and 1980s. Gauthier (1991) used multivariate analyses of OECD countries to investigate the effect of family benefits on fertility. Economists and statisticians have analysed the cost of raising children in an attempt to assess the extent to which the financial impact of offspring on families may be attenuated by policy measures. For example, Joshi and Davies (1992), in a study of selected EU member states, used econometric modelling to look at the effects of the level of wages and, more especially, of women's forgone earnings on fertility.

Policy simulations have been applied by Jeandidier (1997) to test the possible effects of family benefits on behaviour in four EU member states. He used the technique in a comparison which identified as a key feature of policy in France the level of benefits accruing to French mothers who are economically active. Grignon and Fagnani (1996) have exploited micro-simulations in a comparative study of selected EU member states to determine whether net income from female economic activity – financial rationality – is the only factor determining the elasticity of women's labour market behaviour.

Gauthier (1996a) criticizes much of the quantitative analysis for its methodological limitations, commenting, for example, on the problem arising from the use of aggregate rather than individual data and the consequent failure to capture the full extent of the population entitled to receive benefits, the impact of actual take-up rates and the full range of services made available to families. These are issues which research like that by the Social Policy Research Unit (SPRU) has tried to overcome by taking account of a broad range of factors.

The studies presented here provide an indication of the large body of material available to those interested in the comparative dimension of family policy. They cover a variety of methodological approaches and of country mixes, but few of them set out systematically to test comparative hypotheses or to develop typologies. A more common objective is to identify trends in a number of countries enabling them to be ranked according to different indicators, to determine, for example, where policy measures appear to be most generous and whether signs of convergence can be detected as far as policy instruments and outcomes are concerned.

Two conclusions can usefully be drawn from this review for the purposes of comparative studies. First, given the number of contextual factors involved in family policy research which crosses national boundaries, the most satisfactory results may be obtained by combining several methodological approaches (Hantrais and Mangen, 1996b). Second, the findings from comparative studies are likely to differ according to the mix of countries involved. When studies are commissioned at European level, generally researchers are not free to select the countries for inclusion, but it is clear that any similarities and differences identified and their intensity and the degree of complexity of the analysis will vary if other subsets or combinations of countries are contrasted, such as the Nordic with the Mediterranean states, or EU member states with Northern America, Eastern Europe or Asian countries.

Conceptualizing Family Policy in European Contexts

Despite the attempts made at international level to standardize the collection of data, statistics remain conventional constructs, which can only be fully understood in a cross-national context if deconstructed and reconstructed in such a way as to reveal the interactive relationships involved in the process. The same limitation applies to institutional and public policy definitions of families. Institutions are not only the producers of statistical definitions and categories, they also provide legal and administrative frameworks, each with its own agenda and its own logic.

Studies of families and family policies which do not seek to unravel this process or to come to terms with the many conceptual issues associated with the family indicators used by policy makers may have difficulties in understanding and interpreting the information collected (Hantrais and Letablier, 1996; van Solinge and Wood, 1997). This section is devoted to an analysis of the ways in which the family policy process has been conceptualized by different actors – statistical agencies, policy makers, public administration – to illustrate the conceptual issues involved.

Statistical definitions of families in Europe

The European observatories, like most institutions studying sociodemographic trends, rely heavily on Eurostat, the Statistical Office of the European Communities created in 1958, for annual demographic data relating to families. The socio-demographic data used by policy makers in predicting the needs arising as a result of trends in family building and structure and to justify policies that may have an impact on families are not unproblematic since statistical categories and concepts are dependent on national traditions and conventions (Desrosières, 1996).

In addition, national data refer to territorial boundaries that are identified for administrative purposes, and which may, or may not, represent a certain degree of cultural identity. Within-country differences can be greater than those between countries, as is the case for Italy, where the northern regions display patterns of economic and social development that are very different from those in the south, or in Germany, where regional administration enjoys a relatively high level of autonomy, and where the social structures of the two Germanys diverged as a result of very different economic and political regimes. The territorial unit is particularly problematic in a policy area such as that of the family where local administration has a high degree of discretion, with the result that access to benefits and take-up can vary significantly from one area to another.

The exercise of producing data at national and, even more so, at supra-national level is premissed on the assumption that they have been collected according to uniform criteria, are measuring the same phenomena and are fit for the purpose of informing policy. The harmonization process that data must undergo if they are to be homogeneous and, thus, comparable involves removing, or eroding, much of the finer contextual detail. Researchers wishing to exploit the output are, thereby, distanced from the object of study and the underlying concepts on which it is founded, and need to return to the broader societal context to locate their findings.

Eurostat has adopted the United Nations' (1987) definition of the family unit based on 'the conjugal family concept'. The UN definition presents the family as a sub-category of a household, composed of couples or singles and the children to whom they are biologically related, generally for so long as these children remain unmarried. It distinguishes between couples living in consensual unions and those who are legally married. The Belgian, German, Greek and Dutch censuses have not, however, included consensual unions, and the age of children is an important source of discrepancies in the absence of a common age limit for childhood (Eurostat, 1995).

Data collected in national censuses generally take private households rather than families as the unit of measurement. Most EU member states adopt the housekeeping unit, but Denmark, Finland,

France and Sweden use the concept of household dwelling which tends to underestimate the number of households. Germany counts twice individuals occupying more than one dwelling, thereby inflating the number of single-person households. Ireland and Greece count everyone present in a dwelling on the census date rather than all persons normally resident. Different practices are followed to identify the reference person: the wife is, for example, taken as the reference person in Denmark for households with children.

According to the definitions used, consensual unions may or may not be recorded. Statistics on lone-parent families are unreliable, both because they form a particularly unstable and heterogeneous category and because they are conceptualized differently from one society to another. If information about the age of children is not provided, the data can be extremely misleading, and it is not always possible to distinguish between different categories of lone parenthood (unmarried, divorced, widowed) (Bradshaw et al., 1996). Statistical tools have also proved inadequate for identifying multiparental families, step-families, reconstituted, blended or re-ordered families, as they have been described, since most national censuses do not provide information about biological relationships (van Solinge and Wood, 1997).

The conclusion can be drawn that cross-national comparisons founded on statistical data for families and households need to be handled with extreme caution for several reasons: differences occur in the construction of the statistical apparatus due to national conventions; social statistics are a response to a specific demand and are constantly being reviewed; the categories adopted may be based on criteria that are not applied uniformly. The family itself should, therefore, be seen not as an immutable and monolithic statistical concept, but rather as a generic term concealing a plurality of family forms.

Public policy definitions of families in Europe

Public policy definitions of the family and of family relationships also reflect differences in national, philosophical and religious traditions and in the legal obligations and responsibilities of family members towards one another (Ditch et al., 1996; Dumon, 1994; Hantrais and Letablier, 1996; Millar and Warman, 1996). As both the commissioners and users of statistical data, policy makers are responsible for formulating definitions of families and households which can be applied in the administration of public services. They must also respond to shifts in socio-economic behaviour and to the demands of pressure groups. The conceptual issues underlying the policy-making process and the political forces influencing decisions are particularly salient from a comparative policy perspective (Hantrais and Letablier, 1996).

Social policy is generally described as family policy when the family is the deliberate target of specific actions, and the measures initiated are designed to have an impact on family resources and, ultimately, on family structure. If the definition of family policy as measures with the family as their target population is applied strictly, it could be argued that many of the provisions monitored by the European Observatory, including child care, parental leave and income tax arrangements, are not properly speaking family policies (Hantrais, 1995). Differences in statistical and administrative definitions of families from one country to another will also affect the applicability of the definition of family policy, and it may be more appropriate to refer to family policies in the plural.

The minimalist view adopted in some countries (Ireland, Italy, the Netherlands and the United Kingdom) is that the state should provide no more than a safety net and that families might be expected to have primary responsibility for their own well-being. When external support is necessary, local communities are the first port of call, and collective provision of welfare may come into conflict with informal support structures. At the other extreme, intervention may be legitimized by the national constitution, which places an obligation on the state to support and promote family welfare, or the policy-making process may be used to encourage a particular family type, such as large families in Greece.

By introducing or modifying legislation that affects the status of individuals within families and households, the state has been encroaching further into family life. Such intervention may be justified on the grounds that rules are needed for governing families in a context of rapidly changing social values (Commaille, 1994), to protect members of the family unit from one another (child abuse), or to oblige them to fulfil their obligations to each other (absent father) (Lefaucheur and Martin, 1995), while also carrying out what may be a constitutional duty towards the family as a basic social institution. Policy makers may be faced with the choice of trying to preserve the legitimate family at all costs, or they may be seeking to protect the interests of individual family members, and in particular those of children (Meulders-Klein, 1993).

Thus, lone parenthood and reconstituted families have progressively become topics of social policy interest (see also chapter 10 of this volume). From being considered as a deviant family form in some countries (Nordic states and France), lone parenthood has been ac-cepted as innovative and deserving of public support (Lefaucheur and Martin, 1993), while recognizing that needs will be different depending upon whether lone parenthood involves a single, divorced, separated or widowed parent. Increasingly, attention is being focused on measures to enable lone parents to become financially independent of the state (Bradshaw et al., 1996). Lone parenthood is often a transitional phase into a new relationship, generally involving a reconstituted, blended or re-ordered family. The phenomenon of family reconstitution has also become a subject for concern among policy makers. The available literature (e.g. Meulders-Klein and Théry, 1993) has provided some valuable insights into the complexity and diversity of reconstituted families and has shown the extent to which they have been recognized and accepted as legitimate concerns for public policy in different national contexts.

Although many of the policy issues are common to most countries in the European Union, marked differences remain in the policy objectives pursued by individual governments. A distinction is often made between policies designed to redistribute resources horizontally and vertically and those intended to affect behaviour, including decisions about the timing and number of child births, and the management of family life (Hantrais and Letablier, 1996). Resources may be redistributed horizontally from individuals or couples without children to those with children in the same income brackets through child benefits and taxation, or vertically from individuals and families on high incomes to those with low incomes, often targeting families most in need through taxation and means testing. In the early years of social security, horizontal redistribution was generally taken for granted. Progressively, awareness has developed of the link between family responsibilities and hardship or poverty, resulting in policies to ensure vertical redistribution to low-income families, particularly in situations where national governments are seeking to reduce welfare spending.

While the principles of horizontal and vertical redistribution have been readily accepted as a family policy objective, attempts to influence family size or structure have met with considerable resistance in many countries. Although differential benefits for children in larger families may be justified and accepted on economic grounds, pronatalist reasons are also evoked for supporting larger families as a means of stemming population decline. Belgium, France, Francoist Spain and Sweden have all followed pronatalist policies at particular times in their history, whereas pronatalism has been rejected in Germany, post-Franco Spain and the United Kingdom.

Another dimension of the family policy debate which is relevant here concerns the extent to which the state should intervene to support different family forms: consensual unions, lone-parent families and reconstituted families. While Germany and Ireland are bound by their constitutions to support the legitimate married couple and Greece focuses on the legitimate child, other countries have progressively been removing the distinction between married and unmarried couples and their children (Ditch et al., 1996). In some cases, support for lone parents may help to ensure that mothers are not excluded from the workforce, as in France or the Nordic states, whereas in Ireland or the United Kingdom (at least until the late 1990s), the intention has been to enable lone mothers to raise their own children (Bradshaw et al., 1996). Less attention has been paid to the needs of reconstituted families.

Overall, Belgium, France, Luxembourg and Germany have been identified as countries with relatively consistent and coherent family policies (Barbier, 1995). The first three have ensured both horizontal and vertical distribution of resources, while Germany has focused on vertical distribution, like the other EU member states, except for the Nordic countries, where more attention has been devoted to equality policies and the interests of children. In the mid 1990s, the main trend was towards increasingly targeted policies, in an effort to make policy more accountable, efficient and open to public scrutiny.

A growing focus of attention among policy makers has been the efforts to ensure that parenting and female economic activity are compatible. The family–employment relationship has been on the political agenda at European level since the mid 1970s, both explicitly as an area targeted in policy and indirectly through measures to protect women as working mothers. Proposals for measures to ensure that family responsibilities can be reconciled with job aspirations have been a recurring theme in EU policy documents, including the 1989 Community Charter of the Fundamental Social Rights of Workers, and the 1994 White Paper on European social policy, which addressed the issue of how to manage caring tasks.

Despite the interest shown in political discourse and the creation in 1986 of the European Childcare Network, subsequently renamed as the Network on Childcare and other Measures to Reconcile Employment and Family Responsibilities, consensus over Community action was for a long time elusive. Even when policy objectives are agreed at European level, they may still be conceptualized differently from one country to another reflecting differences in the patterning of factors, such as the extent and pace of change in behaviour and attitudes towards women as mothers and workers, the wider policy environment, the state of labour markets and national trends in family building and structure.

Analysis of caring arrangements for children and older people brings out differences between member states in the conceptualization of the relationship between the public and private spheres. In Belgium, France and the Nordic states, public provision of child care is relatively generous, whereas it is relatively poor in Ireland, Luxembourg, the Netherlands, Portugal and the United Kingdom. The de-institutionalization of care for disabled and older people in many member states, largely for economic reasons, is found to place a heavy burden on family carers. In the Nordic countries, the state has continued to recognize its responsibility for making formal provision for caring, whereas in Germany and the Netherlands there has been a shift towards care insurance as a means of relieving the pressure on both state and families. In the Mediterranean countries, caring has largely remained a duty expected of family members, with relatively little state support (Attias-Donfut, 1995; Lesemann and Martin, 1993).

In some EU member states, public policy would seem to assist parents in combining paid and unpaid work, either as an equality measure or through a commitment to family well-being and to women as mothers. In Denmark, Finland and Sweden, where women display high levels of continuous economic activity, though often on a part-time basis, governments have introduced a range of provisions as equality measures and in recognition that the state has a duty to support children. As a result, employment and family life are seen as complementary. In France and Belgium, parents are also supported in their efforts to combine employment and child rearing, but patterns of female employment are less continuous, and state provision, in this case, is primarily family centred.

In most of the countries at the geographical centre of Europe, the state has supported mothers who leave paid work to raise children, with the objective of maintaining the family unit as a social institution rather than safeguarding the individual rights of its members. Austria, Germany, Italy, Luxembourg and the Netherlands have all introduced policies that help parents to combine paid work outside the home with child raising, on the basis that one or both parents, most often the mother, will momentarily cease or reduce their economic activity to stay at home and look after young children, with limited state support for child-care provision and, often, with adverse consequences for career progression.

In countries where the level of state support is low, a distinction can be made between those where governments have deliberately avoided interfering in the private lives of individuals, as in Ireland and the United Kingdom, and those where financial constraints and a relatively undeveloped system of social protection have meant that priority has been given to more pressing social problems, despite supportive policy statements, as in the case of Greece, Portugal and Spain. In these two sub-groups, market forces or family networks have generally served as a substitute for state support. Cutting across the two categories are countries where low levels of state intervention have not, however, prevented women from displaying relatively high economic activity rates, either on a full-time continuous or a part-time interrupted basis, as in Portugal and the United Kingdom.

When the combined impact on the family of a whole range of policy measures is considered, an indication can be gained of the apparent effectiveness of policy in bringing about a redistribution of resources towards families and in changing behaviour by creating a family-friendly environment. Austria, Belgium, Denmark, France Germany and Luxembourg emerge as the member states where policy is most supportive of families; Ireland, the Netherlands and the United Kingdom are characterized by their selective support for families in particular circumstances; the Mediterranean countries are shown to concentrate their efforts on low-income families; and the Nordic states seem to provide a supportive environment sensitive to the needs of children and their parents, but without the focus being on the family unit.

Administrative definitions of families in Europe

Even if some measure of agreement can be reached at international level about policy objectives, implementation is likely to take very different forms from one national context to another, due to variations in administrative structures.

In Finland, France, Germany, Greece, Ireland, Italy, Luxembourg, Portugal and Spain, the constitution makes reference to the family. In some cases (Finland, Greece, France and Portugal), the state is committed to supporting family members. In other EU member states (Germany and Luxembourg), it may define the legitimate family, or (Ireland) assign to the state the role of protecting the family unit against outside intrusion. In Italy and Spain, the state is empowered to intervene in family life only if other (private) sources of support prove to be inadequate.

Few countries within the European Union (France, Germany and Luxembourg) have consistently given a high profile to family affairs through designated ministerial appointments. Italy and Spain can be quoted as examples of countries where the backlash of authoritarian regimes has been that family policy has tended to be sidelined (Del Re, 1995; Valiente, 1995).

In most countries, a shift has occurred in civil law concerning the legal rights and duties of family members, with the intention of ensuring the rights of children irrespective of whether they are born in or out of wedlock. Differences can be found in the pace and timing of the liberalization of the laws on divorce, as well as the legal recognition of consensual unions which, in a few cases, includes same-sex relationships. Comparative analysis shows that the Nordic states have tended to lead the way in legitimizing non-traditional family forms (by institutionalizing non-institutional relationships), but the Netherlands were among the first member states to introduce legislation allowing homosexual couples to enter into a cohabitation contract covering property rights and taxation, and the United Kingdom and France have more readily recognized consensual unions and extra-marital births than Ireland, Italy, Luxembourg and the southern European countries (Hantrais and Letablier, 1996).

Analysis of laws on contraception, abortion and medically-assisted reproduction reveals not only national differences but also the impact of cultural and ideological factors and points to the disputes that can arise over the rights of family members or which may bring civil law into conflict with the constitution.

The right of children to have two biological parents, the right of women to procreate a fatherless child and the concept of parental authority and responsibility have been the focus of policy debates in most EU member states. The trend has been towards the removal of the legal subordination of women and children within marriage. In the case of unmarried cohabitation, divorce or separation, consensus has been more difficult to achieve with regard to custody, maintenance and property, not only between countries but also within them. Legal obligations towards stepchildren can involve a moral contract to ensure the upkeep of children, as in Germany, and joint parental authority may be awarded even if the parents are not cohabiting, as in Finland and Sweden (Ditch et al., 1996; Meulders-Klein and Théry, 1993; Millar and Warman, 1996).

Within social security systems, institutions may adopt the 'benefit family' as an administrative unit. Responsibility for administering family affairs (in particular family/child benefits) is dispersed across different government departments (ministries), generally subsumed within social affairs or social security/welfare. Maternity benefits are more likely to be grouped with sickness/health and, in some cases, invalidity and old age. Local governments are generally charged with providing services for families (housing, community and child care), with the result that provision may vary from one area to another. In some countries (Belgian, France, Italy and Luxembourg), family associations provide a powerful lobby for protecting the interests of families. The French case is frequently cited as an example where family movements have grouped together to form a recognized and active social partner (Dumon, 1994).

Eligibility for social protection may vary, depending on how relationships within the family are conceptualized, particularly in the case of non-contributory benefits. From a situation, in the immediate postwar period, when the 'preferred' model of the family among policy makers seemed to be the married couple living together with their children, where the husband was the sole or main breadwinner (Lewis, 1992), progressively women have gained entitlements in their own right, and in some cases (Austria, France and Germany) these rights are extended to recognize unpaid work, for example in pensions, or to cover cohabiting partners (Netherlands).

The definition of dependent children for the purpose of paying out benefits varies from one country to another and is affected by factors such as family size (France, Greece, Ireland, Luxembourg), the rank of the child (France, United Kingdom), age (ranging from 15 in Portugal to 19 in Austria), the length of time spent in education (up to 27 in Austria, Germany and Luxembourg), or the needs of children in particular circumstances (disabled children), to the extent that not all children can be said to have the same value.

The liability to maintain relatives is another area where laws and practices differ: in sum, it can be said that the state assumes much greater responsibility for individual family members (older people, children of lone parents) in the Nordic states. At the other extreme, the wider kinship network is expected to provide support for family members in the Mediterranean countries, again raising the issue of the division between public and private spheres (Millar and Warman, 1996).

For the purposes of levying taxes, the unit of assessment may be the household (Netherlands), the family (France, *quotient familial*) or the legally constituted married couple (Germany, *Ehengattensplitting*). Increasingly, married couples can elect to be taxed separately, although in most cases tax relief is granted for spouses, thereby recognizing the marital relationship. The individualization of tax liability emphasizes the productive capacity of family members and can be considered as an inducement for women to enter paid employment and gain control over their earnings.

Children may or may not be recognized for tax relief. At one extreme, no tax relief is granted (Denmark, Ireland, the Netherlands and the United Kingdom), while, at the other, in addition to tax relief, allowances are granted towards child-care costs (Belgium, France, Greece and Spain).

Non-marital cohabitation has been recognized to different extents in tax law. The shift towards individual taxation has removed or reduced disparities between married and unmarried partners, but in most cases unmarried cohabiting couples continue to pay more than married couples, particularly when only one partner is an earner (Ditch et al., 1996).

In sum, a few countries (France, Germany and Luxembourg), conceptualize the family as an administrative unit to be supported and promoted by the state. Another group of countries pledge themselves, in their constitutions, to support the family unit (Greece, Italy, Ireland, Portugal and Spain), but they may not possess the means required to do so (Mediterranean countries), or they may be reluctant to intervene in private affairs (Ireland, Netherlands and United Kingdom). The Nordic states tend to focus on individual needs, rather than on the family as a unit. Paradoxically, as social protection budgets have become stretched, emphasis has been placed increasingly in many countries on the responsibilities of biological parents to maintain their children and on family means, irrespective of formal relationships, as a substitute for public provision, thereby reinforcing the importance of the family as an administrative unit.

The Value of Comparative Family Policy Analysis

The international studies of family policy undertaken in the 1980s and 1990s have undoubtedly contributed to the body of knowledge about changes in family structure and the relationship between the patterning of family life and employment in EU member states. Such studies have demonstrated the need to develop social indicators to assist policy makers in assessing the policy responses required to meet new social contingencies, for example due to the growth in de-institutionalized family forms (consensual unions, lone parenthood, reconstituted families). Comparative analysis of the interaction between socio-demographic trends and family policy, while producing inconclusive and sometimes contradictory findings, has encouraged speculation about the potential for developing policy diffusion and policy transfer and for promoting convergence of policies, under the impetus provided at supranational level by European legislation. Comparative family policy analysis has also made a valuable input to the public versus private debates and to discussion about the indi-vidualization of welfare benefits and taxation (Luckhaus, 1994), in a context where the family offers a prime example of the operation of the subsidiarity principle. The family as a provider of welfare has been identified as a missing, or underrated, dimension in much of the analysis of welfare regimes, although typologies have begun to be developed which rank or cluster countries according to their family policy solutions to social problems (e.g. Bradshaw et al., 1993a; Millar and Warman, 1996; Neubauer et al., 1993). Finally, and perhaps most importantly, comparative family policy studies have confirmed the interest of exploring the socio-cultural contexts in which policy is embedded and of tracing its historical roots.

Further reading

The main body of literature on comparative studies of family policy is reviewed at the beginning of the chapter. On cross-national comparative methods, see the chapters on statistical traditions (Desrosières, 1996), policy simulation (Eardley, 1996b) and models of welfare mix (Schunk, 1996) in Hantrais and Mangen (1996). For an analysis of the application of the comparative method to the study of families and family policies, see the essentially French perspective presented in the introduction by Commaille and de Singly (1997) to their edited collection of texts by authors from several EU member states, Australia, the United States, Japan and Rumania. On the methodology used in a study of family obligations and responsibilities in EU member states and Norway, see Warman and Millar (1996). For an analysis of concepts and contexts in the study of families and family policies in Europe, see Hantrais and Letablier (1996), and the contributions to *Cross-National Research Papers* vol. 4 issues 1–4, in particular no. 3, which is devoted to 'The family in social policy and family policy'.

For a historical overview of family policies, see Gauthier (1996b). On recent developments/trends in family policies in Europe, see Dumon (1994) and Ditch et al. (1995, 1996). These publications also provide information on the child benefit package for model families. Five of the seven volumes in the series of publications on family change and family policies, produced by the thematic network co-ordinated from the University of Mannheim, provide extensive coverage of different groups of countries: Great Britain, Canada, New Zealand and the United States; Belgium, Switzerland and the Netherlands; France and Southern Europe; Austria, East and West Germany, Hungary and Poland; and the Scandinavian countries.

The two remaining volumes examine the family in industrial society and family policies from a comparative perspective.

A valuable addition for comparative policy analysts to the stock of information on trends in the living conditions of families in the European Union is provided by the European Community Household Panel (ECHP) survey, which was carried out for the first time in 1994 on a sample of some 60,000 households and 170,000 individuals in the then 12 European Community member states. The ECHP yields micro-level data on the population aged 15–84 years to supplement the larger-scale demographic and labour force surveys regularly processed by Eurostat. The early findings from the first wave of the ECHP were published in 1996 by Eurostat in their series *Statistics in Focus. Population and living conditions*, and similar outputs can be expected at regular intervals as subsequent waves are analysed, in addition to more detailed specialized reports and studies. Although the results may be subject to bias due to sample size and variations in response rates, the surveys should come to serve as an important database for comparative analysis over time and space.

7

Full Circle: a Second Coming for Social Assistance?

John Ditch

Introduction

This chapter will look at the development of social assistance programmes, in an international context, since the end of the Second
World War. Every effort will be made to refer to the key studies, data
sources and methods. The dominant characteristics of social assistance provision, in terms of objectives, conditions of eligibility, interactions with other parts of the wider social protection context,
delivery mechanisms, value of benefits and behavioural effects will be
described. Even allowing for the diversity of schemes with the OECD
it is possible to categorize provision according to selected criteria: a
framework for analysis will be presented and discussed.

If the study of social security is located at the more empirically
enriched and theoretically impoverished end of the intellectual spectrum the study of comparative social assistance is rough fodder indeed. Despite there being an enormous literature on social assistance
schemes within a national context, and an almost equally voluminous
literature on poverty, work incentives and living standards (see Ditch
et al., 1998 for a 1,200-item bibliography) there has been surprisingly
little attempt to review structures and trends in the development and
delivery of social assistance on a comparative basis. This is not for
want of importance or even endeavour: it is because the task is
difficult and the results necessarily inclined to description rather than
deep analysis. Before the theoreticians can take off someone has to
put fuel in the tank and ensure that a flight plan has been prepared.
These necessities have now been, more or less, completed: but how
was this task undertaken?

As the saying goes, 'the devil is in the detail', and this is especially true when researching social assistance. No individual, or small team, trained in the traditions and values of one or at most two countries can be completely knowledgeable about the history, structure and impacts of social assistance in more than, say, four or five countries. This is a common and necessary constraint on the comparative method. In large part this practical barrier is breached by recruiting experts from each of the countries to be involved in a given study. A technique used by Eardley et al. (1996a, 1996b) was to establish two panels of experts; a group, one from each of 23 countries, who were officials of the relevant government department or agency and who completed a detailed schedule of questions about the legal basis, administrative structure and general functioning of social assistance; and a second group, composed of researchers who were asked to provide a critical perspective on the strengths and weaknesses of social assistance in their own country. A central team was responsible for appraising the resulting documentation and writing the final reports.

Social assistance systems change with alarming rapidity and it is therefore necessary for research documentation to be updated. This has been regularly undertaken for the European Union countries for only the past three years, by MISSOC (1997) which is contracted by the European Commission to report, descriptively, on developments in social protection on an annual basis. Ditch et al. (1998) have constructed a computer database containing full details of social assistance in 24 OECD countries accurate up to May 1996: the potential exists to revise this material on a regular basis. The longer-term challenge is to reflect on these trends and to theorize the development of social assistance in an international perspective: a task for another day.

What is Social Assistance?

There is no single or universally accepted definition of social assistance. One possible approach is to specify what it is not and then to elaborate what it is. There are three basic methods by which any state can allocate resources to individuals, families or households. These are, first, the 'universal', categorical or contingency benefits, not related to either income or employment status, but allocated to citizens falling within a specified social category. Second, there are social insurance benefits which are related to employment status and contributions record. Third, there are the means-tested or income-related benefits, where eligibility is dependent on an assessment of current or recent income and/or assets. This last category includes a cluster of social assistance programmes and may be further sub-divided.

First, there are general assistance schemes which provide cash benefits for all (or almost all) people below a specified minimum income standard – for example, Income Support in the UK, or Minimex in Belgium, or the Social Assistance and Solidarity Scheme in Turkey. Second, there are categorical assistance schemes which provide cash assistance for specified groups. These are of growing importance and examples include Family Credit and Disability Living Allowance in the UK; Family Income Supplement in Ireland; unemployment assistance in Germany and the Netherlands; social pensions in Italy, almost all New Zealand and Australian benefits, and the Old Age and Disability Assistance scheme in Turkey. Finally, there are the tied assistance schemes which provide access to specific goods or services in either cash or kind. One sub-category, of very great importance, is the range of housing benefits, which have been devised to deal with the long-standing and otherwise intractable problem of housing costs. The other sub-category includes, in the British context, Council Tax Benefit, free school meals, waived prescription charges; in the USA it would include Medicaid.

In any event, and in all contexts, social assistance is a benefit of 'last resort' within social protection systems – but they are not benefits which exist in isolation from other benefits. Their importance within national systems of social protection will be contingent upon the structure, characteristics and success of the economy as indicated by levels of male and female economic activity, employment and unemployment levels, the existence of a minimum wage. The other elements in the social protection system, including the existence and scope of social insurance provision, are also of critical importance.

A Brief History

Almost all countries have developed schemes to provide support and assistance for individuals and their dependants who are otherwise unable to provide for themselves. Historically, these arrangements are often linked to a Poor Law tradition, rooted in the twin principles of less eligibility and workhouse test and came into effect when three other systems of support were shown to have failed: the market which may be expected to provide income through paid activity; the family which may be expected to provide support on the basis of kinship and obligation; and charity, often associated with religious belief and order, providing help as an expression of human solidarity, sometimes on a conditional basis. The expansion of state-provided schemes of assistance was closely associated with the industrial revolution and the need for structures which could respond to the needs of those who were displaced from traditional systems of support while at the same ensuring the creation, transmission and enforcement of a value system which emphasized self-reliance, family obligation and work.

As the nineteenth century progressed so new forms of solidarity developed which were linked to friendly societies and the broader concept of social insurance. The so-called Bismarckian paradigm embodies assumptions about the centrality of work and the practice of complementary contributions linking employee, employer and the state in a binding relationship. In the United Kingdom the principle and practice of social insurance came later, in the early part of the twentieth century, and even then its application was more piecemeal. It was not until the publication of the Beveridge Report in 1942 and the revision and extension of what in Britain was called National Insurance, together with the introduction of categorical benefits, that the character of the social security system was shaped. It was in the immediate post-war period that the values associated with the locally provided Poor Law were formally disavowed and a new system of national assistance introduced (Hills et al., 1994). Critically, it was hoped and expected that this would be little more than a residual safety net for those who (for whatever reason) were either without or had exhausted their entitlement to National Insurance benefits. In the event, and over the next half century, the means-tested social assistance programme became the primary source of income for over 15 per cent of the British population. This growth in dependency has been mirrored in most other industrial countries.

The end of the Second World War stimulated many countries to redesign their social security programmes and in so doing it appeared that two complementary but contrasting models of social protection were consolidated. On the one hand were predominantly European systems based on social insurance and on the other those, for example in the United States, where the market and private insurance prevailed. But dichotomies of this kind are too simplistic. Social security systems mesh with other elements in what have become styled 'welfare regimes' (Esping-Andersen, 1990) to configure more complex and distinctive clusters of provision. This mid-range mapping of social policy is a form of meta-theory which may not fit the specifics of sub-system arrangements such as social assistance. Starting with Titmuss's three (rather) abstract models which distinguish 'institutional', 'residual' and 'achievement–performance' types and move forward to consider Esping-Andersen's more empirically derived categories of 'Conservative/Corporatist' (Austria, France, Germany and Italy), 'Liberal' (Australia, Canada and the USA) and 'Social Democratic' (Scandinavian countries) it is nevertheless impossible to assign social assistance systems on a corresponding basis.

The quest for 'models' and 'welfare regimes' is both fashionable and flawed. Esping-Andersen's framework has been an immense stimulus to research and has become the focus for much criticism. Castles and Mitchell (1991) re-examined empirical data from the Luxembourg Income Study and found, on the basis of achieved outcomes rather than system characteristics, that both Australia and the United Kingdom had been mis-assigned by Esping-Andersen. Lewis (1992) was in the first wave of critics and argued, with some justification, that the central concept of 'de-commodification' (the basis for allocating countries to regime type) was gender biased and ignored the status and contribution of women; moreover, by concentrating on workers, Esping-Andersen privileged the significance of social insurance transfer mechanisms over categorical and assistance-based schemes. Bradshaw et al. (1993a) conducted an international study which examined the package of support for families and arrived at a quite different configuration of welfare types to those identified by Esping-Andersen. The insensitivity of existing models was a stimulus, among others, to the emergence of comparative studies of social assistance in the early to mid 1990s. But this concern needs to be placed in context.

An interest in selective benefits, and by definition this includes social assistance programmes, was given intellectual stimulus during the 1970s and 1980s when the first systematic challenges were made to the dominance of so-called universal values in social provision. Almost imperceptibly there had been a shift towards more means testing, greater conditionality and more targeting. The fiscal consequences of the 1973 oil shock for the major Western economies brought into focus debates about the macro- and micro-economic significance of social security: its affordability on the one hand and its behavioural impacts on the other. Leaving to one side the extent to which debates around the principles of universality and selectivity were a form of shadow boxing, an indulgent intellectual exercise which did not equate to the realities of the real world, there was a clear growth in international concern about the capacity of social insurance schemes, and the appropriateness of categorical benefits, to meet the challenges posed by rising levels of unemployment, new forms of poverty and changing family structures.

The ensuing international debate has been shaped by a belief that the costs of social security have increased to almost unsustainable and certainly uncompetitive levels. Not a universally held commitment, it is one which was advanced throughout the 1980s by the governments of the United Kingdom and the United States. It was also a powerful theme which runs through successive analyses conducted by the OECD (1994c) and although the European Union has not fully bought into this analysis there has been a visible shift in emphasis with policy pronouncements (European Commission, 1995c; Luxembourg Summit, 1997) aimed at increasing competitiveness and employment by reducing non-wage costs on employers and promoting work incentives through detailed changes to the structure and functioning of social security programmes. There are two implications to this trend: first, the assertions and arguments have encouraged a contraction in the scope and duration of social insurance programmes and this, in turn, has contributed to a displacement of 'business' from insurance- to assistance-based systems. Second, within social assistance schemes, there has been a manifest shift in favour of tougher eligibility criteria, more exacting job-search behaviour and attempts at controlling aggregate budget levels.

But if an interest in social assistance has been stimulated by debates about the form and effects of other components of the social protection arena (what might be called the 'push' factors) then there has also been a remarkable growth in the demand for social assistance (the pull factors). Two reinforcing and international trends can be observed. First, there has been a growth in the numbers of unemployed claimants. The impact of new technology on production processes, aligned with a general shift towards employment contraction in the tertiary sectors, reinforced by a marked expansion in female economic activity has altered the composition of the labour market and contributed to higher levels of unemployment. Each cycle of economic recession has resulted in an increased stock of unemployed claimants. Second, there has been a change in the composition, and not just the number, of poor people. Indeed, this trend has been styled the emergence of 'new poverty'. Estimates of the number and characteristics of the new poor do vary and are sensitive to data source and statistical approach used (see Bardone and deGryse, 1994; Bradshaw and Chen, 1997; Ramprakash, 1994). These apparently methodological concerns do interact with substantive policy issues in at least one important sense: in many countries the social assistance rates become the *de facto* poverty lines. That there is an important conceptual and substantive distinction to be drawn between poverty measures and minimum income standards is well explored by

Veit-Wilson (1998) who tersely notes: 'Minimum income standards and benefits may reflect official views about poverty, but they are not scientific facts about it' (p. viii).

Changing family forms, associated with changes to traditional family structures – more lone parents, more cohabitation, less family stability, more divorce – are all contributing to new demands on social assistance schemes. In response to these trends some new policy initiatives are being developed such as family maintenance (child support) programmes which enforce the obligations of absent parents to support their ex-partners and children when they are in receipt of social assistance (see Ditch et al., 1997a and Bradshaw et al., 1996).

All the evidence suggests, however, that it is the same categories of people who are most likely to experience poverty. Eardley et al. (1996a) report that 'households headed by lone parents, by unemployed people, by women, by older people, large households, those without any member in employment or headed by a person with a low level of education, households in certain regions and, in some countries, those working in farming and agriculture, are all more at risk of relative poverty, as measured in studies, than other groups' (p. 22). There is a clear link between poverty and dependence on social assistance mostly because its recipients do not have access to social insurance benefits.

The overall significance of social assistance has been given impetus by international institutions and agencies including the World Bank and the European Union. The former has linked the provision of development aid to emphasis on targeted social protection schemes: 'a comprehensive approach to poverty reduction . . . calls for a program of well-targeted transfers and safety nets as an essential complement to the basic strategy' (World Bank, quoted in Atkinson, 1993, p. 1). The EU has approached the issue from a different perspective, emphasizing the potential for social assistance schemes to provide a guaranteed minimum level of income. Such schemes were already in existence in several countries: in Denmark since 1961, Germany since 1962 and the Netherlands since 1963. Belgium introduced their Minimex scheme in 1974, Luxembourg in 1986, France (the *Revenue Minimum d'Insertion*) in 1988. The United Kingdom has had a general social assistance scheme since 1948. Against this background, in 1992, the European Council adopted a Recommendation (on common criteria concerning sufficient resources and social assistance in social protection systems) which encouraged all EU countries to include a minimum income scheme in their portfolio of social protection programmes. Indeed, Guibentief and Bouget (1997) argue that 'guarantee of resources can be definitively regarded as having become a new element in the "social contract" in Europe' (p. 109).

The growth in social assistance, and the adoption of the European Council Recommendation, does not obviate any of the problems and deficiencies inherent in means-tested programmes. Whereas the International Monetary Fund and the World Bank see only virtue in a well-targeted social assistance programme there is a library of empirical research which records the problems. For example, the mechanics of means testing result in low take-up (van Oorschot, 1995), intrusive enquiries, stigma, poverty and unemployment traps, high administrative costs and the creation of social divisions. Equally, social assistance programmes focus on poverty relief rather than on some of the other legitimate objectives which may be set for social security policy: protection against risk, horizontal equity, redistribution over the life cycle and the promotion of social cohesion (Eardley et al., 1996a, p. 23).

The European Commission's Annual Report on Social Protection for 1995 (European Commission, 1995c) has summarized governments' responses to these challenges in the following terms: in respect of expenditure on social security that there has been a growth in targeting, means testing, taxation of benefits together with tighter and more exacting rules of eligibility and conditionality. In a wider frame there have been efforts to displace costs from the state towards private-sector initiatives – especially in the field of pensions – with a view to encouraging self-reliance. Equally, and reinforced at every European Council meeting, is an emphasis on active as opposed to passive measures to prevent long-term benefit dependency.

What Policy Objectives for Social Assistance?

In an international context there are two key aims for social assistance. First is to prevent extreme hardship among those with no other resources. Almost all OECD countries (the only exceptions being Greece and Turkey) have some form of scheme which seeks to achieve this objective. A major problem rests, of course, in attempting to define, in operational terms, what constitutes the minimum level to be guaranteed (Veit-Wilson, 1998). Such measures vary within as well as between countries: in some contexts budget surveys or other cost of living measures are used (the Australian government is currently pursuing a review of adequacy using this methodology); there are technical issues to do with the definition and measurement of poverty or inequality and the refinement of equivalence scales to take account of households (benefits units) of different size and

composition. Being able to focus (target) resources on specific categories and then monitor/evaluate the effectiveness with which resources can be transferred and with what outcomes for recipients is a
key challenge for policy makers and researchers alike. The second
aim is to prevent social marginalization and exclusion. Although
there have been difficulties in defining these concepts they have
gained currency in both continental Europe and the UK: emphasis is
placed on the capacity of individuals to participate in society and fulfil
their individual potential.

Although there is not necessarily incompatibility between these
aims (financial adequacy and integration) it is clear that although the
latter is logically contingent upon the former, it is not an inevitable
consequence of it. In other words, in some predominantly Anglo-
Saxon countries greater emphasis is placed on the relief of hardship
than may be placed on the promotion of social integration. However,
the second aim can be viewed in two ways: positive and negative.
Measures can be taken which actively encourage and facilitate individual growth, development and social integration (linked to notions
of social cohesion, solidarity and stability) or, on the other hand,
measures which are seen to minimize the disincentives to paid employment and the promotion of independence and individual (or
familial) responsibility. Those pursuing growth place emphasis
on education and training, social services and community work.
Those wishing to avoid disincentive effects focus on conditions
of eligibility, the interaction of social assistance rates with earnings
levels and opportunities (and costs) associated with moving to either
part-time or full-time work.

Finally, overlaying almost all schemes, irrespective of policy objectives, has been an international concern to contain or restrain total
expenditure on social assistance to a level which can be financed
without risking the consensus required for the funding of social protection schemes. There is clear evidence that policy change is being
driven by expenditure constraint. However, as is so often the case,
these objectives are rarely articulated in an unambiguous manner;
moreover, they are neither congruent in or through time.

Trends in Expenditure

Allowing for definitional uncertainty and problems about the availability of comparable data the research found that in 1992 the level of
funding on social assistance, expressed as a fraction of GDP, ranged
from 0.1 per cent in Greece (which has no general assistance scheme)
to 13 per cent in New Zealand, where almost all benefits are resource

Table 7.1   *Cash assistance as a proportion of GDP 1980–1992*

Country	1980	1985	1992	Change 1980–92 (% of GDP)	Index 1992/1980 1980 = 100
Australia	5.4	6.0	6.8	1.4	126
Austria	1.0	1.0	1.3	0.3	124
Belgium	0.4	0.6	0.7	0.2	156
Canada	1.6	2.0	2.5	0.9	156
Denmark	n/a	0.9	1.4	n/a	n/a
Finland	0.7	1.1	0.4	0.3	438
France	0.6	1.0	1.3	0.7	205
Germany	1.0	1.6	1.6	0.6	160
Greece	0.1	0.1	n/a	0.0	100
Iceland	n/a	n/a	0.2	n/a	n/a
Ireland	3.0	4.5	5.1	2.2	174
Italy	1.1	1.3	1.5	0.4	135
Japan	0.4	0.4	0.3	−0.1	60
Luxembourg	n/a	n/a	0.4	n/a	n/a
Netherlands	1.7	2.5	2.2	0.5	133
New Zealand	8.6	9.2	13.0	4.4	151
Norway	0.1	0.3	0.7	0.5	486
Portugal	0.2	0.6	0.4	0.2	22
Spain	0.3	0.8	1.2	1.0	473
Sweden	0.8	1.2	1.5	0.7	186
Switzerland	n/a	n/a	0.8	n/a	n/a
Turkey	n/a	n/a	0.5	n/a	n/a
UK	1.8	3.0	3.9	2.1	212
USA	1.1	1.0	1.3	0.2	115

based (table 7.1). Categorical assistance for specific claimant groups is more important than general programmes in most continental EU member states, while tied (housing) assistance is especially important in the UK, France and Sweden.

Four countries exhibited an increase in social-assistance spending over the period of more than one percentage point of GDP: Australia, New Zealand, Ireland and the UK (over two percentage points when housing assistance is included). Japan is the only country to have registered a declining share. When proportionate increases are examined, the picture changes. The English-speaking countries operate the most extensive social assistance programmes and the smallest assistance schemes are found in Greece, Japan, Portugal, Spain and Switzerland. When categorical schemes are included, Australia and New Zealand predominate and Ireland also joins the high-coverage group. In most countries, but especially the UK, Canada, Ireland, Germany and the Nordic countries between 1980 and 1992, there was a significant expansion in the number of recipients of social assistance. Disaggregating the data into specific claimant groups is not easy but the clear indications are that old age has become less important as a trigger for claiming assistance, while disability, unemployment and lone parenthood have become more significant. In most countries, between one-half and two-thirds of claimants are single people and only one-third (on average) have children.

Operating Principles

All social assistance schemes operate with the same underlying rationale: that eligibility for benefit should be established on the basis of an assessment of means, taking into account established conventions of family obligation and reciprocity. Attempts to shift responsibility for support on to the extended family have been mostly unsuccessful just as attempts to individualize entitlement and payment has been mostly frustrated. As ever, a complicating factor in the administration of social assistance is the treatment of housing costs: in some countries it is included within general social assistance and in others there is a separate, and general, housing benefit scheme. Only three countries (Italy, Spain and Turkey) do not have either a generalized scheme for housing assistance or an element within social assistance payments to meet housing costs. However, there are also differences between countries in whether the housing element of social assistance is paid as a specific supplement or is meant to be met out of the standard assistance payments. Belgium and The Netherlands are the two main examples of the latter approach, although where claimants face particularly high housing costs any extra help is purely discretionary in Belgium, whereas there is access to a regulated housing benefit scheme in the Netherlands. Switzerland also has a largely discretionary approach to the treatment of housing costs, and this varies according to individual cantons.

There is no avoiding administrative complexity in assessment and delivery of social assistance. A key difference is between countries which are organized on a centralized, integrated and national basis (like the UK and Australia) and where there are common conditions of eligibility and payment and those countries (like Italy, Norway and

Switzerland) which have structures which allow for the devolution of responsibility for combinations of policy and administration to the local level (Ditch et al., 1997b). A frequently observed pressure is experienced in those localities where demand for social assistance is high but where capacity to fund schemes is limited. Although there is diversity of policy objectives and delivery structures there is common concern to streamline administration and to increase the role of computers in assessment, payment and the detection and prevention of fraud. Non-governmental organizations (NGOs) play an uneven role in the administration of social assistance. In some countries, such as the UK, they are predominantly styled as a 'poverty lobby' seeking to campaign and influence policy; in others, such as Switzerland, they are a form of shadow social assistance structure offering an alternative to the highly stigmatized formal arrangements; in other countries, and there are examples in Canada and New Zealand, NGOs are organized to provide supplementary assistance in the form of food banks. In many countries, especially those with a Catholic tradition, charities have a special role in responding to urgent and exceptional needs.

Conditions of Eligibility

The situation is necessarily very complex: in general it is unusual to guarantee minimum income through one generalized, all-encompassing, means-tested benefit. Indeed, this is an arrangement mostly confined to the Nordic countries (Ditch et al., 1997b). In an international context the majority preference is for separate coverage by population category, but here a number of approaches must be distinguished from one another. One group, principally the Southern Mediterranean countries (Greece, Italy, Portugal, Spain and Turkey) organize a limited minimum income protection scheme principally in relation to specific groups, such as older or disabled people, families with children or unemployed people (with unemployed assistance usually available on a temporary basis). In some of these countries there is then a discretionary local assistance back-up (see Ditch, 1996). Another group, including the UK and the other Northern European countries, have one primary and inclusive national assistance benefit, together with a number of other categorical benefits serving different functions. In the case of the UK, for example, Family Credit and Disability Working Allowance have specific functions in relation to work incentives and low pay, and thus potentially reach further up the income scale than the general social assistance benefit (Income Support).

Minimum age thresholds

In most countries entitlement to benefit can only be established after an individual reaches the age of 18 years. Australia and New Zealand both differ in making special unemployment or training benefits available from the age of 16, and Germany and Japan have no specific lower age limit, though the assumption is still that parents would normally support children at least until they leave school. France and Luxembourg stand out in restricting access to the *Revenu Minimum d'Insertion* (RMI) and the *Revenu Minimum Garanti* (RMG) to those aged at least 25 and 30 respectively (though minimum-age thresholds are generally not applied to persons looking after dependent children). While in France some unemployed people under 25 may have access to insurance benefits on the basis of previous work, or to training courses and special employment schemes, it is clear that young people are relatively lacking in support through social assistance compared to those in most other countries with general schemes.

In general, while comparison shows that restricting access to benefit in normal circumstances to those over 18 is not unusual, this policy also has to be seen alongside broader policies on youth training and employment, and on access to non means-tested unemployment benefits. In a number of other countries, including Belgium, Denmark, Finland, Norway and Sweden, if young people are unemployed they may have access to non-contributory unemployment benefits, even if these are sometimes set at a level below that of social assistance. Others, such as Germany, the Netherlands and the UK, attempt to meet this need through special training or employment schemes, but with varying degrees of success.

Residence and nationality conditions

As discussed in chapter 11 of this book, entitlement to social assistance is often contingent upon either a test of nationality, citizenship or residence. The European Union's policy of free movement of workers in a single market makes this a live issue at present, particularly in the light of controversy over immigration from outside the Union. More than half the countries in the OECD require some period of prior residence, in addition to citizenship of the relevant country or of another with which there is a reciprocal agreement. Within the European Union, the main exceptions are Belgium, Germany, Ireland, Italy, The Netherlands and Portugal. The most restrictive are, again, France and Luxembourg, where eligibility for the main assistance benefit is limited to those with ten years residence (or three years continuous, employed residence), and ten years residence out of the previous 20 years respectively. In Luxembourg, registration with a municipality is also required. Until 1992 Belgium required five years recent residence or ten years over a lifetime, but this was abolished as a result of a ruling in the European Court. Now only formal registration with a municipality is required, though this can still act as a further restriction – particularly for homeless people or others without fixed addresses. Denmark requires three years' residence from EU citizens, while some regions in Spain impose their own varying prior residential conditions. The UK introduced an 'habitual residence' test in 1995 which brought provisions into line with those prevailing elsewhere in the EU.

One of the groups most likely to face exclusion from or separate treatment in social assistance are recent migrants from outside the EU, especially refugees and asylum seekers (see also chapter 11 of this volume). The economic vulnerability of refugees and other recent migrants means that in some countries they make up a substantial part of the social assistance caseload. There is clearly a tension between principles of inclusiveness, which are often expressed in policy statements, and anxieties about immigration, dependency and abuse of welfare benefits. In principle, the majority of countries take a broadly similar approach to this question, which gives people accepted as refugees, and accorded rights of residence, the same eligibility for assistance benefits as other citizens or legal residents. During the period of adjudication most countries apply special (temporary) provisions to meet the need of refugees. It is often the case, however, that these arrangements do not carry legal entitlement or rights of appeal. In Sweden, where local authorities have to meet most of the costs of providing assistance, central government provides extra funds to meet the expenses of help for refugees during the first three years of their residence in the country.

The economic and political pressures arising from both legal and illegal immigration have led some countries in the last few years to place further restrictions on benefit entitlement. Germany, for example, which has accepted substantially higher numbers of both war refugees and economic migrants than most European countries since 1989, faces particular pressures both from re-unification and from its geographical position on the borders of the Union. Since November 1993 asylum seekers have lost eligibility for general assistance and have to rely on special, reduced cash or in-kind payments. Debates in a number of other countries too have focused on apparent cases of fraud among immigrants, or special treatment accorded to them, though frequently the real situations turn out to be less dramatic than suggested by newspaper reports. Overall, the question of inclusion or exclusion within eligibility for social assistance benefits by age and by residential or nationality conditions is likely to remain a live issue in many of the countries in the study. This was highlighted by the Proposition passed in 1994 in the US State of California, which denies illegal migrants access to welfare and other social services.

Value of Benefits

Eardley et al. (1996a) collated detailed information about the value of social assistance benefits for different types of claimant using a 'model families matrix' methodology. All income and expenditure data (relating to May 1992) were converted using purchasing power parities. Common assumptions were specified with respect to housing costs, local taxes, health costs and education and child care costs. There was immense variation in the levels of payments: for example, after housing costs, and for a couple aged 35 years with two children (aged 7 and 14), the value of benefits ranged from £222 per month in purchasing power parities in New York to £607 per month in Sweden. For a retired couple the value of the social assistance package (after housing costs) ranged from £139 per month in Italy to £546 in Denmark. For a lone parent with one child (aged 7) the range was from £80 in New York to £513 in Switzerland.

The apparent generosity of one country when compared to another varies according to precise location of benefit recipient, his/her age, status and family responsibilities. For example, most countries provided relatively larger assistance to people over retirement age: this is especially the case for Canada, France, Greece and the USA. Only a few appeared to pay higher benefits to working-age single people and couples than to pensioners. A composite ranking, based on percentages from the mean for nine family types, puts Iceland at the top, after housing costs, heading a group which includes the Nordic countries, Luxembourg, The Netherlands and Australia, all with levels of more than 20 per cent above the mean. The next cluster of countries, led by the United Kingdom, includes the USA (New York), Japan, France, Canada and Germany. The third, and final group, with social assistance levels more than 10 per cent below the mean, included Belgium, New Zealand and the Southern European countries. (See table 7.2.) When the level of social assistance is compared with average gross wages (before housing costs), the relative position of France, Finland and Sweden improves – countries where

Table 7.2 *Social assistance: percentage difference from the mean – all cases after housing costs (1992)*

Country	%
Iceland	50
Switzerland	41
Luxembourg	35
Netherlands	33
Finland	31
Denmark	29
Italy	28
Norway	25
Sweden	24
UK	11
Japan	8
USA (New York)	6
France	4
Ireland	2
Canada	2
Austria	−2
Germany	−5
Belgium	−12
New Zealand	−18
Spain	−41
Portugal	−90
Greece	−119

average gross earnings are relatively low due to high social insurance contributions from employers constituting a deferred wage.

The countries with the very highest levels of payment such as Switzerland (Canton of Fribourg), Luxembourg, The Netherlands, the Nordic countries and Australia share certain characteristics in common: relatively high levels of GDP per capita, traditionally low levels of unemployment and social assistance schemes which are both residual and locally administered. Moreover, they also have strict means tests and in the Nordic countries there are limited capital and earnings disregards and a firm emphasis on claimants returning to the labour market. In summary, there would appear to be a relationship between generosity of benefit and small numbers of claimants.

Conditionality Rules

In the great majority of countries, there is a work test in operation which usually requires that recipients register as unemployed and establish that they are actively looking for work. There is nothing unusual about this for recipients of working age: indeed, this is a principle rooted in the Poor Law tradition. The exceptions to this include Greece, where the only general payments are made on a one-off basis, and a work test for recurrent eligibility is not relevant. In addition, in Japan, outside Reykjavik in Iceland, and in Switzerland it appears that the requirement to seek work is not a formal rule, but that there are very strong expectations that individuals will make full use of their capacities.

The past five to eight years have seen a systematic and almost universal extension of the work-test rules. To the forefront of these developments have been, for example, Ontario (Canada) where a workfare programme has been implemented requiring employable claimants to work for their social assistance benefits. The United Kingdom introduced a Jobseekers' Allowance in October 1996 which is paid on the basis of an unemployed person being available for, and actively seeking, employment. In the United States the Personal Responsibility and Works Opportunity Act (1996) ended the Aid to Families with Dependent Children programme and replaced it with the Temporary Assistance for Needy Families block grant programme to states. Although arrangements differ from state to state there are some, like Wisconsin, which has replaced its entire welfare assistance programme with a scheme which requires all recipients, with the exception of those with children under three months, to be engaged in work-related activities in return for assistance.

In virtually all countries, work tests are not applied, or are more relaxed, for people who are ill or experience disabilities, or who are over or approaching retirement age. The major variations relate to lone parents, in particular to the age of children who exempt lone parents from the requirement actively to seek work. The most liberal provisions apply in Ireland, the United Kingdom, Australia and New Zealand, where lone parents are not required to seek work until their youngest child is 16 years (or older). Germany is also relatively liberal in this respect, as lone parents must normally seek part-time work when their youngest child is at school, and full-time work when the child is 14 or over. In Norway, lone parents receiving the Transitional Allowance are not required to seek work until the youngest child turns ten years of age. In Luxembourg and the Netherlands, the qualifying ages are six years and five years respectively. In Austria and Finland, the qualifying age is three years, while in Sweden the age is being liberalized from about 15 months to three years. In both Sweden and Denmark, however – the two countries with the strongest expectation of work or work seeking – municipalities are required to provide child care for lone parents looking for work. In France, the extent to which lone parents receiving the RMI would be expected to engage in 'insertion' activities varies both by *départements* and according to individual circumstances. Those with children under three receiving the *Allocation de Parent Isolé* are not required to seek work (see Bradshaw et al., 1996).

Most social assistance schemes employ sanctions against those who fail the work tests and these range from full loss of benefits either through ineligibility or suspension, or loss of part of benefits for defined periods. There are also schemes offering incentives to return to work, or to set up as self-employed. Specific incentives were identified in Australia (from March 1995), Ireland, Luxembourg, the Netherlands, Norway, Sweden, the United Kingdom, and the United States. In most cases these appear to be small extra supplements, or lump-sum grants, although a number of countries also made available loans and grants under their various special assistance arrangements for people wanting to start up in self-employment.

Income Tests and Related Arrangements

Most countries appear to provide 'free areas' under which benefits are not reduced, or provide equivalent disregards of income or earnings. The situation is not entirely clear in the case of Iceland, Italy, Japan, Spain, Sweden, Switzerland and Turkey. The rules in Denmark and Finland also appear to allow for some discretion in the provision of disregards, although they are apparently not often applied. Where levels are stated clearly, disregards were lowest in the United States (apart from for food stamps), followed by Belgium and the United Kingdom. The disregards were most generous in Ireland, Australia and New Zealand, as well as in Luxembourg. The disregards are set as percentages of earnings in Canada, France and the Netherlands, and as a percentage of the minimum wage in Portugal.

In the majority of countries, social assistance is reduced in relation to net income, although in Australia, Denmark (from 1994), Luxembourg, New Zealand and Portugal it is gross income that is taken into account. Virtually all social assistance schemes operate an income test with a withdrawal rate of 100 per cent. The exceptions are Australia, New Zealand, and Ireland for lone parents since July 1994 and Portugal for social pensioners. It is evident that arrangements in

Australia and New Zealand are the most liberal, although this reflects the absence of social insurance benefits. It should also be noted that in these countries the income taken into account is gross and not net of tax, so that the effective withdrawal rate will be increased over income ranges where income is also subject to tax. The income test – or rather the tax surcharge – is most relaxed in the case of recipients of superannuation in New Zealand.

Conclusion

Can any order be adduced from this diversity of policy and experience? The answer rather depends upon the criteria to be applied: legal frameworks or entitlement rules would give one set of groupings (Lødemel and Schulte, 1992); administrative systems and the extent of national or local responsibility would give another, as would a framework based on the value of benefits or the effectiveness of poverty alleviation (Leibfried, 1991). In the mid 1990s and on the basis of data collected earlier in the decade, Eardley et al. (1996a) identified no less than seven categories or types; they are reported here. A later article deriving from the same research (Gough et al., 1997) presented no less than eight (broadly similar) social assistance regimes.

1.   Selective welfare systems: Australia and New Zealand
These countries remain unique in that all benefits are means tested. There are several categorical programmes, nationally organized, inclusive and rights based. The means testing is carefully constructed and monitored and is implemented in a consistent way. Assets and earnings disregards are relatively generous. Although principles and structures are similar the value of benefits vary, with Australia being relatively generous and New Zealand relatively parsimonious.

2.   The public assistance state: USA
In the early 1990s the USA exhibited an extensive set of means-tested benefits, arranged in hierarchy of acceptability and stigma. Assets tests were generally tough, but there were in-built earnings disregards and work incentives in every scheme. Benefit levels varied from state to state but tended to be low both in comparison with other countries and in relation to domestic poverty lines. Procedural rights, on the other hand, were well entrenched.

3.   Welfare states with integrated safety nets: Britain, Canada, Ireland and Germany

This is a varied group of countries, but in the early 1990s they had several common features. Income Support in the UK had become a large, national, general programme providing an extensive safety net at or below social insurance levels. After housing costs were taken into account the levels of payment were above the OECD average. Rights to benefit are relatively well entrenched and the means test continues to contain important disregards, with some work incentives for people with children through Family Credit. Ireland is at first sight a mix between this and the antipodean pattern. There are numerous categorical assistance schemes covering a high proportion of the population with means tests and entitlements on a par with those in Britain. But even in the early 1990s it was moving towards a more integrated system.

Both Canada and Germany are federal states and thus exhibit regional variations. These are considerable in Canada, but in other respects the Canadian Assistance Plan had much in common with Britain. However, the Canada Health and Social Transfer which came into effect in April 1996 inaugurated a new and more devolved pattern of relationships. Germany has also developed in a similar way, though from different historical antecedents: *Sozialhilfe* is, despite its federal-Länd structure, geographically equitable, codified, rights based, extensive and of average generosity (see Ditch et al., 1997b).

4. Dual social assistance: France and the Benelux countries
These countries provide categorical assistance schemes for specific groups, but have supplemented these with newer programmes providing a general basic safety net. Local discretion remains, but is now firmly placed within a national regulatory framework. Assets tests are moderately flexible, as are earnings disregards. But benefit levels vary considerably between generous Netherlands and Luxembourg, and below-average Belgium.

5. Rudimentary assistance: Southern Europe and Turkey
National categorical assistance schemes covered specific groups, mainly elderly and disabled people. Otherwise there was local, discretionary relief provided by municipalities or religious charitable bodies (nationally regulated in Greece and Turkey). Means testing was not especially stringent and, apart from Turkey, obligations do not extend beyond the nuclear family. Money assistance was often linked to the provision of social work and other services. Benefits remain very low and for some groups and geographical areas, non-existent.

6.   Residual social assistance: the Nordic countries
Historically social assistance was a residual component of the wider
programme of social protection. However, the growth in unemployment in the late 1980s and early 1990s posed a considerable challenge. Each country has a single general scheme with relatively high
benefit levels. Though there are national regulatory frameworks (to
varying degrees), the role of local authorities is substantial and links
with social work and social care persist. Strict means tests combine
with a view of family financial responsibilities which place more
emphasis than in most countries on the individual, particularly in
relation to cohabitation. General citizenship-based appeal systems
modify the discretionary aspects of assistance in all countries except
Norway.

7.   Highly decentralised assistance with local discretion: Austria and
Switzerland
These countries contain elements of both the Nordic and Southern
European models. In the Alpine countries, assistance consists of
localized, discretionary relief, linked to social work and with wider
kin obligations. However, benefit levels are significantly above average – but are claimed by small numbers. This is partly because of a
record, at least until recently, of full male employment. However,
take-up also appears to be low, which is attributed to stigma and the
substantial powers of intervention accorded to local social welfare
workers.

The past half-decade has seen further developments in the form and
extent of social assistance within the OECD countries. There are
indications that three categories of countries can now be discerned
(see Ditch and Oldfield, 1998). One group, 'the consolidators' have
not engaged in any significant policy developments beyond the rou-
tine uprating of benefit levels and other minor administrative changes
(Austria, Belgium, France, Germany, Greece, Italy, Norway, Spain,
Sweden and Switzerland). Although debates are underway in both
France and Italy the capacity for change is limited. Two countries,
Portugal and Turkey, however, might be styled 'extenders' because
they have introduced or substantially extended what were previously
meagre social assistance schemes. The predominantly English-
speaking countries of Australia, Canada, New Zealand, the UK and
the USA – the 'innovators' – have all introduced radical changes to
key benefits or operating systems. New conditionality rules, a
refound concern to administer schemes via local providers and a
commitment to contain benefit expenditure against the background

of rising benefit dependency: precisely the issues which fired debates about Poor Law provision about 200 years ago. *Plus ca change*!

Further reading

Despite the importance of social assistance there have been few international studies of its growth, current structure and effectiveness. The most comprehensive and detailed was undertaken by Eardley et al. (1996a, 1996b) and subsequently updated by Ditch et al. (1998). Guibentief and Bouget (1997) undertook a review of minimum income policies in the European Union and Veit-Wilson (1998) has examined the ways in which the governments in ten countries define minimum incomes. Descriptive information on EU social assistance programmes is now to be found in the MISSOC Reports (annual).

The research conducted by Eardley et al. (1996a, 1996b) specified three broad aims: first, to compile, on a country-by-country basis, descriptions of the structure and functioning of social assistance schemes; this was to be illustrated by data on funding, expenditure and claimant numbers, recent policy developments and an assessment of overall performance. Second, on a more thematic and comparative basis, the aim was to analyse trends over time and to seek similarities and differences, strengths and weaknesses; and third, to compare the value of assistance payments for different types of claimant by examining the replacement rates, implicit incentive structures and behavioural effects. Particular attention was paid to the following topics: conditions of entitlement, coverage, benefit levels, means testing, fraud control, emergency and exceptional payments, help with housing costs, benefits 'in kind', interaction with other social security benefits and the role of non-governmental organizations. This chapter draws heavily on that work which was conducted under the direction of the author.

8

Comparative Approaches to Long-term Care for Adults

Susan Tester

Introduction

Although long-term care for adults is a key social policy issue in the late 1990s, until recently the topic has been neglected in comparative social policy. This may reflect policy makers' and policy analysts' lack of priority for the groups concerned, as well as difficulties in defining and analysing forms of care which cross organizational and professional boundaries. Long-term care has gained prominence largely because of politicians' alarm over increasing costs in an area of risk inadequately covered by the welfare states and social insurance systems developed in many industrial societies earlier in the twentieth century. Demographic aging resulting from falling mortality and fertility rates, and increasing numbers of people with disabilities in adulthood and later life, have focused attention on potential rising needs for care and on seeking new methods of paying for long-term care (see, e.g., Vincent, 1996). Long-term care is not only a key political issue, but also an appropriate current focus for comparative social policy. Cross-national research on long-term care reflects shifts in emphasis in social and economic policies, social welfare provision, social policy analysis and the comparative study of social policy.

A useful introduction to the topic is provided by Laing's (1993) definition of long-term care as embracing 'all forms of continuing personal or nursing care and associated domestic services for people who are unable to look after themselves without some degree of support, whether provided in their own homes, at a day centre, or in an NHS or care home setting' (p. 18). The terminology used in discussing this topic area in the United Kingdom includes 'long-term care', 'continuing care', 'community care' and 'social care'. The question of defining such terms in a comparative context is discussed later in the chapter. Adults with long-term care needs include those with physical disabilities and illnesses, mental health problems and learning disabilities; older people with such disabilities and health problems will be the main focus of this chapter. Examples are drawn mainly from Europe, with some references to member countries of the Organisation for Economic Cooperation and Development (OECD).

The aims of the chapter are: to identify key policy issues and trends in the topic area; to discuss the advantages and disadvantages of comparative approaches to this topic; to identify and discuss key conceptual, theoretical and methodological issues in comparative research in this area; to review theoretical, conceptual and methodological approaches used in cross-national studies; and to identify issues for comparative social policy research on long-term care for adults in the twenty-first century.

Key policy issues and trends

Key policy issues on paying for and on delivering long-term care should be considered in the context of cost-containment policies of recent decades, following periods of economic recession, and of reduction in the role of the state particularly by governments with New Right ideologies, such as the Thatcher and Reagan governments in the United Kingdom and United States in the 1980s (Tester, 1996, p. 15).

Politicians and policy makers are concerned about increasing costs of social protection, including pensions, disability benefits, health and social care, for older people with long-term care needs (OECD, 1988, 1996a). Debate continues on issues such as who should pay for long-term care; what should be the relative contributions of public and private sources of finance; whether to introduce compulsory care insurance; whether support for individuals should be in cash or in care services; whether family carers should receive payment for care; and to what extent limited resources should be targeted at those in greatest need (Pacolet et al., 1994; Richards, 1996; Joseph Rowntree Foundation Inquiry, 1996; Glennerster, 1997). Issues in the delivery of long-term care are debated in the context of humanitarian policy aims of caring for people in their own homes and providing appropriate services. Major issues include the balance between sectors of the mixed economy of welfare; the co-ordination of health, social and housing services, and whether to separate housing and care (Houben, 1997); and how to tailor services to the needs of individuals and support their carers (Baldock and Evers, 1992; Evers and Svetlik, 1993; Hugman, 1994).

Such policy issues have been addressed since the 1980s in cross-national research on the care of older people, particularly in Europe, reflecting the development of the European Union and the focus provided by the European Year of Older People and Solidarity between the Generations, 1993. Several projects reviewed older people's living conditions and the provision of services in different national contexts. Some of these projects formed part of large-scale research programmes. For example, Age Care Research Europe (ACRE) conducted a programme of research on home care delivery systems for older people in nine countries (Illsley, 1987; Jamieson and Illsley, 1990; Jamieson, 1991). The European Centre for Social Welfare Policy and Research in Vienna undertook a project on shifts in the welfare mix, including national studies of health and social care in 14 countries (Evers and Svetlik, 1991). The European Centre also co-ordinated a study on innovations in care for older people in three European countries (Kraan et al., 1991). The European Foundation for the Improvement of Working and Living Conditions undertook research on family care of dependent older people in 11 countries (Jani-Le Bris, 1993; Steenvoorden et al., 1993). The European Commission's Observatory on Older People carried out research on social and economic policies in 12 member states (Walker et al., 1993; Walker and Maltby, 1997). The OECD undertook a review of policies on caring for frail elderly people in member countries (OECD, 1994b, 1996a).

Other research examined specific topics such as paying for care. Glendinning and McLaughlin (1993) focused on support for informal care in six countries and the UK. A study of payments for care in 16 countries compared payments to recipients of care, informal carers and paid volunteers (Evers et al., 1994). Comparative research on social protection for older people in need of long-term care developed an earlier study of services and policies in 12 EC countries (Nijkamp et al., 1991). A study of systems of support in six member states (Pacolet et al., 1994) was followed by a study of all 15 member states (Pacolet et al., 1998). The organization and financing of home care in 15 EU countries were compared by the Netherlands Institute of Primary Health Care (NIVEL) (Hutten and Kerkstra, 1996). Studies drawing mainly on secondary sources and the authors' research experience include Davies's (1992) study of care management; Giarchi's (1996) comparison of care for older people in 29 countries;

a study of social care in Europe (Munday and Ely, 1996) and an earlier directory of European social services (Munday, 1993); and studies of caring for older people in Europe (Hugman, 1994; Tester, 1996).

Cross-national trends in responses to the issues on paying for and delivering care are identified through such research (see, e.g.: Baldock and Evers, 1992; OECD, 1996a). Economic and humanitarian aims are combined in the trend towards caring for people in their own homes rather than in institutions, providing social rather than medical care, informal rather than formal care, as seen for example in the principle of 'substitution' in the Netherlands (Baldock and Evers, 1992, p. 302; Tester, 1996, p. 20). The main trend in welfare pluralism has been a shift in the balance between sectors away from state-provided services towards increased use of the private (profit and non-profit) and informal sectors. Governments have sought to increase choice and participation of service users through increasing diversity of service providers and have promoted support for informal carers and encouraged self-help (see, e.g., HMSO, 1989). A trend away from standardized services has led to systems such as care management which attempt to co-ordinate flexible packages of care across service boundaries to meet the needs of individuals (Davies, 1992).

Although these trends may indicate some tendency to policy convergence at macro-level, other approaches focus on the differences between and within countries at micro-level. Smaller-scale, more qualitative studies compare the outcomes of health and welfare systems for people with care needs and their carers at a local level, contextualized within the broader national policy situation (Schunk, 1996; Chamberlayne and King, 1996; Hantrais and Mangen, 1996a, p. 5).

Advantages and disadvantages of comparative approaches in this area

Through using comparative approaches to long-term care, it is possible to identify broad trends and to understand the wider context in which individual countries' policies are developed. Further, since long-term care embraces different systems and sectors which form the network of care available in a particular setting, comparisons at local levels can increase understanding of the outcomes of systems for individuals with disabilities. In a policy area of such complexity (Baldock, 1997, p. 82), the need to define concepts and components of care for comparative purposes helps to develop analytical categories, theories and models of care, and to increase understanding of long-term care both generally and in a specific context. Through cross-national comparisons policy analysts can learn how other countries respond to common issues such as paying for long-term care. Comparative studies can thus facilitate the transfer of policies and practice and their adaptation for adoption in other settings (Higgins, 1986, p. 225; Teune, 1990, p. 58; Tester and Freeman, 1996). Comparisons can also be made between countries at different stages, for example of population aging, allowing lessons to be learned or predictions to be made.

The complexity of the policy area, however, entails conceptual and methodological difficulties, particularly those of definition and equivalence. Further disadvantages arise from the paucity of research, until recently, in the area of long-term care and the lack of availability of comparative data, particularly on areas of care which are difficult to identify and quantify, such as community-based non-medical services (Doty, 1988, p. 146), and on differences in outcomes of long-term care by class, gender, ethnicity and disability (Ginsburg, 1992, p. 19). To compound the above disadvantages, there are practical difficulties in the management and financing of cross-national research (Hantrais and Mangen, 1996a, pp. 6–7).

Conceptual, Theoretical and Methodological Issues

These key conceptual, theoretical and methodological issues are now reviewed and potential approaches are identified; then later in the chapter actual approaches used in comparative cross-national research on long-term care for adults are discussed.

Conceptual and theoretical issues

The specification of research questions, concepts and terms is essential in the design of any social policy research. In comparative research, this is particularly important because of the need for equivalence, or comparing like with like. Thus in comparative approaches to long-term care for adults it is necessary to specify, for example, which aspects of long-term care will be studied and which categories of adults will be included, and to define key concepts and ways of measuring them. This, however, is not a simple matter as questions, concepts and terminology are 'culture specific' (Jones, 1985, p. 6). Even when countries use the same language, concepts and terms must be understood in their particular context. Achieving equivalence becomes increasingly difficult the more different languages and cultures are involved. Non-equivalence in terms and concepts used has been found in many cross-national studies (Hantrais and Mangen, 1996a, p. 9). As Bennett (1991, p. 218) points out: 'in comparative analysis policies adopted by different governments frequently do not fit into the same conceptual categories'.

The complexity of the policy area of long-term care and difficulties of defining key concepts such as social care, community care, or home care are recognized (see, e.g., Jamieson, 1989, p. 446; Munday, 1996, p. 5). Definitions acceptable in one country, for example Laing's definition of long-term care cited above, would need further explanation for use in a comparative context, since terms such as 'day centre', 'NHS or care-home settings' may not be understood outside the UK. Comparative policy analysts recognize that it is rarely possible to achieve exact linguistic equivalence in concepts and that their aim must be to devise functional equivalents (Bennett, 1991, p. 219; Teune, 1990, p. 54).

Further conceptual difficulties arise because the concepts and terms for which functional equivalence is sought must also be seen in the context of particular ideological discourses and value systems used by policy makers and researchers (Evers, 1994, p. 20; Hantrais and Mangen, 1996a, pp. 7–9). Therefore the wider political ideology and welfare regime type in which a policy or institution is set will influence meanings attached to it. Where long-term care is concerned, the discourse of welfare pluralism and shifts in the balance of the welfare mix (Evers and Svetlik, 1993) is crucial to understanding policy developments in response to current issues of paying for and providing care.

Theoretical and policy issues

Approaches taken to the conceptual and theoretical issues discussed above are influenced by the purposes of the research and the perspectives of those involved. Research aims in this field usually include description, mapping or review of different long-term care policies and systems and the provision of basic comparative information, to be used for policy development and/or further research. Evaluation of the current arrangements and lesson learning may be further aims. The more theoretical aims of comparative studies of long-term care include explanation and theory building. Combinations of descriptive, evaluative, lesson learning and explanatory aims are often stated.

The researchers' theoretical perspectives and values, whether explicit or implicit, are important in the design and conduct of the research, but other interests are also often involved. Funding bodies which commission comparative social policy research, such as the Commission of the European Communities (CEC), usually influence the aims and perspectives of the research, which may be designed to fit a particular funding programme. The interests of other stakeholders may also be influential, including those of the users of the research, such as policy makers, service providers, managers and practitioners, and the users of long-term care services, their carers and non-governmental organizations (NGOs) representing users and carers. In designing or using comparative social policy analysis it is therefore important to take account of these perspectives and to identify the interests served. One pitfall to be avoided is ethnocentricity, where the perspective of one country or culture detracts from the understanding of other cultures, is inappropriate in other contexts, and limits the wider relevance of the research.

When formulating research questions and selecting concepts and terms for comparative research on a topic such as long-term care, various aspects of social policy are usually taken into consideration. The aims of the research will affect the extent to which it focuses on each of the key components of social policy: the origins, substance and outcomes (Ginsburg, 1992, p. 2). Where the origins component is considered, the emphasis has tended to be on the development of policies in different contexts and, sometimes, on the extent to which broad policy trends may be explained by convergence of welfare states at a macro-level (see, for example, Abrahamson, 1992, p. 10). Less attention has been paid to the process of policy implementation and to explanations for policy transfer or diffusion of policy ideas at a micro-level; research on these issues is, however, being developed in the policy area of innovations in care for frail older people (Tester and Freeman, 1996). Similarly, comparative research has focused on the origins and substance, rather than the outcomes of policy (Schunk, 1996, pp. 87–8).

Further considerations in comparative research are the variables of space and time. The geographical location of the study in a selection of countries, areas or cultures relevant to the aims of the research is important for both theoretical and methodological reasons. Similarly the time span for the research is crucial in that this embraces the legislative and policy time frame. Further, an adequate time span can allow the comparative analysis of policy development, the implementation of innovations, policy transfer, and the outcomes for users and carers, particularly of policy innovations over a period of time. Ideally, longitudinal studies would be undertaken comparing the development of long-term care policies and their outcomes for users over an extended period, although funding implications are likely to be prohibitive. Outcomes of long-term care policies could also be traced longitudinally through official statistics, but these are rarely available on the topic.

In the study of long-term care the level of analysis is another key variable, since social care policy and practice are often determined at a local level, while health care policy may be made at a different, more centralized level. The relationships between levels are crucial to effective co-ordination of long-term care which crosses organizational boundaries (Tester, 1996, p. 81). Key aspects of such co-ordination are the medical/social divide and the power of professionals. The governmental structure of a country, the extent of centralization or decentralization, and the implementation of principles such as subsidiarity, will also affect the level at which policy decisions are made, including national, federal, regional, state or local levels. To compare only national-level data would provide a very misleading account of different countries' long-term care systems and conceal wide differences within countries. Diversity within populations and among users or potential users of long-term care services and their carers is another key theoretical issue to be recognized by including the effects of social differentiation by gender, class, race, disability and age in the analysis.

The development of theoretical frameworks for the comparison of long-term care systems, taking account of the conceptual, theoretical and policy issues discussed above, has until recently been neglected by comparative social policy research. Mainstream comparative studies have focused on welfare states, social protection systems and paid work. For example, Esping-Andersen's (1990) influential categorization of three welfare regime types: 'liberal', 'conservative–corporatist' and 'social democratic' (1990, pp. 26–8) is based on measures of social security programmes and the extent of 'de-commodification'. Such categorizations, while useful for long-term care research in indicating the context of broad systems and analysing class and power differences, have been criticized for failing to address issues of gender, race and age (Ginsburg, 1992; Orloff, 1993; Sainsbury, 1994, 1996). Feminist social policy analysts, concerned with gendering welfare states, emphasize the relationships between paid and unpaid work, gender and caring. In the study of long-term care gender differences are particularly significant because such care is mainly provided by women, as paid or unpaid carers (Langan and Ostner, 1991; Taylor-Gooby, 1991; Lewis, 1992; Tester, 1996). Models and frameworks for the comparative study of social care have begun to emerge (Alber, 1995; Anttonen and Sipilä, 1996).

Methodological issues

Opinions differ as to whether there is a distinct methodology for comparative research (see, for example, Øyen, 1990, pp. 10–11). Methodological approaches and methods available for comparative studies are essentially the same as for any social research. There are, however, more difficulties in their application, taking account of the conceptual and theoretical issues outlined above, and of differences between countries in disciplinary and interdisciplinary approaches to social policy analysis. As in any research, it is important that the methodological approach is appropriate to the theoretical perspectives and aims of the study, that theory and data are linked, and that issues of validity and reliability and ethical considerations are addressed. The need for comparability is an additional dimension.

Language is a key issue since the functional equivalence sought in definitions and concepts should be maintained throughout the data collection, analysis and dissemination stages of the research. Difficulties in collecting and analysing primary data often mean that researchers rely on existing data from comparable or comparative sources, including factual data such as cross-national statistics and commentary such as research studies (Jones, 1985, pp. 20–6). However, the paucity of such data has been an obstacle in the policy area of long-term or social care (Doty, 1988, p. 146; Jani-Le Bris, 1993, pp. 6–7; Nijkamp et al., 1991, p. 4; Munday, 1996, p. 11). Comparative social policy has tended to focus on areas that are easily quantifiable, such as social security or health care expenditure. Where quantitative, comparative data are available, for example aggregate statistics collected by supranational bodies such as the OECD or the EU (Eurostat), they rarely include analysis by variables such as gender, class, race, disability, age or marital status, necessary for the study of outcomes of long-term care for different social groups (Ginsburg, 1992, p. 19; Jani-Le Bris, 1993, p. 7). Even at national level, reliable data on social care services are not always available, and rarely include evaluation or studies of outcomes (Glendinning and McLaughlin, 1993, p. 135; Tester, 1996). Particular substantive areas relevant to long-term care, such as day care and transport services, have been neglected by national and cross-national research. Similarly, a policy and research focus on aging populations has meant a lack of information and research on other groups of adults with long-term care needs (Glendinning and McLaughlin, 1993, p. 12).

The selection of countries or other units of comparison is ideally based on theoretical considerations such as the inclusion of different types of welfare regime or geographical areas. In a study of long-term care it would be useful to include countries with different proportions of people with long-term care needs, both in the population and in institutional or community-based care, and different policies and cultural traditions in relation to responsibilities of family, state and private sectors of the mixed economy of care. In practice, research has tended to focus on North West Europe and North America; countries for study are often selected for pragmatic reasons such as language, availability of data, access through existing contacts, and availability of funding (see, e.g., Tester, 1996, pp. 2–3). Criteria of funding bodies may mean the inclusion of countries for reasons of little theoretical relevance to the study.

The selection of units of comparison and the methods of data collection and analysis for comparative research on long-term care will ideally take account of the considerations discussed above. In practice, however, a purpose-designed, fully comparative, cross-national study entails a high level of financial support and the resources to surmount the many barriers involved. For such reasons comparative researchers find that 'cross-national research by its very nature demands greater compromises in methods than a single country focus' (Hantrais and Mangen, 1996a, p. 10).

Conceptual, Theoretical and Methodological Approaches to Long-term Care in Comparative Perspective

As comparative research on long-term care is a developing area, existing studies tend to be exploratory, building on the limited data available. This section reviews examples of conceptual, theoretical and methodological approaches taken in comparative policy analysis, ways of addressing some of the issues outlined above, and the compromises made in attempts to open up this increasingly important field of study.

Aims and perspectives, policy issues covered

Most studies of long-term care aim to provide basic information on the care systems, to give an overview or a review of services, to document existing arrangements, and to fill or reveal gaps in knowledge. Many studies also aim to evaluate the arrangements reviewed, usually so that other countries may learn lessons from them. Some studies aim to formulate explanations or theories. For example the ACRE programme's aims include description, evaluation and explanation. The researchers formulated the problem in terms of blockages in pathways through services; they hypothesized that these difficulties were attributable to over-use of institutions and to fragmentation in service provision. This formulation led to a set of research questions aimed at explanation and understanding of the blockages (Illsley and Jamieson, 1990, p. 84).

Such projects are based not only on the researchers' theoretical perspectives and values, but also on the interests of the users of the research and other stakeholders. The negotiation of the research process is thus more complex than it would be for a single-country study. Important aspects of negotiation and compromise between interested parties concern the policy focus on specific issues in long-term care. To ensure that the same issues and areas concerning aspects of paying for or delivering care are addressed in each country or setting, one main approach used is to draw up a list of questions. For example, in the ACRE study of home care, contributors from each country addressed the same set of nine questions (Jamieson, 1991, p. 10). A second, similar approach is to provide a framework of headings to be covered (see, e.g. Giarchi, 1996, p. 37; Jani-Le Bris, 1993, pp. 4–5). For a study of community care a framework was devised with topics under the headings origins, substance and outcomes; this was applied in chapters on different areas of care such as accommodation and domiciliary care (Tester, 1996, p. 25).

In taking such approaches, comparative policy analysts recognize that different issues may be more salient in some countries than in others, and that countries will vary in the amount of information available on each topic. Therefore compromises have to be made between setting out the discussion in a consistent way to facilitate cross-national comparison, and leaving scope for focus on country-specific issues from which other countries can learn. This is clearly more difficult when there are different contributors and different approaches taken in each country than when a single researcher or research team from one country undertakes all the research.

Concepts and definitions

A further area for discussion is the definition of concepts. The difficulties of achieving equivalence in cross-national research on long-term care are well recognized. Doty (1988), for example, found 'a wide variety of terminology used to label long-term care institutions' (pp. 145–6); terms such as 'nursing home' convey widely different meanings in different contexts. Therefore, rather than referring to institutions such as 'nursing homes', Doty's questionnaire defined long-term care institutions 'in terms of generic facility categories (i.e., medically oriented versus nonmedical residential care) and presented examples of what such facilities might be called' (p. 146). Similarly, writers comment on the difficulties of defining 'community care' for cross-national study, and stress that this Anglo-Saxon concept must be defined in a way that will be understood in languages which do not use 'community' in this sense (Jamieson, 1991, pp. 6–9; Glendinning and McLaughlin, 1993, p. 12; Tester, 1996, p. 5).

Various approaches are taken to defining key concepts relating to the aspects of 'care' to be covered in comparative studies, such as listing services that are included and discussing the meanings of terms. Munday (1996), for example, in discussing 'social care' distinguishes this from the British term 'personal social services' and stresses that social care includes both formal and informal support (p. 6). An effective way of seeking functional equivalence consists of breaking down the more general terms into components or categories which do not relate to a specific country's systems and so are more readily understood cross-nationally. Jamieson (1991) approaches difficulties over terminology such as 'home help' by first identifying and describing three core types of help: 'nursing help', 'personal care' and 'home making', considering the services involved, then defining the key terms to be used in the study (p. 9). A further approach is to provide precise definitions of key concepts, for example the comprehensive list of definitions of terms relating to categories of care and services given by OECD (1996a, p. 4).

Definitions of groups to be studied, for example 'older people', are mainly in terms of chronological age, such as over 65 years. This group is sometimes divided into 'young' and 'old' categories of older people with the age cut-off point at 75, 80 or 85. 'Frail' older people are also defined in terms of health problems, and 'dependent' people in terms of need for help with activities of daily living (e.g. OECD, 1996a, p. 4). Pacolet et al. (1994) adopt and discuss a broad definition of dependence, using four dimensions, physical, mental, social and economic (p. 5). 'Informal carers', or 'family carers', a term more widely understood in Europe, are usually defined according to their relationship with the person cared for, for example: 'the family carer is a person who is related to the person he or she is caring for either by blood or by marriage' (Jani-Le Bris, 1993, p. 4). The wide use of this definition in Europe means, as Glendinning and McLaughlin (1993, p. 12) point out, that there is little research on the broader concept of informal care as understood in the UK, including care by friends and neighbours. The concept 'care' in the British social policy context has been associated with unpaid care, but recent feminist approaches stress the importance of focusing on all forms and dimensions of care and on caring relationships (Ungerson, 1995).

This review of approaches to terminology demonstrates the difficulties involved in comparative studies of such a complex area of social policy, and the importance of compromise between giving as much specification and explanation as possible using a combination of approaches, and being able to make meaningful generalizations. Further development work is needed to formulate definitions and categories for this area of study which would be broadly comparable and comprehensible in different countries, languages and cultures.

Ideological and theoretical contexts

Such definitions and concepts must be understood in the context of policy debates and discourses on topics such as ideologies and principles of care; the welfare mix; organization of formal care; and family and informal care. These debates reflect shifts in policy emphasis towards the non-state sectors of the mixed economy of welfare, and the increasing importance of feminist perspectives in social policy.

Most researchers outline the broader socio-economic and demographic factors and political ideologies which underpin long-term care policies in countries studied (e.g., Jamieson, 1991, pp. 286–92; Tester, 1996, pp. 13–15). Values and assumptions about the roles of the family, state, market and non-profit sectors of the mixed economy of care are particularly relevant in this field. Long-term care policies are influenced by economic principles such as cost effectiveness and efficiency, which may conflict with humanitarian principles concerned with improving service users' and carers' quality of life.

Key economic concepts in comparative research on long-term care include 'substitution' and 'subsidiarity'. Substitution of community care for institutional care, less formal for more technical care has been a key principle in long-term care in The Netherlands since the 1980s (Tester, 1996, p. 20). Subsidiarity is a central principle in countries such as Germany, Spain and Italy, ensuring that responsibility for care rests first with the individual and family, then local, non-state organizations, and as a last resort with statutory organizations (Tester, 1994, p. 254; Giarchi, 1996, p. 32). Humanitarian concepts on which many countries' long-term care policies are based include independence, social integration, inclusion, participation, choice and empowerment, discussed for example by Glendinning and McLaughlin, (1993, pp. 9–11) and Walker and Maltby (1997, pp. 33–4).

The concept of welfare pluralism, crucial to long-term care policies, is discussed to some extent in most comparative studies on the topic. The key issue is the changing balance and interaction between sectors in a system's 'welfare mix', a concept developed through studies on innovative welfare mixes in care (Evers and Svetlik, 1991,

1993; Evers and Wintersberger, 1990). A full discussion of the analytical and conceptual aspects of the welfare mix approach is given by Evers (1993) who summarizes the difference between welfare pluralism and welfare mix concepts: 'While both are concerned with the historical, conceptional and value dimensions of pluralism . . . it is the welfare mix approach which centres on questions of interlinkages, interactions and balances between sectors of pluralistic welfare systems' (pp. 27–8).

The theoretical context of comparative studies thus focuses on the organization of formal systems of long-term care and the relationship between these systems and their users and informal carers. For example, for the ACRE policy study on the effects of health and social care systems on services for older people, Illsley and Jamieson (1990, pp. 85–6) select as key variables for their analytical framework the structural and procedural factors in the systems, the 'system characteristics', which they consider in the wider context of 'non-system' factors. Another approach to conceptualizing the organization of care is taken by Pacolet et al. (1994, p. 8) who distinguish between 'assistance in kind (services provided) or in cash', and provide a matrix of organizational forms of care through informal and formal, private (for profit and not-for profit) and public sectors, and financing methods in the informal and formal sectors.

Comparative studies focusing on informal and voluntary care are set within contexts of wider debates concerning gender and caring, labour market participation, and the interests of carers and those cared for. Such research draws on UK literature on informal care and on feminist critiques of community care policy in the 1980s and 1990s and more recent critiques by the disability movement arguing for people with disabilities to have more control over their own care (Morris, 1993). Useful reviews of these issues are given by Glendinning and McLaughlin (1993), Evers (1994), Ungerson (1994) and Twigg (1996). More specifically the structure and role of the family are reviewed, for example by Jani-Le Bris (1993, pp. 18–21), who discusses changes in family structure and features of modern and traditional family models in European countries. Theoretical frameworks or models for comparison are based on such debates, and are devised as a basis for a deductive approach, or built from the observations of comparative research, using inductive methods.

Theoretical frameworks or models for comparison

Comparative analysis of long-term care may be set in the context of models or typologies of welfare state or welfare regime, such as those devised by Esping-Andersen (1990), Abrahamson (1992) and

Leibfried (1993). These models, based mainly on social protection systems, and usefully enabling broad categorizations and comparisons, have been criticized, first, for their limitations in describing the current situation in social welfare systems (Spicker, 1996, pp. 70–2; Bonoli, 1997, pp. 352–9). Second, the models are based on Western capitalist systems and may not be applicable to post-communist regimes in Eastern Europe (Deacon, 1993, pp. 190–7), nor to the Confucian welfare states of the Far East (Jones, 1993, pp. 214–15). Third, they have neglected Southern European welfare states (Ferrera, 1996, p. 18). Fourth, and most important for our topic, feminist critiques stress that the models have limited relevance to the complex areas of long-term care and social care, particularly since they neglect gender differences and unpaid work.

Models and frameworks for the comparative study of social care (an important constituent of long-term care) have begun to emerge. Alber (1995) draws on reports to the European Commission's Observatory on Older People (Walker et al., 1993) in seeking to develop a framework for the comparative study of social services. He argues that cross-national variations in social services for older people cannot be explained by conventional variables used in comparative welfare state research. Alber (1995) identifies four key explanatory factors: the regulatory structure, the financing structure, the delivery structure and the degree of consumer power (pp. 135–6). He argues for a shift in theoretical approaches and research agenda to make them more appropriate for social services and to recognize the importance of relations between centre and periphery at different levels of government and between church and state (pp. 145–6).

Similarly Anttonen and Sipilä (1996), in seeking to identify models of European social care services, analyse the limited data available on children's day care services and welfare services for frail elderly people in EU countries. These services are considered important in the relationship between the state and the family, and for women's personal autonomy. Anttonen and Sipilä (1996) identify social care models which are similar to Leibfried's (1993) models for income support systems, but also find variations in social care in central Europe between models of care for children and for frail older people. They conclude that 'it seems that in the European context it is legitimate to speak of European social care regimes with their own distinctive constructs' (p. 98).

Thus it seems possible to build on the welfare regime approach to incorporate social care services that are relevant to women's position in the family and the labour market, and to the situation of service users and carers outside the labour market. Further development of the exploratory work of Alber and of Anttonen and Sipilä will be important in shifting the focus of welfare regime theory. The approach would need to be adapted for the specific area of long-term care.

Since welfare pluralism is an important feature of social care services, other theoretical models focus on the sectors of the welfare mix in relation to care services. The concept of the welfare triangle, based on the division between market, state and civil society, was devised in the 1980s by researchers at the University of Copenhagen and the European Centre, Vienna (Abrahamson, 1992). In developing the concept of the welfare mix, the European Centre emphasized the importance of the voluntary/non-profit sector as an intermediate area within the triangle (Evers, 1993). Further development, reflecting the increasing importance of the voluntary sector, produced the 'welfare diamond', with the care recipient at the centre, and four sections representing the state, voluntary, informal and market sectors. The diamond can also be divided into formal/informal and non-profit/for-profit dimensions. This model is used for the 'Payments for care' project, interested mainly in the non-profit, informal and voluntary sectors (Pijl, 1994, pp. 4–6).

The various approaches reviewed reflect a growing concern to develop conceptual frameworks more relevant to social care or long-term care than the established comparative welfare state models based on social protection systems.

Methodological approaches

Methodological approaches taken to the comparative study of long-term care are influenced by these theoretical concerns; and by an increasing emphasis on qualitative methods in comparative social policy, reflecting a shift away from the identification of broad trends and towards a recognition of diversity and the importance of outcomes for individuals. More pragmatically, approaches are influenced by the practical difficulties which often preclude use of the ideal methods for a particular research problem. Compromises are therefore necessary to keep the research within resource constraints (Øyen, 1990, p. 15).

Most cross-national studies on long-term care and related topics use a range of complementary quantitative and qualitative methodologies and methods. Typically, the larger cross-national studies use existing data such as official statistics, policy documents and reports, combined with some new empirical research involving cross-sectional surveys, interviews and documentary analysis in each of the participating countries. Smaller-scale qualitative projects tend to take a case study approach to local areas within two or more countries.

Most researchers, especially in the larger projects, rely on contributions to the study from other sources, particularly independent experts or research teams in each country included. The co-ordinators provide an overview of the research, giving broad comparisons and trends; to address the problem of over-generalization, detailed descriptions of individual countries or areas are also published as separate chapters or reports (see, e.g., Walker et al. 1993; Hutten and Kerkstra, 1996). The 'safari' approach, in which a researcher or team from one country undertakes the research in all the countries, is more feasible in smaller-scale studies (Hantrais and Mangen, 1996a, p. 4).

The larger-scale design is exemplified by the ACRE study undertaken by teams in nine countries, which had three complementary strategies. The first consisted of surveys of representative samples of older people, their needs and services, in the areas where fieldwork was undertaken for the second approach: a study of pathways into and through services, looking at 'key points in the service system' and the interactions between older people and the services, using case studies. The third approach was a study of policy development and implementation which, together with the surveys of older people, provided context for the study of outcomes (Illsley, 1987, pp. 341–2; Jamieson, 1991, p. 4).

In contrast, a recent small-scale study in two countries focused on one locality in each country and first charted patterns of welfare mix, then examined characteristics of service providers and delivery, using documentary analysis, participant observation and interviews. National-level data were collected to contextualize the case studies (Schunk, 1996, pp. 88–9).

The other studies reviewed use a range of combinations of research strategies, comparing different groups of countries, drawing on existing material and collecting new data using methods discussed below.

Use of existing data

Comparative studies thus draw on available statistics, documents and literature to maximize their use of existing resources and reduce the need for expensive primary data collection. In any research a major drawback of the use of data from secondary sources is that these were collected for different purposes from those of the current study. A new field of comparative research has additional problems of limitations in the amount and comparability of material available, necessitating the time-consuming process of collating as much information as possible in a piecemeal way from numerous sources.

The difficulties of using official statistics are well recognized (Hantrais and Mangen, 1996a, p. 8). Attempts to collate statistics on specific variables may reveal more gaps than data (Alber, 1995, pp. 134–5). Where long-term care is concerned, the few comparative statistical sources such as those from OECD only partially cover the information required and rarely differentiate between social groups. Data on social security and on some aspects of health care are much more likely to be available than those on institutional social care, home care, day or respite care, sometimes only accessible at local level. Data from national sources are rarely comparable. Where aggregate data are available at national level, they may be based on inadequate sources, and therefore not reliable for cross-national comparisons (Schunk, 1996, p. 88). Different sources within countries may give varying figures for a particular measure; for example, rates of institutionalization in different types of facility vary according to the definitions used (Doty, 1988, p. 147; Walker et al., 1993, p. 110). Similarly, definitions of dependence vary between and within countries (Jani-Le Bris, 1993, p. 4).

Policy documents at national, regional or local levels, and the procedural documents used by service-providing organizations, can provide useful information on aspects of long-term care systems. However, as with any documentary analysis, careful interpretation and an understanding of the policy and cultural contexts are necessary, as well as familiarity with terminology in different languages (Øyen, 1990, p. 16). This means that it is advisable for such analysis to be undertaken by a researcher from the country concerned, or to be supplemented by observation, interviews or consultation with key informants, as in the study of community care (Tester, 1996).

Existing research studies and reports can provide fruitful sources to build upon in spite of their inadequacies. Alber (1995), for example, re-analyses the country reports for the EC Observatory in applying his suggested framework for comparative study of social services. Glendinning's and McLaughlin's (1993) study of paying for care relies mainly on existing cross-national studies and published literature; however, there are limitations in that the definitions used and material covered are not closely enough related to their topic of support for informal carers (pp. 11–12). The difficulties are compounded when more qualitative approaches are taken. For their qualitative study of 'cultures of care', for example, Chamberlayne and King (1996) found that 'very little primary, cross-national, qualitative research has been conducted into the dynamics of the informal sector' (p. 95).

This brief review of some implications of drawing on existing data for the comparative study of topics such as long-term care demonstrates the need for the development of cross-national comparative datasets on these topics, as well as for primary research into the various aspects of long-term care on which existing information is so sparse.

Collecting new data

Methods of collecting and analysing new data used by comparative approaches include a range of traditional methods as well as more innovative ones, as illustrated below.

Kerkstra and Hutten (1996) used a postal questionnaire which was sent to identified experts on home nursing and on home help in each of 15 countries, requesting details of organization and funding of the services. The problem of incomplete data was experienced, with differences between countries and difficulties obtaining national level data in some countries (pp. 4–6). Possible misinterpretations of the data were minimized by asking experts to comment on draft chapters, as well as using interviews with experts in some countries to supplement the information.

Interviews were carried out to supplement desk research in a study of family care (Jani-Le Bris, 1993, pp. 3–6). In each of six countries, 24 'semi-directive' interviews were held with a sample of carers designed to include differentiation between rural and urban areas, gender, marital status and employment of carers. The interviews provide a rich source of qualitative data focusing on the carers' experiences. Schunk (1996) also used semi-structured interviews with service providers at different levels, combined with participant observation in provider agencies to complement the understanding of local welfare mixes gained from documentary sources (pp. 89–90). Other studies drew on key informants or experts in various ways, through interviews, written consultations, or contributions to reports or seminars (e.g., Evers et al., 1994, p. ix; OECD, 1996a, p. 14).

Innovative approaches to comparative social policy research in this area include the construction of typical cases for which the mix of available services can be described and compared. Pacolet et al. (1994) use this approach to supplement their full description of social protection services. They define 12 cases on the basis of disability, income, living arrangements and social network, their aim being 'to distinguish . . . a limited number of categories of elderly people, on the basis of which the differences in social protection arrangements for the elderly in the six countries . . . should become clear' (p. 67). Similarly Schunk (1996) uses a 'model case' approach for the evaluation of care options of frail older people, constructing models of people with different health and social care needs, and including differentiation by 'age, gender, race, wealth/income, education and family type' (pp. 90–3).

Biographical interpretative methods, used by Chamberlayne and King (1996, p. 96), contribute a further innovative approach to the comparative study of informal care, allowing 'an interpretation of underlying personal meanings and family dynamics' (pp. 97–8). The approach involves a 'case reconstruction' method of analysing and interpreting biographical data (pp. 98–9). The conceptual framework developed from the interviews enabled the researchers to emphasize differences by generation, class and gender, to identify 'traditional' and 'modern' modes of caring, and to distinguish between the results of 'system effects' in East and West Germany (p. 101).

Thus in spite of the difficulties both of using existing data and of collecting new data, comparative researchers have found ways of reducing these limitations by using combinations of complementary methods. Qualitative methods are being developed appropriate to the search for increased understanding of long-term care in the context of different welfare mixes and their implications for people with care needs and their carers. The range of methods may be enhanced by further use of model case and vignette techniques, and by the use of new technology to increase efficient communication through video-conferencing, e-mail and the Internet.

Conclusions: Future Approaches to Comparative Study of Long-term Care

This overview has examined selected studies on long-term care, including closely related areas such as social care, home care and informal care, for adults, and particularly for older people, the focus of much policy and research attention in industrial societies. Although this is a fairly new area for comparative social policy, the review shows that a considerable body of literature has been built up in the past decade. The chapter reviews approaches to the comparative study of this topic, rather than the substantive findings on long-term care issues, which readers may follow up from the suggestions for further reading below.

In developing this new area of comparative study, researchers have encountered problems common to most cross-national studies, compounded by particular difficulties relating to the topic. Equivalence of concepts and terms is difficult to achieve in a complex area of study where boundaries are unclear and there are wide variations in cultural and organizational contexts. There is a shortage of existing data on which to build the development of theories and methodologies appropriate to this field. Variability and lack of comparability of the data available are further problems. Practical difficulties over management and funding of research in this area must also be overcome. However, this review shows that, through compromise, researchers have largely achieved their aims, although most recognize the limitations of their studies. As the body of knowledge is increased, these difficulties will diminish; they should not constitute a reason for not taking a comparative approach to long-term care. Although comparative studies are more difficult to conduct than those in a single country or area, they offer added value not achievable without comparative cross-national research. For example, at a macro-level, broad trends can be identified and concepts such as shifts in the welfare mix can be developed; while at the micro-level the effects of different organizational systems and differences in individual experiences of the care systems can be identified and explained.

The development of comparative social policy analysis in the field of long-term care is important for several reasons. First, with increasing globalization of communications and markets, industrial societies recognize long-term care as a common policy issue to be addressed in the context of socio-demographic factors such as aging populations. Policy learning from the insights gained through comparative studies can contribute to the policy development process. Networks of researchers, policy makers, service providers and users formed through cross-national projects also promote the transfer of effective policy ideas and innovations, as well as the development of future research on issues perceived as salient by those involved. Such communication is likely to be particularly effective between people in local areas in different countries rather than at national level (Tester and Freeman, 1996), and is facilitated by new information technologies.

Second, long-term care is potentially a key focus for comparative social policy, since it is consistent with shifts in emphasis of social policies towards the non-state sectors of the welfare mix, towards community-based care for people with health and social care needs, and towards individualized care offered by a diversity of care providers.

Third, as a topic for social policy analysis, long-term care is central to the issues of gender and caring and relationships between public and private spheres, highlighted by feminist critiques of social policy in the 1980s and 1990s.

Fourth, in the comparative study of social policy an emphasis on welfare regimes theory, based on social protection systems and paid work and quantitative data, has been challenged by feminist critiques stressing the gender implications of welfare states and the effects of care systems and informal caring on the lives of people with care needs and their carers who are outside the labour market. Thus the comparative study of long-term care is central to an emphasis on the voluntary and informal sectors of the welfare mix and to research interest in the outcomes of different welfare mixes at a local level using qualitative methods, rather than in broad trends at national level. It provides a way of broadening comparative social policy to include less easily quantified areas and more qualitative approaches to issues relevant to the lives of diverse groups.

Since definitions and concepts differ between countries, there is need for more work on clarifying definitions of the types of care involved as well as of care recipients, as a basis for comparative data collection to fill the many gaps identified. Such gaps include research on social care for groups other than older people, and on informal care by carers other than close family members. To broaden the existing statistical data, comparative data sets on health and social care are needed to complement those on social security and health care expenditure. It is also necessary to collect such data at national level. Where qualitative data are concerned, a useful contribution can be made by small-scale qualitative studies such as those by Schunk (1996) and Chamberlayne and King (1996). Further development of their methodologies and of the theoretical insights gained from such studies would make a valuable contribution to research on long-term care which would not necessitate expensive large-scale studies.

The various approaches reviewed show the need to build conceptual frameworks more relevant to the study of long-term care than the established comparative welfare state models. A common component of such approaches is the recognition that a number of different dimensions must be included. For the comparative study of long-term care the following components could contribute at different levels:

- broad welfare/social care regime models, building on the approaches of Anttonen and Sipilä (1996);
- types of welfare mix, adapting the welfare triangle or diamond approaches;

- more specific focus on health and social care systems in which long-term care operates, building on Alber's (1995) key variables: regulation, financing, delivery and consumer power;
- more specific focus on relationships between long-term care providers in different sectors and organizations at different levels, and between these providers and the service users and their families;
- dimensions of the organization and purpose of long-term care, such as institution/community, medical/social, formal/informal, maintenance/rehabilitation.

The further development of such models of long-term care, together with the formulation of definitions of key concepts, and an increase in the availability of comparative and comparable data, will add to the considerable progress made in this field in the past decade, and help to establish long-term care at the forefront of comparative social policy in the next century.

Further reading

On the substantive issues and findings in relation to long-term care, the most recent studies provide current information; see, for example, OECD (1996a) or Hutten and Kerkstra (1996). Two studies on paying for care provide detailed coverage and discussion of these issues: Evers et al. (1994) and Glendinning and McLaughlin (1993). For a basic introduction to community care or social care in Europe, see Tester (1996) or Munday and Ely (1996). Examples of methodological approaches in large-scale studies are provided by Jamieson (1991) and Jani-Le Bris (1993). To follow up the discussions on conceptual frameworks, see the articles by Alber (1995) and Anttonen and Sipilä (1996). For further reading on methodological and theoretical approaches see Hantrais and Mangen (1996b), particularly the chapters by Hantrais and Mangen, Schunk, and Chamberlayne and King.

9
Unemployment Compensation and Other Labour-Market Policies

Jochen Clasen

Mass and long-term unemployment have been characteristic of many countries for two decades or so and there is ample evidence that joblessness has remained a major cause of income inequality, poverty and social exclusion. Consequently, as a social problem, unemployment has been a genuine concern for social policy research and teaching. Yet labour market schemes, as a potential means to overcome or tackle the problem, rarely figure in British textbooks on social policy – or are paid much less attention than income maintenance, social services, health or housing policies. Although this seems to be changing (Alcock, 1996; Hill, 1996; Alcock et al., 1998), the fact that employment policies are somewhat neglected might indicate that training, job creation and other programmes are primarily regarded as ways of improving economic efficiency and thus as belonging to the field of economic rather than social policy (Deacon, 1998). The administrative separation, in the UK at least, between benefits for the unemployed on the one hand and labour market policies on the other, has probably been an additional factor. Such a division has been less marked in many other countries or where only one common legal, financial and administrative basis of these two forms of public interventions exists.

In the UK, and in other countries, there is a fairly extensive body of literature on labour market policies such as training or job creation, or other programmes which are often referred to as 'active' labour market policies. There are also reviews of country-specific schemes and cross-national analyses (see Fay, 1996) and a few explicitly comparative studies which rely on econometric modelling and highly aggregated data aiming to measure the effectiveness of labour market policy across countries (Kraft, 1994; Aarnio, 1996). Overall, however, there is relatively little systematic cross-national comparative research in this area, perhaps because of methodological difficulties, some of which will be discussed in this chapter. As far as unemployment compensation is concerned, the situation is slightly better. This is reflected in this chapter which discusses theoretical, conceptual and methodological aspects which are specific to comparative research in labour market policies. It begins with a brief discussion of the definition and conceptualization of the topic which, here, covers both benefits for the unemployed, often referred to as 'passive' measures, and other forms of labour market schemes which are conventionally regarded as 'active', a characterization which is questionable. There then follows a section reviewing existing comparative studies in the field, distinguished by analytical aims. A further section considers some methodological aspects of comparative research in this particular policy area.

Labour Market Policies – a Note on Concepts and Definitions

Labour market policies, understood in a very broad way, can be regarded as any form of public intervention which aims to reach, or maintain, a high and stable level of employment (Beveridge, 1944). In principle this covers a wide range of public programmes, some of which are primarily directed at stimulating labour demand such as subsidies to particular industries, investment in infrastructure, a ban on overtime working or the promotion of part-time work or work sharing. Recent studies have focused on some of these policies within a more or less explicit comparative framework (Symes, 1995; Compston, 1997). However, they are not considered in this chapter, which adopts a narrower definition of labour market, rather than employment, policies by concentrating on programmes which are primarily aimed at facilitating labour market transitions (such as transitions from unemployment to employment, from school to work, from family formation to paid employment or from the latter to early retirement and other types of labour market exit). A cursory cross-national glance reveals that such a definition still covers a vast array of policies ranging from unemployment benefits and alternative forms of income transfers to fully or partly unemployed people, to placement services, parental leave schemes, training and work experience programmes and so on. A two-dimensional classification could be made between policies aimed at particular social groups on one axis (long-term unemployed, school leavers, older workers, immigrants, 'women returners', etc.) and particular directions of labour market transitions on the other. This is a perspective which has been adopted by Schmid et al. (1996) in an exhaustive compilation and evaluation of different types of labour market policies within an international and comparative framework.

The focus on labour market transitions facilitates the avoidance of the by now conventional distinction made between 'passive' and 'active' labour market policies. Such a distinction has become a back-cloth for international debates on (allegedly passive) unemployment benefit systems, the reformulation of which should make 'social protection more employment-friendly' (Bosco, 1997). Although a sharp distinction between active and passive labour market policies is contestable (see Sinfield, 1993, 1997) a number of supra-national organizations (OECD, 1994c; European Commission, 1995a) have repeatedly recommended a so-called 'activation' of benefit payments, i.e. promoting programmes such as training and work experience at the expense of 'passive' forms of income support for the unemployed. It is interesting to note that this provides a marked contrast with the 1960s when the same organizations, such as the OECD for example, picked up the Swedish focus on 'active manpower policies' which included benefits as part of the 'active' response to unemployment (OECD, 1963). This illustrates that the conceptualization of labour market measures such as training as 'active' and those which provide benefits as 'passive' has to be regarded as historically contingent and as dependent on economic contexts and prevailing political ideologies at the time.

A narrow definition of active labour market policies consists of placement, job creation and training programmes in particular (Calmfors, 1994) and excludes 'unemployment insurance, early retirement and other passive policies that do not move people into jobs' (Janoski, 1996, p. 705). However, while early retirement policies are clearly aimed at removing people from full-time employment, unemployment benefits are not. Instead, the payment of benefit not only provides income maintenance as replacement for lost earnings but has also economic functions. These include maintaining aggregate consumer demand and enabling job search activities, which not only 'move people into jobs' but facilitate an improved match between labour supply and demand because job seekers, depending on the level and duration of benefits paid, will be able to select jobs more suitable to their skills and experience. Benefits thus reduce the chance of future unemployment and increase productivity (Sinfield, 1997).

While unemployment compensation has an active rationale, it can be argued that some so-called active programmes such as training or work experience schemes are passive in the sense that they potentially foster apathy, resignation and inactivity on the part of participants if they are not tailored to individual needs. This, at least, is how some Swedish experts, and participants, perceived particular national programmes which arguably tended to lock people in a merry-go-round of periods of benefit receipt and labour market measures rather than leading to re-employment (Clasen et al., 1998). What is more, most schemes combine, at least implicitly, both primary and secondary economic and social policy objectives. Training and work experience schemes, for example, are conventionally regarded as aiming to lead to employment. While this has an economic aspect (increasing or maintaining total employment), employment for former participants is a social policy aim in itself (income security). Beyond that, training programmes can also have an impact on social equity by, for example, promoting the integration of socially disadvantaged groups such as immigrants or people with disabilities, or functioning as a social equalizer by providing targeted support to regions heavily affected by unemployment (Schmid, 1996).

There is also the problem of the unambiguous classification and thus operationalization of the concepts of 'passive' and 'active' across countries. For example, in Belgium and Norway claimants seeking full-time work but accepting part-time employment can receive unemployment benefit (Grubb, 1994, p. 192). Adminstratively these are counted as expenditure on passive transfers but a case could equally be made to regard those as active policies in a sense that they keep people in jobs and thus maintain a given level of employment. What is more, a similar employment effect could be achieved through wage subsidies paid to employers who take on certain target groups such as long-term unemployed people. While this would most probably be budgeted as spending on an active labour market programme, it is questionable whether tax expenditure which would be functionally equivalent to wage subsidies, such as exemptions from employers social security contributions, would as readily be accounted for in the same way. Finally, as Sinfield (1997) points out, the label 'passive' demotes those functions of unemployment benefit which are not economic, such as the provision of an income as a social right which prevents or alleviates hardship, poverty and processes of social marginalization or exclusion. A reductionist conceptualization of so-called passive measures in national and international debates ignores these aspects of unemployment compensation and thus facilitates a preoccupation with the topic of work incentives in relation to benefit levels (see below 3). Therefore, it is important to take a broad rather than narrow perspective, especially in cross-national comparative research. Rather than characterizing different labour market policies as either passive or active *per se*, it seems more sensible to consider positive and negative aspects of any form of labour market policies and to realize that all have an economic as well as a social role. Since economic or social theories do not provide unambiguous predictions as to the quality and impact of specific labour market policies, both these roles need to be carefully identified and evaluated through empirical research.

Analytical Aims and Research Foci

Comparative cross-national research on labour market policies can be categorized by their respective focus of research and primary objectives. On a broad level, studies can be distinguished as mainly interested in policy description, explaining policy change or policy evaluation. Of course, these aims are not mutually exclusive and many studies, sometimes implicitly, address two or even all three of these aims.

Policy description

The study by Kaim-Caudle (1973) was one of the first systematic attempts which aimed to describe the history and dimensions of provision, social and economic implications and general direction of social security schemes, including unemployment compensation, in a number of advanced countries. Similarly descriptive, yet critical and comprehensive cross-national reviews of particular labour market policies and particular groups of unemployed people were conducted by Reubens (1970, 1977). The work conducted by both these authors is not only informative but illustrative as an exercise of early comparative work which, when set against more recent studies, provides a sense of change and stability of cross-national patterns of policy and provision. It also highlights the relevance of socio-economic contexts as an influencing factor on policy formulation – as well as on comparative social policy research. This is reflected in Kaim-Caudle's (1973) description of policies adopted in many countries during the 1960s which actually improved provision for the unemployed as an attempt to adapt benefit levels to rising living standards and to increase the acceptance of temporary lay-offs at a time when rapid economic restructuring was expected.

Compared with the 1960s, and even 1970s, there is now a much larger body of literature which provides information on current policies, programmes and institutional arrangements, either at a particular point in time or on a periodic basis. Examples would include sections within *The OECD Jobs Study* (OECD, 1994c), *Employment in Europe* (European Commission, 1996), single-country labour market studies published by the EU (e.g. European Commission, 1997b), annual reports on institutional designs and tax benefit calculations within social security systems in six European countries (see Hansen, 1997) or the regularly updated MISSOC publications on social security programmes including unemployment compensation and MISEP which concentrates on changes in labour market policies and programmes in member countries of the EU.

Explaining policy change

Selective articles found in MISEP go beyond a mere description or reporting of policies and adopt a more analytical or evaluative cross-national approach reflecting, for example, on differences and trends of policy convergence or divergence (e.g. Mosley, 1993; Höcker, 1994; Schömann and Kruppe, 1996; Schmid, 1997). A much more explicit theoretical emphasis, however, is displayed in a body of literature which aims to explain policy change as the 'dependent variable', such as variations in programme expenditure or changes in administrative structures, benefit arrangements, entitlement criteria, financing methods, etc. Applying a quantitative methodology, Janoski's (1994, 1996) work on determinants of variations of expenditure on labour market policy across industrialized countries would be an example of the former. Research within the latter category has tended to be more qualitative and, depending on the prominence of explanatory variables, can be located with the larger body of literature on welfare state expansion, which can be separated into three different phases and strands of thinking (see Pierson, 1991; van Kersbergen, 1995, ch. 2); structural explanations of welfare development, stressing changes in industrialization and degrees of need (e.g. Wilensky, 1975); political explanations – and the power resources model in particular which was largely associated with neo-Marxist thinking (e.g. Korpi, 1983); and statist (Weir et al., 1988) and 'new institutionalist' (Steinmo et al., 1992) approaches which became influential in the 1980s. Research within the latter framework has been conducted to explain changes in welfare policies cross-nationally (Pierson, 1994, 1996) but proliferated also in other disciplines and fields of study. Indeed, analyses adopting new institutionalist perspectives can be subdivided into distinct theoretical schools of thought (Hall and Taylor, 1996).

Since different theoretical approaches of comparative welfare state research have been addressed elsewhere in this volume (see chapter 3), here it is sufficient to note that there are some early studies on labour market policies which can be loosely subsumed under the heading of 'new institutionalism' even before the label was invented. For example, in his seminal work on the historical origins and development of income maintenance policies in Sweden and the UK, Heclo (1974) rejected both functionalist and labour movement theories and stressed the role of 'political learning' on the part of bureaucratic elites as crucial determinants for policy direction. Alber (1981) emphasized the importance of early policy choice and institutional design influencing the development of unemployment insurance systems with regard to control mechanisms, generosity and redistributive impact in 13 advanced capitalist countries. The relevance of forms of governance or types of benefits, and thus the path dependence of unemployment support policies, has also been highlighted in more in-depth comparative studies of only a few countries, such as Germany and the UK (Clasen 1992, 1994) and Germany and Japan (Seeleib-Kaiser, 1995) or, from a different angle, England, France and the US (Cohen and Hanagan, 1995). Yet studies of this type are not restricted to unemployment compensation. Schmid and Reissert (1988; see also Schmid et al., 1992) illustrate that the mode of financing of labour market policies, a variable which has often been ignored or neglected (Fay, 1996), is a crucial variable in the determination of policy direction. Regarding training and placement schemes, the importance of early policy choices and institutional parameters in the formation of preferences, strategies and negotiations between collective actors and thus historical trajectories of labour market policies has been stressed in comparisons between Sweden and the UK (King and Rothstein, 1993) and between Great Britain and the USA (King, 1995).

A sub-theme within the debate on causes for the expansion and contraction of labour market programmes has been to focus on the policy mixes applied in different countries and to develop typologies based on these. For example, Schmid (1996) has put forward a complex typology of 'organizational regimes' of national labour market programmes, each consisting of different mixes of 'policy regimes' (according to modes of social co-ordination: social values, associative structure, market, law), 'implementation regimes' (according to parameters such as competence, decision making, financial and legal structures) and 'incentive regimes' (distinguishing between moral, status, financial and political incentives). As far as characteristics of unemployment compensation systems in particular are concerned, two-fold or three-fold typologies are conceivable. For example, Reissert (1994, 1997; see also Schmid and Reissert, 1996) categorizes programmes as either primarily 'insurance oriented' or 'welfare oriented' systems, that is as programmes which emphasize the link between earnings and benefits by providing wage replacement transfers which maintain accustomed living standards (for a time at least) on the one hand, and others which primarily aim to prevent poverty by providing moderate or low, and often means-tested, benefits only. Drawing on the distinction between types of welfare capitalism (Esping-Andersen, 1990, 1996a), Ploug and Kvist (1996) develop a three-fold categorization in relation to degrees of benefit generosity and universality, and distinguish between countries with 'selective' forms of unemployment insurance (e.g. Germany), comprehensive models (e.g. Denmark) and residual systems (e.g. UK).

The feasibility, and indeed usefulness, of creating typologies of entire welfare states (for an overview see Kvist and Torfing, 1996) has recently been questioned (Baldwin, 1996), and similar reservations can be expressed about the attempt to typecast particular policies, such as national unemployment benefit or labour market policy systems. Broad typologies are in danger of down-playing the fact that each national unemployment system is made of different mixes between insurance and assistance principles and that there can be enormous differences even between national systems of the same type in regard to institutional structures, financing mechanisms and the ways in which they interact with other types of public policies (Pennings, 1990; Ministerie van Sociale Zaken en Werkgelegenheid, 1995). On the other hand, carefully researched, historically sensitive and conceptually derived categories have the potential to provide researchers with a frame of reference and thus a platform on which to build empirical research leading to explanatory accounts of policy change. However, there are a number of conceptual and methodological aspects which have to be considered, such as the selection of appropriate parameters as the building blocks of typologies. These are discussed later in the chapter.

Policy evaluation

Although it should be noted that a definitive line is not always easy to draw, one can distinguish between policy outputs, i.e. the impact of policies on a particular target group in terms of policy objectives, and policy outcomes, the impact of a policy on society as a whole. For example, evaluations might be interested in the effectiveness of national unemployment compensation regimes on living standards of unemployed claimants (a policy output) or, more widely, on patterns of social stratification, poverty or inequality in the wider society over longer time spans (a policy outcome). Regarding labour market measures such as training or job creation schemes, a primary output indicator would be whether participants entered regular employment and the level of earnings they receive once a particular programme has been completed. Outcome studies might go beyond this by considering the quality of jobs entered and the effect on overall employment, taking account of the interaction with other policies and possible side effects such as deadweight losses (a company would have hired a person even without training), substitution (does the employment of the trained person lead to redundancy of existing staff?) or displacement effects (a company with subsidized workers reduces output among firms who do not have subsidized staff).

Within this context a large number of studies have been carried out, mainly by economists applying numerous indicators measuring the performance and diverse set of effects of different types of labour market schemes based on different theories and techniques (for an overview, see Calmfors, 1994). However, as a recent EU publication confirmed, the literature on labour market policy evaluation 'tends to be highly heterogeneous and disparate in scope and method' (European Commission, 1996, p. 127). What is more, very little of this work has been truly comparative and only recently has there been a move towards an internationalization of these studies, illustrated in publications on particular types of programmes based on chapters on a country-by-country basis (OECD, 1991, 1993, 1995; Jensen and Madsen, 1993). Collectively, these publications indeed display the 'state of a complex art', as an OECD (1991) title suggests. Nevertheless, a few studies have adopted a more explicitly comparative approach. For example, Disney et al. (1992) compare a range of labour market policies in Germany and Britain by reviewing single-country evaluation results, followed by a re-evaluation based on a commonly applied technique. Leigh (1995) concentrates on a comparison of programmes which assist 'displaced workers' (that is those who are unlikely to be recalled to their former job or to a similar job in the same industry) in seven industrialized nations. Van Doorn (1997) investigates differences and common features of the mix and extent of particular active labour market policies in three countries by setting them in a wider policy context which allows a more differentiated cross-national comparison.

All three studies stand out since they provide systematic overviews of national labour market institutions, or even a description of their historical evolution and interaction with other policies, and thus a framework for policy evaluations which is not only international in nature but, at least to some extent, comparative. However even those studies which are sensitive to differences in institutional contexts and customary practice are confronted by methodological and conceptual problems if their aim is to compare the effectiveness of particular policies. Those include choosing an adequate measure for effectiveness, taking account of the time horizon (when benefits are assumed to occur), considering the occurrence and distribution of costs as well as benefits for participants, the local economy, employers and the public sector.

While those problems are not specific to cross-national research, Schömann (1995) illustrated that they can be more difficult to overcome than in single-country studies. For example, there are potential trade-offs, or conflicts, between policy objectives. Given that the chances of re-employment decline as the length of unemployment increases, early labour market intervention might prevent long-term unemployment but might also be accompanied with effects of deadweight loss. There might be similar trade-offs between small programmes for particular groups (better targeted yet proportionally more expensive and with a marginal impact on total unemployment) and large schemes (more people with a chance of success, yet potentially lower programme quality and efficiency and decreasing returns). Recent reviews (Fay, 1996) indicate that labour market intervention which concentrates on particular groups needs more evaluation in the context of institutional frameworks of national, and regional, labour markets (considering that this is just one of the factors which impacts on unemployment). This means that a generalization of results across countries, or even regions, is often difficult because of programme-related differences (attributes of target group, size of programme, etc.), as well as external differences (local labour market conditions, interaction with other policies).

As far as unemployment compensation schemes are concerned, policy evaluations might be concerned with a programme's impact on providing a minimum or 'adequate' income for claimants or on the level of benefit take-up, but also on other aspects such as psychological well-being and self-esteem of those in receipt of benefits. Comparative studies interested in the wider effects might for instance consider the role of national unemployment compensation in allowing for an effective job search, preventing or alleviating processes of social marginalization, exclusion or social disintegration (Kronauer,

1993). Perhaps because of methodological problems involved in measuring these effects cross-nationally, the most interesting comparative research of this kind has so far been confined to single-country studies, such as Engbersen et al. (1993) who compared the situation of long-term unemployed people in neighbourhoods in three Dutch cities. Of course, unemployment compensation can mediate the influence unemployment might have on aspects such as on health, psychological well-being or crime, and there is a large body of literature on these and other issues which attempts to gain a better understanding of the social and personal impacts of unemployment (McLaughlin, 1992; Wilkinson, 1996). However, since labour market policies are generally not the focus of this type of research, a discussion would go beyond the scope of this chapter.

The issue of disincentives

Before concluding this section, one particular policy effect deserves to be mentioned since it has frequently been a central concern in both single-country and cross-national studies and to researchers from different academic disciplines. This is the question as to how far labour market policies, and unemployment compensation in particular, might exacerbate the problem of unemployment by providing disincentives to work. These might be distinguished between policy outputs (e.g. discouraging or lengthening a job search) and policy outcomes (e.g. inducing current workers to take greater risks of dismissal). Linked to the notion of work disincentives is the suspicion of benefit fraud and the question of responsibility for self-maintenance. In comparison with other social security schemes, this is particularly pertinent in unemployment compensation and has been so ever since public support programmes were introduced, as many single-country studies have illustrated (Pankoke 1990; Bryson and Jacobs, 1992). Cross-national comparisons of administrative control mechanisms and eligibility criteria with regard to receipt of unemployment benefits illustrate this (Pennings, 1990).

There is hardly any systematic cross-national research on the ways in which unemployment benefit arrangements or other labour market programmes strengthen or weaken the work ethic. Yet the topic of work disincentives has been a domain especially for economists who tend to conceptualize work–welfare choices as preferences of utility maximizing individuals who weigh up monetary gains with loss of leisure time. Reviews of largely single-country studies indicate that the evidence of such effects is either inconclusive or that labour market policies and benefits have an insignificant or small influence on flows between unemployment and employment (Atkinson and

Micklewright, 1991; Layard et al., 1991; see also Atkinson and Mogensen, 1993 for an international perspective).

Nevertheless, based on regressional analyses of a number of labour market programmes and institutional variables in 17 OECD countries, Scarpetta (1996) claims that 'generous' unemployment benefit schemes in particular, but also employment protection systems, tend to raise the level of structural unemployment. On the other hand, studies based on panel data have indicated a positive relationship between unemployment compensation and job search behaviour. Panel data allow researchers to evaluate the effects, and effectiveness, of labour market policies in a broader sense and thus to be more sensitive to cross-national differences in, for example, unemployment insurance arrangements, the design of certain training or job creation schemes or the incidence and heterogeneity of unemployment across countries. They are also more capable of capturing the multitude of transitions between labour market states over a longer period of time. However, firm cross-national conclusions based on these types of studies are hampered by a lack of comparability due to differences in relation to methods and data (Pedersen and Westergård-Nielsen, 1993). A relatively new data set (Eurostat, 1996) might improve the situation for comparative research in this area somewhat, as shown by Gallie and Alm (1997) who examined gender differences on attitudes to work.

Sociologists and social policy analysts have attempted to broaden the discussion on incentives and disincentives by taking account of aspects such as job and income security and also of the need to focus on households, rather than individuals, in order to further the understanding of decisions about labour market participation (Millar, 1994). The significance of such a shift is indicated when jobless rates for individuals are compared with those for households which throws a different light on cross-national patterns of employment and unemployment (Gregg and Wadsworth, 1996). Unemployment compensation schemes might have an impact on those patterns by, for example, fostering or weakening 'unemployment traps'. This has been confirmed in empirical comparative studies which indicate that families in receipt of means-tested transfers face greater obstacles in making the transition from benefit receipt to paid work than those who are, at least partly, in receipt of insurance-based transfers (Evans, 1996a, 1996b). What is more, explorative comparative studies indicate that particular types of benefit and labour market programmes can provide positive employment incentives. This seems to be the case especially in corporatist–conservative welfare states where access to benefits such as pensions is largely determined by labour market participation and thus reinforces the search for regular paid work (Clasen et al., 1998).

Finally, rather than merely concentrating on flows between unemployment and paid work, it is important to note that in a broader perspective a number of other transitions are conceivable which might be influenced by labour market policies. For example, Schmid and Reissert (1996) discuss 16 possible types of transitions between employment, unemployment, labour market programmes and forms of 'inactivity' such as early retirement. However, many of those are under-researched even within the context of single countries and more comparative and longitudinal studies are needed in order to improve our understanding of the impact different labour market policies can have on labour market transitions and, in a wider perspective, on processes of social marginalization and social integration.

Some Methodological Considerations

Cross-national studies in social research have to grapple with a number of methodological problems (Hantrais and Mangen, 1996b) and comparative research in social policy is no different in that respect. However, there are some issues which are specific to the area of social policy, as discussed in chapter 3 of this volume, and some which apply to labour market policies in particular. Some of the latter are common to studies on unemployment compensation schemes, aiming, for example, to measure the impact of benefit systems in terms of material living standards, and to other types of labour market programmes which might intend to evaluate the effectiveness of training schemes on job reintegration rates or post-programme earnings. Most comparative research in these areas is either based on real cases, that is on actual interviews with particular groups such as long-term unemployed people (e.g. Clasen et al., 1998), or on hypothetical or model cases as applied by Evans (1996a, 1996b; Hansen, 1997) who examined the effects of means-tested unemployment programmes in relation to their interaction with other forms of income maintenance and potential earnings for individuals and families. Both types of studies have to address questions of cross-national conceptualization, equivalents and the choice of parameters for comparisons.

Cross-national conceptualizations

Today there are perhaps fewer difficulties with data availability than a decade or two ago. However, problems remain in the sense that, for example, statistics on labour market policies might be centrally available from one institutional source, as is the case in Sweden, or scattered around a number of ministries, and available only from a multitude of central, regional and local sources. What is more, in some countries, such as Italy, there is no clear distinction between expenditure for different types of programmes.

But even comparisons between countries with reliable data sets are hampered by a number of conceptual difficulties regarding the meaning of central terms such as employment, unemployment, households, benefits levels and income. While a discussion of those issues would go beyond the scope of this chapter, a few considerations with respect of the conceptualization of unemployment will be made here in order to illustrate some of those difficulties. A broad distinction can be made between data based on registered unemployment on the one hand and data provided by labour force surveys, which rely on observed or self-reported perception and behaviour, on the other. Both leave out certain groups: the former those who are ineligible for benefits and thus might not register as unemployed; the latter those who work part-time for economic reasons, or those who might not actively be looking for a job and thus might not consider themselves to be unemployed but are in fact discouraged from seeking work because of care responsibilities, sickness, participation in training schemes or simply because of adverse labour market conditions (OECD, 1995). What is more, surveys may be based on households, or at least dwellings, and thus may miss out homeless people and those in institutional or even boarding-house settings.

Whereas these considerations are important for any research on unemployment, there are additional problems for comparative studies because of diverse national statistical traditions and conventions in the generation of indicators of employment and unemployment stocks and flows. International surveys, such as the European Community Labour Force Survey, attempt to overcome these diversities by applying the same (or at least fairly similar) concepts and definitions across countries. Other organizations, such as the US Bureau of Labor Statistics, adjust or standardize national statistics to common concepts. Both of these are useful for comparativists, but it should not be assumed that data produced in these ways are either fully comparable or necessarily of a better quality than those produced on a national basis, because a number of premises must be made in order to harmonize nationally produced figures or adapt surveys to national circumstances. What has to be recognized is that unemployment data can reflect different aspects of unemployment and serve different purposes. This has been the approach adopted by the US Bureau of Labor Statistics which has published seven alternative international unemployment indicators since 1976 (Sorrentino, 1993). For comparative research, it is important to realize that these different conventions can have significant impacts on comparing, for example, beneficiary rates between countries (OECD, 1994c) or on assessing the extent of long-term unemployment which tends to be under-estimated in both national and international data (Karr, 1997).

Questions of equivalence

In order to measure like with like, the equivalence between national programmes such as income maintenance or retraining programmes needs to be considered. A comparative study of the former, for example, would have to recognize that in addition to unemployment insurance, in many countries there are supplementary unemployment assistance schemes for those who have exhausted, or never gained access to, insurance benefits (Kvist and Ploug, 1996; Schmid and Reissert, 1996). In addition, the continuous mass and high levels of long-term unemployment in most countries has increased the number of unemployed who rely solely, or additionally, on means-tested minimum income provisions such as social assistance and other forms of support such as housing benefits and family allowances. These transfers can supplement unemployment benefits and thus point to the need to focus on income maintenance for unemployed people in the context of their families, rather than as individual claimants, in order to evaluate the adequacy of benefit provision cross-nationally (Fawcett and Papadopoulos, 1997). This could be extended to other types of public interventions given that some countries (and sometimes particular regions or municipalities within countries) provide assistance in the form of, for example, free or subsidized public transport and other Republic services and facilities. Thus, rather than merely focusing on, say, benefit replacement rates, a cross-national comparison which intends to analyse the generosity of unemployment compensation would have to look at the structure and level of the package of unemployment support as a whole.

Depending on the particular focus and aim of comparative studies, certain alternatives to unemployment support mechanisms might also have to be considered. For example, as a form of part-time unemployment benefit short-time work allowances are payable to workers in some countries, allowing companies to reduce the hours of work during periods of economic downturn and thus prevent full-scale redundancy. This scheme was extensively used after the collapse of the East German labour market in the wake of German unification but is also common in other countries such as Belgium. Bad weather allowances function in a similar way by compensating workers in certain industries (such as construction) for temporary lay-offs during the winter months.

Compensating those who have left paid work can take other forms. For example, countries such as France and Germany have facilitated labour market exit in the form of easier access to retirement and incapacity pensions instead of, or following receipt of, unemployment benefits, especially during the 1980s and early 1990s (Esping-Andersen, 1996b; Casey, 1996). Other alternatives to unemployment benefits which allow wage earners to leave jobs temporarily include parental leave schemes, sabbaticals or grants for taking time off for education or training (such as in Denmark). Finally, different types of public intervention in labour markets might have the same objective. In one country subsidies might be paid to avoid layoffs and closure of firms, in another the same outcome might be achieved via tax exemptions on employer social security contributions, and in a third by regulations which simply prevent firms laying off workers, or make it difficult for them to do so. In sum, comparative research on labour market policies requires careful consideration not only of similarities and differences between national programmes of the same type of policy but also of functional equivalences of what appear to be different types of public intervention into the labour market.

Which parameters?

We discussed above the trend to create frames of reference based on generating typologies and policy regimes. One of the difficulties in such attempts is the lack of an a priori parameter which should be the basis for typologies or for ranking national systems (Gallie and Alm, 1997). Apart from broad distinctions based on benefit organization and financing, one commonly applied parameter is the replacement ratio, i.e. the level of benefit in relation to previous earnings. This, however, is by no means an unambiguous concept (see Martin, 1996). For example, within the EU unemployment compensation is generally calculated on the basis of gross earnings, it is calculated on net earnings in Austria, and on adjusted net earnings, i.e. excluding certain components of wages, in Germany. Furthermore, the effect of minimum benefits, benefit ceilings and contribution thresholds and ceilings is often ignored in cross-national comparisons, although those can have significant distributional impacts (Hansen, 1997) by, for example, passing on, exacerbating or reducing the effect of earnings differentials on replacement rates for men and women

(Grimshaw and Rubery, 1997). Another parameter which is often referred to in comparative evaluations is the beneficiary rate, or coverage, i.e. the number of unemployed actually receiving support. However, to compare the quality of unemployment compensation merely on the basis of this variable has the potential of hiding rather than revealing cross-national variation not only because of the problem of programme equivalence but also because such a procedure would ignore the possibility that benefit eligibility (as well as the duration and the level of benefit) can depend not only on the period of insurance or the participation in paid work prior to unemployment but on a variety of additional factors such as family status, age and dependants (Kaim-Caudle, 1973).

Provided these conceptual and methodological problems can be adequately addressed, the difficulty of selecting the most useful parameter for comparison remains. Some countries might, for example, provide relatively generous benefits but limit access through strict entitlement criteria, while others might favour modest levels of maintenance but grant support for a relatively long duration. Combining two or more parameters might thus be the way forward for evaluative comparisons. This has been advocated by Grimshaw and Rubery (1997) who have shown that a combination of replacement rate and level of coverage produces a picture of the relative degree of social protection for male and female unemployed across the EU which is significantly different from evaluations based on replacement rates alone. However, one could go further. National tax regimes can have an impact on the actual net disposable income of claimants and would thus have to be included in order to arrive at the ratio of after-tax benefits to net earnings for particular groups of unemployed people and their families at a particular point in time. Some recent studies have tried to take account of this (OECD, 1994c, p. 225; Ministerie van Sociale Zaken en Werkgelegenheid, 1995; Evans, 1996b; Hansen, 1997). Of course, one could further include other types of public intervention which could reasonably be regarded as components of national unemployment support packages, as suggested above. However, because of methodological difficulties of clearly identyfying those subsidies and computing their value, such comparisons stretch the limits of what is currently feasible in cross-national research of this kind.

Conclusion

This chapter has attempted to underline that unemployment compensation can be regarded as but one type of labour market policy which has economic as well as social aspects. Rather than trying to distinguish between allegedly passive and active programmes, a more fruitful approach would be to identify those aspects and to evaluate the direction and scope of their impact. Such an approach might help to bridge a disciplinary division between, on the one hand, economists who tend to be concerned with assessing the effectiveness of active labour market schemes and the disincentive effects of benefit payments and, on the other, social policy analysts who have tended to ignore or neglect labour market policies at the expense of concentrating on systems of unemployment compensation as a mechanism to prevent, or failing to prevent, processes of social exclusion and poverty. Of course, such an approach would require a greater openness of theoretical and conceptual thinking on both sides. This, however, might be what is required, especially in comparative research in the area, in order to tackle methodological difficulties of evaluating national labour market policies across countries and thus to further the understanding of both policy development and the micro- and macro-impacts of those policies.

Further reading

From an international and comparative perspective, perhaps the most authoritative and exhaustive current overview of labour market policies and policy evaluation which attempts to take account of the interaction between different types of policy intervention is Schmid et al. (1996). Good international overviews of labour market policies in a number of countries, and difficulties in evaluating them, are also provided by OECD (1991) and Jensen and Madsen (1993). A good starting-point for an assessment of, and theories underlying, European labour markets and labour market policies is Adnett (1996). OECD (1993), Fay (1996) and Pedersen and Westergård-Nielsen (1993) review country-specific and cross-country evaluative studies and panel-data research on the impact of different types of labour market programmes in OECD countries. Grubb (1994) concisely demonstrates differences between concepts and design features of national labour market programmes and thus highlights the need for sensitivity towards those in comparative research.

Legal structures of provision and institutional frameworks are constantly changing but excellent starting-points for a comparative study on unemployment compensation schemes, taking account of the interaction with other policies, would be Pennings (1990), Ministerie van Sociale Zaken en Werkgelegenheid (1995) and Hansen (1997), all of which discuss systems within a limited number of European countries and are sufficiently detailed. Current institutional and other characteristics of unemployment benefit systems and other types of social security support for unemployed people in the EU are monitored within MISSOC. MISEP focuses on developments in labour markets and labour market policies generally. A good recent and comparative account of basic types of unemployment compensation systems and a number of related aspects within systems in EU countries is provided by Schmid and Reissert (1996). King (1995) illustrates the importance of a detailed historical perspective for the theoretical understanding of policy change in this field.

Acknowledgement

I would like to thank Fiona Clasen, Bent Greve, Jon Kvist and Adrian Sinfield for valuable comments on an earlier draft of this chapter.

Part III

Themes and Topics in Comparative Social Policy

10

The 'Problem' of Lone Motherhood in Comparative Perspective

Jane Lewis

The debate over lone motherhood has been particularly ferocious in Britain since the late 1980s, and in the USA since the early 1980s. Depictions of lone mothers in the British press have been extremely hostile during the 1990s, playing chiefly on the idea that these mothers and their children are an economic burden for the taxpayer. As political parties increasingly chose to enter the moral arena, lone mothers became a favourite target for criticism, notably during the Conservative Party's 1993 'back to basics' campaign, which lauded traditional family values and portrayed lone mothers as undermining them. As Edwards and Duncan (1995) have remarked, in Britain (and the United States) lone mothers passed from the status of 'social problem' to that of 'social threat', as they were charged with economic dependency; with responsibility for the bad behaviour of children and, in the case of unmarried mothers, of young men; and with moral fecklessness. Since the election of a Labour Government in May 1997, lone mothers have continued to be singled out as a particularly acute example of 'welfare dependency'.

A reasonable point of departure for comparative work on this subject is the nature of the contemporary debate and the reasons for it. The first discovery for an English speaker will be the shock and incomprehension of continental European audiences in response to the tone of the debate in Britain and America. Continental Europeans find the iconography that has accompanied the debate in the press repellent. For example, a *Sunday Times* cartoon (11 July 1997) of a blousy bride marrying a man whose face is blotted out by pound signs and the words 'social security payments', and trailing a group of children, obviously intended it to be understood that lone mothers were deliberately choosing their way of life and were probably contemptuous of traditional family life and values. Lone mothers are, first, not the subject of so much comment on the part of press and politicians in other European countries and, second, the tone of the debate is quite different. Why should this be so?

This is a reasonable comparative question and one that is likely to occur to many students wishing to investigate the subject of lone motherhood. It is not necessarily an easy one to answer, because it requires that attention be paid to a large number of cultural, political, social and economic variables. The most difficult task in comparative work is to choose what to measure. The importance of contextualizing comparative research on welfare states has been widely acknowledged, but is very difficult. Esping-Andersen (1990, p. 106) has commented:

> It is analytically difficult to confront detailed historiography with a table of regression coefficients. The former paints a dense portrait of how myriads of events impinged upon social policy formation; the latter seeks economy of explanation, and reduces reality to a minimum of variables. From the former, it is difficult to generalize beyond any particular case, in the latter, we have no history.

Most comparisons of welfare states and welfare regimes begin with a data set that measures inputs or outputs and then deduces the explanation for the observed differences. For example, Bradshaw et al's (1993) study of child benefit packages compared outcomes for children in 15 countries, but as soon as the authors sought explanations for the differences between countries they reached for inputs in the sense of how policies have been structured in the different countries. To do this properly would involve an extraordinary amount of empirical work (in the manner of Baldwin, 1990) and thus Bradshaw's team hypothesized the importance of particular variables to an explanation of the differences. The results are not, as they admit, altogether satisfactory. The demographic variable did not turn out to prove significant, and yet we know that in regard to France, where the child benefit package was shown to be very generous, pro-natalism has driven family policy and that provision of particular family benefits have been absolutely central to the French welfare regime in a way that they have not in Britain (e.g. Dawson, 1979).

This chapter begins with a question centred on the debate about lone mothers, rather than with a question that seeks to explore some aspect of their relative position (in terms of poverty rates, for example) or entitlements, which would immediately suggest the use of large-scale data sets. All that can be done by way of providing an answer is to lead the reader through the kinds of issues that are appropriate to explore, the aim being to reveal the structure of *an* explanation that does not pretend to be definitive or comprehensive.

The Structure of Lone Motherhood

The first place to look for an answer is in the demographics. The numbers and kinds of people who are being talked about or treated is basic to any area of social policy. It may just be that Britain and the United States have much larger populations of lone mothers. Table 10.1 shows that there is some truth in this. All the European countries except Scandinavia have significantly lower proportions of lone mothers than Britain and the USA.

There are also major differences in terms of what kind of lone mothers predominate in the different countries. As late as the mid 1980s, almost the same proportion of lone mothers were widows as were never-married mothers in the Netherlands. The USA and Britain have the highest divorce rates among the Western liberal democracies and their position contrasts hugely with that of Italy and Ireland, where divorce was legally impossible until recently and where divorce rates are extremely low, even though separation rates are increasing (see table 10.2). There are major differences, too, in the numbers and ages of unmarried mothers. Extra-marital birth rates are high in the Scandinavian countries (table 10.3), but there is relatively little young motherhood in any of the European countries other than the UK.

Table 10.1 *Lone-parent families as a percentage of all families (most recent national sources)*

Denmark (1994)	19
(West) Germany (1992)	19
France (1990)	12
Ireland (1993)	11
Italy (1992)	6
Netherlands (1992)	16
Sweden (1990)	18
UK (1992)	21
USA (1991)	29

Source: Bradshaw et al., 1996, table 1.2, p. 12

Table 10.2   *Divorce rates per 1,000 population*

	1960	*1970*	*1980*	*1990*	*1993*
Denmark	1.5	1.9	2.7	2.7	2.5
France	0.7	0.8	1.5	1.9	1.9
(West) Germany	1.0	1.3	1.8	2.0	1.9
The Netherlands	0.5	0.8	1.8	1.9	2.0
Italy	NA	NA	0.2	0.5	0.4
UK	0.5	1.1	2.8	2.3	3.1
Sweden	1.2	1.6	2.4	2.3	2.5
USA	2.2	3.5	5.2	4.7	4

Sources: *Eurostat Demographic Statistics*, 1995, table F-19; *Statistical Abstract of the United States*, 1995, table 87

Table 10.3   *Extra-marital birth rates, 1960–1990*

	1960	*1970*	*1980*	*1990*
Denmark	7.8	11.0	33.2	46.4
France	6.1	6.8	11.4	30.1
(West) Germany	6.3	5.5	7.6	10.5
Netherlands	1.3	2.1	4.1	11.4
Italy	2.4	2.2	4.3	6.1
Sweden	11.3	18.4	39.7	—
UK	5.2	8.0	11.5	27.9
USA	5.3	10.7	18.4	28.0
Ireland	1.6	2.7	5.0	14.5

Sources: *Eurostat Demographic Statistics*, 1992, tables E.2, E.3. *UN Demographic Year Book*, 1965, table 20, p. 522; 1975, table 32, p. 759; 1986, table 32, p. 857. *Statistical Abstract of the United States*, 1995, tables 89, 94, pp. 74, 77

The vast majority of unmarried mothers in Scandinavia are in cohabiting relationships. The proportion of births registered by two parents has also increased significantly in Britain (table 10.4), although the precise meaning of this statistic remains unknown. It is not necessarily the case that the parents live together all the time.

However, given that young unmarried mothers will usually be dependent on the state, and given the particular anxiety about both the sexual morality of young women and about the fate of the

Table 10.4   *Registration of births outside marriage, England and Wales, 1964–1994*

	1964 %	1971 %	1981 %	1994 %
Sole registration	60	55	42	26
Joint registration	40	45	58	75
Births outside marriage (% of all births)	7	8	13	32

Sources: OPCS, *Birth Statistics: Historical Series 1837–1983*, tables 1.1, 3.7, Series FM1 No. 13 (London: HMSO, 1987); *Population Trends*, No. 81, autumn 1995, table 10

Table 10.5   *Live Births to teenagers in selected countries, 1971, 1980, 1990. Births per 1,000 women aged 15–19*

	1971	1980	1990
USA	66.1	53.3	59.4
England and Wales	50.8	30.9	33.3
Sweden	34.6	15.8	12.7
Denmark	29.3	16.8	9.8
France	27.7	17.8	9.1
Netherlands	22.2	9.2	6.4

Source: Selman and Glendinning, 1996, table 14.3, p. 203

children concerned, their numbers acquire special significance when it comes to understanding the degree of moral panic that has characterized the British and American debates (table 10.5).

It is also the case that the large numbers of unmarried mothers in Scandinavia on the whole share the characteristics of married mothers. In a relatively homogenous population, they are white and usually in the labour market. In the United States, unmarried mothers are disproportionately black and on benefit. In Britain, they are disproportionately poorly educated and unskilled and also on benefit. As McLanahan and Booth (1989) have observed for the USA, the debate about lone mothers has focused on other major c~ about women's roles as mothers and as workers, about rac and the relationship between the state and the family. A similar point could be made about Britain although, as Phoenix (1993) has observed, lack of official data in respect of race has to a large extent stopped it becoming central to the debate in the manner of the USA or, to a lesser extent, The Netherlands.

It is probably also important that the change in family structure in Britain has been both dramatic and rapid. By the 1960s there was evidence of the separation of sex from marriage and an increase in sexual activity outside marriage that resulted in a high pre-marital pregnancy rate. However, the vast majority of births nevertheless took place inside marriage. Only since the mid 1980s has the second major change in the marriage system taken place, with increasing evidence of a separation of marriage from parenthood. On the one hand, there is less marriage and older marriage, and on the other there is a high divorce rate, the emergence of widespread cohabitation and a dramatic increase in extra-marital births, all of which have resulted in a high incidence of lone motherhood. High rates of cohabitation emerged earlier and somewhat more gradually in the Scandinavian countries.

Nevertheless, differences in the demography of lone motherhood alone cannot explain the profound differences in the nature of the debate about lone mothers in Britain as opposed to the other European countries. Everywhere the numbers of lone mothers have risen. It is important first to return to the content of the concern about lone motherhood in the English-speaking countries.

The Nature of the Debate about Lone Motherhood in Britain and the United States

Like so many social policy ideas during the 1980s, the analysis of the problem of lone motherhood travelled from the United States to Britain. Major American polemicists such as Charles Murray were given platforms in this country and also influenced British commentators, who repeated many of their arguments in the 1990s. When Britain reached for policy solutions it also looked to the United States (and to some extent to Australia), for example on the matter of securing more financial support for lone mother families from absent fathers. The policies operated in the other European countries remain largely unknown. Castles and Mitchell (1993) have put forward the idea that there is an 'English-speaking family of nations' on the basis of their work comparing welfare outcomes, but it seems that it is also the case that 'policy transference' is much more likely between the English-speaking countries, for simple reasons of language but also, during the 1980s, for reasons of political affinity between the American and British Governments.

In the United States, Gilder (1981) spoke out early against:

the benefit levels [that] destroy the father's key role and authority. He can no longer feel manly in his own home. At first he may try to maintain his power by the use of muscle and bluster. But to exert force against a woman is a confession of weakness. Soon after, he turns to the street for his male affirmations. (p. 114)

Thus Gilder blamed the state's willingness to support lone mothers for the bad behaviour of young men. Without the 'steadying' effect of family life, Gilder feared that young men would turn eventually to crime. However, other, in the end more influential, voices from the political Right in the United States put forward rather different arguments. Murray (1984) stressed the extent to which in a society where birth control techniques were advanced, unmarried motherhood was a question of choice. Given this, the drain on public funds represented by the welfare bill for unmarried mothers was unacceptable. Murray argued that the moral hazard of providing welfare benefits was too great, they created more of the problem they set out to solve. It would therefore be better to cut off welfare benefits to unmarried mothers altogether. Murray pointed out that most married women participated in the labour market in late twentieth century America and that there was therefore no reason why unmarried mothers should be exempt. Gilder (1987) and Carlson (1987), who saw women's wage earning as part of the problem rather than the solution objected, preferring to focus on social policy solutions that gave incentives to marriage, for example via the tax system, and which forced fathers to maintain their biological children. However, both strands in the debate could agree that state benefits for lone mothers were not the answer.

In Britain, similar strands of argument could be identified in the polemical literature by the 1990s. Dennis and Erdos (1992), writing from a traditional left-wing perspective sought to trace the rise of the 'obnoxious Englishman' to family breakdown. Just like Gilder, Dench (1994) warned that:

The current attack on patriarchal conventions is surely promoting almost the exact opposite, namely a plague of feckless yobs, who leave all the real work to women and gravitate towards the margins of society where males naturally hang around unless culture gives them a reason to do otherwise. The family may be a myth, but it is a myth that works to make men tolerably useful. (p. 17)

British commentators tended to follow the conservative, authoritarian strand within the American literature, meaning that they had more in common with Gilder and Carlson than with Murray. Thus Morgan (1995, p. 75) saw policies to encourage lone mothers to enter the labour market as 'the solution to the wrong problem' in much the same way as had Gilder. Morgan's main concern was to deny that lone mother families had special needs, a view that was increasingly accepted by government in the 1990s.

Thus this debate has focused on the fate of children and the fear that they will in their turn under-achieve, misbehave and possibly become lone parents; on the fact that mothers and children can live autonomously with the result that young men in particular are less likely to be tied into families and are more likely to behave in anti-social ways; and, most important of all, that lone mothers are a heavy burden on public expenditure. It would be useful to compare the discourse in other European countries on all these issues. For example, when Popenoe (1988) investigated what he believed to be the 'decline and fall' of the Swedish family in the mid 1980s, he noted the absence of literature on the effects of divorce on children. Such literature, which stressed the negative effects on children, became very important in the United States from the beginning of the decade (e.g. Wallerstein and Kelly, 1980) and was echoed in later British work (e.g. Richards and Dyson, 1982; Cockett and Tripp, 1994). Similarly, there seems to be little evidence in continental Europe of concerns about the effects on the behaviour of young men if they are not tied into families. However, there is a lively debate in many European countries about fatherhood and the importance of fathers caring for their children. In the English-speaking countries it is still the importance of getting fathers to pay for their children that takes precedence. These differences are important and are worthy of further investigation not least because they indicate the extent to which the whole issue of lone motherhood has been framed differently in different countries. This chapter, however, confines itself to an exploration of the last element in the British and American debate, the drain on public expenditure of supporting lone mother families.

Dependency Patterns of Lone Mothers

There are three main possible sources of income for lone mothers: earnings, men and state benefits. Women have rarely been able to rely entirely on earnings because their wage rates have been much lower than those of men and because their responsibility for the

Table 10.6   *Percentage lone mothers employed full time and part time, most recent national data*

	Full-time	Part-time	All employed
Denmark (1994)	59	10	69
(Unified) Germany (1992)	28 (36+ hours)	12	40
France (1992)	67	15	82
Ireland (1993)	—	—	23
Italy (1993)	58	11	69
Netherlands (1994)	16	24	40
Sweden (1994)	41	29	70
UK (1990/2)	17	24	41
USA (1992)	47	13	60

Note: Part-time = less than 30 hours a week
Source: Bradshaw, et al., 1996, table 1.3

unpaid work of caring has resulted in periods of absence from the labour market or part-time work. Over the past century, married women and single women without children have come to rely rather more on earnings and rather less on male kin, while women with children and without men have been able to rely increasingly on earnings and state benefits. However, the way in which women 'package income' (Rainwater et al., 1986) varies considerably.

It is therefore worth exploring whether lone mothers are more welfare dependent in Britain and the United States than in continental European countries. Table 10.6 shows the labour market participation rates of lone and married mothers.

Britain certainly has an extremely low percentage of lone mothers in employment, something that is all the more striking given the high labour-market participation rate of its married mothers, albeit that the levels of part-time working are also high. The labour-market participation rate of American lone mothers is much higher, but the debate in that country has focused largely on the behaviour of unmarried mothers, who are disproportionately black and reliant on welfare benefits. In all the other European countries, lone mothers tend to have higher labour-market participation rates than married mothers, although in the Scandinavian countries all adult women tend to be in employment and the female labour participation rate is similar to that of men. The pattern of labour participation rates is hard to explain. For example, the fact that large numbers of lone mothers are likely to be in employment in both the United States and in Sweden is likely to be due to quite different reasons, given the very different structure of incentives operating in the two countries.

In all countries the amount of income that lone mothers get from the fathers of their children is but a small percentage. However, it has been a relatively constant figure in most continental European countries, where maintenance orders are attached to earnings, whereas in Britain the amounts gleaned from 'liable relatives' under the social security system during the 1980s fell significantly, something that the 1991 Child Support Act was supposed to rectify. In contrast, the income lone mothers get from state transfers is important in all European countries, even in Scandinavia, where income from earnings is relatively so much higher.

The main difference between countries, therefore, lies in the extent to which lone mothers are dependent on earnings as opposed to the state. In Britain, lone mothers are more visible than in other European countries because their labour market behaviour is so different. This helped to give American arguments regarding the evils of welfare dependency purchase. It is therefore important to pursue the reasons for the different behaviour of British lone mothers.

There are strong beliefs about the causes of what is often termed the 'welfare dependency' of lone mothers in Britain and unmarried mothers in the United States. As we have seen, the polemical literature focused strongly on the role of the state benefits in promoting lone motherhood. American academics attacked this argument, pointing out not only that the real value of benefits declined during the very period that the numbers of lone mothers began steeply to increase, but that one of the major reasons for the rise in the number of lone mother families was the decline in the number of two-parent families, which could have little to do with the supposed incentive effects of the benefit system (Garfinkel and McLanahan, 1986; Ellwood and Bane, 1985; Bane and Jargowsky, 1988; Bane and Ellwood, 1994). This empirical investigation of the quantitative evidence dismissed the idea of a causal relationship between welfare benefits and the increasing numbers of lone mothers, but accepted that state provision facilitated the creation of autonomous households by lone mothers. Most of these critics of Charles Murray would also agree that women's economic independence has contributed substantially to family change. However, there is something problematic about this explanation for the growth in lone mother families in Britain and America when so many of them are patently not reliant on earnings. The fact that lone mothers in other European countries package income rather differently shows that we need a more rounded notion of how lone mothers are positioned within welfare regimes and how policy logics have structured their position. It is after all unlikely that, given free choice, British lone mothers would behave so differently in respect of the labour market from their counterparts in other countries, although culture and identity (for example, as mothers or as workers) may differ between countries and affect labour market behaviour. Hakim (1996) has argued controversially that the large number of women working part-time in Britain do so out of choice rather than because there are impediments to their full-time employment.

Lone Mothers and Welfare Regimes

Esping-Andersen's (1990) influential discussion of different types of welfare regime was based on the nature of the relationship between work and welfare, where work is defined as paid work and welfare as policies that permit, encourage or discourage the decommodification of labour. However, women's contribution to welfare has been both via paid employment – virtually the whole of the increase in British married women's employment in the post-war period has been in the service of the welfare state (as nurses, teachers, social workers, home helps, etc.) – and via the unpaid work of caring for children and other dependent relatives. Indeed, as both Oakley (1986) and Kolberg (1991) have noted, the family has historically been the largest provider of welfare and its importance in this regard shows no sign of decline. The crucial relationship to be considered, therefore, becomes that between paid work, unpaid work and welfare (Taylor-Gooby, 1991). This set of relationships is gendered, because while it is possible to argue that the divisions in paid work have substantially diminished to the extent that greater numbers of women have entered the labour market (although not necessarily in respect of pay, status and hours worked), all the evidence suggests that the division of unpaid work has changed little (Morris, 1990; Anderson et al., 1994).

Most adult women face the problem of combining paid and unpaid work. The position of lone mothers is particularly fraught in this respect and is reflected in the structure of their entitlements to social welfare. Women may qualify for social provisions by virtue of their position in the labour market as workers, or as wives (gaining benefits derived from the husbands), or as mothers. The post-war welfare state was based on certain assumptions regarding the stability of families and full employment for men, and in most Western countries it was also assumed that husbands would be breadwinners and the primary responsibility of wives would be the unpaid work of caring in the home.

As the social reality changed dramatically, with increased family breakdown and extra-marital childbirth, and increased female labour market participation, levels of part-time work and unemployment, so policies based on outdated assumptions became problematic. In Britain, the assumption that married women would be primarily dependent on their husbands for cover under the social insurance system was reformed with the passing of the equal opportunities legislation of the 1970s. However, relatively speaking, it can be argued that Britain, like Germany and Ireland, retained a strong attachment to the male breadwinner model (Lewis, 1992). For example, at the same time as the 1970s equal opportunities legislation was being passed, the British government also decided not to pay the new invalid carers' allowance to married women, the reason being that it was assumed that caring was in any case the job of married women. In other countries, policy logics both operated differently from the beginning of modern social provision and changed more rapidly in line with changes in the social reality. Thus in France, women's roles as both mother and worker were recognized by the state, albeit that the former was received preferential treatment (Hantrais, 1993). In the Scandinavian countries it was increasingly assumed in the post-war period that all adults would be 'citizen workers' and that women and men could therefore be treated as breadwinners. In Sweden, government policy in the form of the introduction of independent taxation, extensive child care, and parental leave during the 1970s drew women into the labour market and ensured almost equal labour market participation with men.

However, the position of lone mothers was more complicated. Within the logic of early assumptions about how the family worked and the respective roles of men and women within it, lone mothers became a social problem because they lacked a male breadwinner and yet had children to support. The terminology used to describe them has often reflected this way of thinking (as well as the level of stigma that lone mothers have faced). Thus in Britain in the 1960s the term 'fatherless families' was often used and in The Netherlands, 'incomplete families'. This kind of terminology contrasts with that used in Sweden, where the term 'solo mother' indicated a measure of support for the idea that lone mothers should be self-supporting. Historically, governments have faced the decision as to how far they should replace the male wage earner – whether, in other words, to treat lone mothers as workers and assume that they would provide cash and care for their children, or to treat them as mothers, with state benefits filling the vacuum of the male earner.

Interestingly, approaches on the part of governments to the other main source of support for lone mothers, the absent father, have varied considerably. In Britain, under the early nineteenth-century Poor Law, unmarried mothers were not permitted even to name the father of their child, the thinking being that it would only encourage women's immoral behaviour if it were to be thought that they could attribute paternity to a man and get him to pay. Something of the same attitude is apparent in German law. The Civil Code of 1900 assumed that an illegitimate child was the offspring of a propertied man who would not wish to acknowledge the child. However, in Norway, machinery to enable women to claim support from the father was set up before the First World War. Because lone motherhood has been seen as a moral as well as a social problem, decisions as to how to treat lone mothers and what structure of incentives and disincentives to provide in the matter of where they should seek support has been far from value neutral. In countries where the moral issue has been strongest, decisions regarding the nature and terms of state support have tended to be harshest. This is certainly the case in the English-speaking countries, where the state has been much more concerned to preserve a strict boundary line between 'private' family matters and public policy than has been the case in the continental European countries (Hantrais and Letablier, 1996), but at the same time has been anxious not to do anything to promote a 'deviant' family form.

Historically, in countries where assumptions regarding the desirability and existence of a male breadwinner have been strong, governments have tended to make a dichotomous choice between treating lone mothers as workers or as mothers. Thus in Britain under the Poor Law (which was finally abolished in 1948), lone mothers tended to be treated as workers and were told to keep as many of their children as they could by wage earning. The rest would be cared for by the state. Widows were treated most leniently, largely because least moral blame was attached to them, separated women were treated with suspicion for fear that they might be colluding with their husbands to defraud the authorities, and unmarried mothers were treated the most harshly. By mid century, in both Britain and the United States, lone mothers were treated primarily as mothers, for reasons that had to do with the increased recognition of the work of psychologists, led by John Bowlby, on the importance of the mother/

child relationship; the realization that providing for mothers and children at home could be cheaper than taking some children into institutional care; and the heightened regard for the welfare of children as a result of the Second World War. Over the past decade in the United States and to a lesser extent in Britain, the pendulum has swung back again to treating lone mothers primarily as workers. 'Workfare' programmes in the United States have obliged lone mothers to work or undertake training in return for benefit. In Britain, earnings disregards for lone mothers have been increased and the eligibility criteria for benefits paid to those in work have been extended. This trend has also been observable in another strong male breadwinner country, The Netherlands, which in 1996 moved sharply away from assuming that lone mothers would stay at home to look after their children, to promoting their labour market participation (Bussemaker et al., 1997). Local discretion over the rate of assistance-based benefits paid to lone mothers has also been increased.

However, while the logic of assumptions regarding men's proper role as providers leads to a common set of decisions regarding the choice to be made as to how far the state should support the lone mother *qua* mother, the patterns of dependency among lone mothers nevertheless varies considerably. Labour-market participation rates differ widely between the UK, the USA, Germany, the Netherlands and Ireland (table 10.6), all countries in which adherence to the male breadwinner model has persisted into the late twentieth century. This is because the reasons for lone mothers' labour-market behaviour has to do largely with the nature and generosity of their other sources of income, particularly state benefits, and also with the nature of the sources of care for their children. In other words, it has crucially to do with the nature of the relationship between paid work, unpaid work and welfare. It may also have to do, as we saw above, with differences in values among mothers in different countries as to the relative importance of their different kinds of work, and with differences in preferences particularly in respect of time versus money. However, there has been little systematic cross-national investigation of these issues.

In the USA, state provision for lone mothers has been stigmatized as a categorical assistance-based benefit and is mean in terms of amount, with the result that lone mothers have been pushed into the labour market. The state provision of child care in the USA is also poor, although there is more state support for child care through the tax system (which favours those in better paid jobs) than in Britain. In Germany, the state benefit system is insurance based. Lone mothers who have to resort to state support must rely on second-class social assistance benefits and their position is very unfavourable compared to that of wives who have not entered the labour market and who rely on insurance-based benefits derived from their husbands. In addition, the jobs secured by lone mothers in Germany tend to pay better than those held by lone mothers in Britain. Thus in Germany too there is a substantial incentive for lone mothers to work, notwithstanding the relatively lower state provision of child care (Daly, 1996; Ostner, 1997). In the Netherlands and in Britain the position is somewhat different. Lone mothers draw social assistance, but in the post-war period this has been a nationally determined benefit, which is drawn by men as well as by women. The stigma attaching to such benefits has lessened substantially in Britain since the 1970s. The Netherlands has historically paid generous benefits, sufficient to replace a male breadwinner's earnings. In these countries lone mothers were not pushed into the labour market until very recently. Nor have they been in Ireland, where assumptions about female dependence on a male wage have been most explicitly embedded in the categorical benefits that are available to lone mothers, which classify them in terms of their relationships, past or present, to men (Jackson, 1993, 1997).

In Britain and Germany lone mothers continue to be treated more as mothers than as workers, largely because of the ambiguous feelings of modern Conservatives in Britain about the proper role of mothers (on this and other tensions between the libertarian and authoritarian wings of the late twentieth-century Conservative Party, see King, 1987), and the traditional attachment to the principle of subsidiarity in Germany. These countries have given rather more attention to developing the only other main source of support for lone mothers: absent fathers. Germany operates a guaranteed maintenance scheme and maintenance payments from fathers are deducted by employers with the result that very few fathers avoid payment. Interestingly, the 1974 Finer Committee on One-Parent Families considered European guaranteed maintenance schemes, but rejected them as being too intrusive for the British population (Cmnd. 5629, 1974). However, in 1991 the UK introduced legislation that was much more severe in its pursuit of the absent father, showing how far the debate on lone mothers has travelled. The 1991 Child Support Act moved child support from the sphere of private law into the sphere of public administration and aimed to make men support all their biological children. The Act places an obligation on women to identify the father of their children, something that was abolished in Sweden in the 1970s at the same time as the UK rejected any form of guaranteed maintenance system that involved pursuit of the father. Protests from mainly middle-class fathers and their second wives has resulted in substantial modifications to the formula governing payment by fathers. This contrasts with Sweden, where proposed legislation to increase fathers' contributions has been broadly accepted. Similar legislation to the British Child Support Act was brought in during the 1980s in the USA and in Australia, although the form of the legislation was substantially different (Millar and Whiteford, 1993). In Australia the main aim was to do something about child poverty, whereas in the UK the aim was largely to bring down public expenditure. In other words, lone mothers should depend on the labour market and on absent fathers for income rather than the state.

In other policy regimes the way in which lone mothers are treated is substantially different. In France, where generous benefits are available to mothers with children under three years old, lone motherhood is conceputalized as a risk rather than social deviance. In fact French lone-mother families rely less on benefits than two-parent families in which the mother is out of the labour market, which is a reflection of the extent to which French social policy has historically redistributed income towards families with children (Lefaucheur, 1995). The Scandinavian countries have moved furthest away from the male breadwinner model towards an assumption that all adults, male and female, will be in the labour market, which means that lone mothers *per se* are not conceptualized as a problem. Rather, it is assumed that all adult women will have different employment profiles and needs for child care over the life cycle. The fault line is thus drawn not between one- and two-parent families, but between single-earner and dual-earner families, which means that the issue of achieving equity between one- and two-parent families which has troubled policy makers in strong male-breadwinner countries is absent. The state provision of child care is high, and lone mothers' labour market participation is, like that of married mothers, high. They have all been pulled into the labour market, rather than pushed as in the USA. But they also have substantial call on citizenship-based state benefits and also on programmes that secure parental leave, which operates in Denmark as a tax-based benefit and in Sweden via the labour market and the insurance system. As Sainsbury (1996) has stressed, mothers' entitlements to benefits and to care services have been universalized in Sweden (and indeed in Denmark), which has proved enormously important for the welfare of lone mothers.

Conclusion

Thus it is possible to see the way in which the treatment of lone mothers and the incentive structures that are given to them to package income in particular ways are profoundly embedded within policy logics. But these logics are far from stable and in the English-speaking countries have been strongly influenced over the last decade by the kinds of arguments that were reviewed above. In Scandinavia, rising unemployment has had a disproportionately detrimental effect on policy towards lone mothers.

Not only have lone mothers in the Scandinavian countries in particular, but also in France and the Netherlands, not become the kind of debating issue that they have in the English-speaking countries, but they have also tended to do better in terms of material outcomes (see Hobson, 1994 for a comparison of poverty levels using LIS data). At first sight, it might appear that this has to do with their relatively higher labour-market participation (the high rate of benefits that has been responsible for this outcome in the Netherlands would be dismissed as undesirable and unachievable in this country). However, lone mothers also draw heavily on state benefits in the Scandinavian countries and it is the high social wage – in the form of child care provision and parental leave – that enables them to enter the labour market in the first place. Martin (1995) has stressed the importance of a commitment to explicit family policies in France in lowering the poverty rate among lone mother families. McFate et al. (1995) also concluded that lone mothers do best in countries where they are both in employment and receive state benefits.

In a recent comparative study of lone mothers' employment patterns, Bradshaw et al. (1996) concluded that the low labour-market participation rate of Britain's lone mothers was attributable to the lack of affordable child care. Because lone mothers in the Scandinavian countries and in France have not been categorized as a social poblem, because it is accepted that women will engage in both paid and unpaid work, and because the state does not feel obliged to draw a firm line between the private sphere of the family and public policy, the problems women face in reconciling paid and unpaid work have been addressed. Unless the state takes some action in respect of child care that makes it easier for women to go out to work, it is likely that they will remain on benefit. What comparison of the debates about lone mothers and their underpinnings shows is that the call further to whittle down state support is part of the problem rather than the solution. In the British case, the welfare dependency of lone mothers has much to do with the poverty of their social wage compared to so many of their counterparts in other European countries. The tendency in British legislation has been further to privatize responsibility for lone mothers and their children, by turning to absent fathers and trying to enforce the traditional roles of husband/ breadwinner and wife/carer even when marriage has ended or never even existed, rather than to take collective action to address the problems of combining paid and unpaid work.

In Britain and America there has been active debate about the fate of children in lone-mother families; however attention has effectively centred on the welfare dependency of their mothers. What has been absent is a commitment to the social inclusion of lone-mother families, whose welfare depends on there being universal, citizenship-based entitlements to benefits and services. Inequality grew fastest of all in the UK during the 1980s (Hills, 1996) and the number of children living in households with below 50 per cent of average income trebled between 1979 and 1991. Research has also suggested that the lack of investment in children in the UK is crucial to explaining the high rate of teenage motherhood (Kiernan, 1996). Thus while policy logics are fundamental for understanding the way in which lone mothers are positioned in different welfare regimes, political ideology in respect of family policy and approaches to social investment and integration are key to understanding national differences in policy towards lone mothers over the past decade.

Further reading

There are now two comparative collections of essays on lone mothers, both of which are useful, even though most of the chapters are single country studies (Duncan and Edwards, 1997; Lewis, 1997a). Indeed, most of the work available on lone mothers concentrates on a single country. Kiernan et al. (1998) have written a history of lone mothers in twentieth-century Britain, with limited comparative reference chiefly in respect of the demographic issues. On the European welfare regimes into which it is important to insert policies towards lone mothers, see especially Esping-Andersen (1990) and the feminist critiques of Lewis (1992, 1997b) and Sainsbury (1996). The literature on welfare regimes is voluminous and students may find other feminist critiques helpful as well, particularly that of O'Connor (1993) and Orloff (1993).

The debate on lone mothers is part polemical and part academic. The American contributions deploring the rise in the number of lone-mother families have been particularly influential in Britain

(Gilder, 1987; Murray, 1984; Popenoe, 1988). It is important to see how American sociologists and demographers have refuted these arguments, albeit while accepting that there is a 'problem' of lone motherhood (Bane and Ellwood, 1994; Garfinkel and McLanahan, 1986). Especially important for understanding policies towards lone mothers are the ways in which the problem of lone motherhood has been constructed over time and in different countries. A piece such as that by Phoenix (1993) is helpful in suggesting how these issue might be framed.

11

Inside Out: Migrants' Disentitlements to Social Security Benefits in the EU

Simon Roberts and Helen Bolderson

Introduction

Chapter 3 in this book showed that the terrain of comparative social policy is contested by different theoretical accounts and by a wide range of methodological approaches. It may be difficult for scholars to locate themselves on this rich but patchy ground: moreover, some areas are well trodden but others are relatively bare.

Researchers who pioneer a particular area of the terrain might most appropriately start by 'mapping' it. Maps provide the essential orientation which enable studies to move on to explanatory work and this is clearly important since the reason for phenomena cannot be explored ahead of knowing how and where they are manifested.

The work described in this chapter maps the legislative arrangements which disentitle migrants from social security benefits in the 15 member states of the European Union (EU). The purpose of the map is to show whether the exclusions are widespread and what forms they take in order to conceptualize their significance. However, mapping is only preliminary to considering bigger questions for which different methodologies, richer in explanatory power, are required.

Some of these 'big' questions are about how and why these disentitlements came about in different countries and whether the various barriers to benefit have been lowered or raised as migration increasingly becomes part of modern living. For example, in a number of the countries of the European Union (EU) (Belgium, France, Germany, Luxembourg, Portugal and the UK) benefits for asylum seekers have been reduced and/or settlement provisions have come under scrutiny since 1993. The timing of more restrictive policies comes after a four-fold increase in the numbers seeking asylum in EU countries between 1985 and 1992 and the harsher policies appear to be part of a downward spiralling caused by countries competing to deter applications. They may also be associated with prejudice against some people/countries of origin of asylum seekers who, in 1993, increasingly came from the Middle East, Africa and Asia as well as the Balkan States (Robinson, 1996).

The assumed connections between exogenous factors and restrictive policies need to be examined much more closely. How, in detail, have each of the countries reacted to the changing nature and increasing number of migrants and asylum seekers? Further, what difference have 'semi-exogenous' factors – such as the EU bloc's favourable treatment of migrant workers from within the EU – made to such policies? Beyond these there are questions about the countries themselves. For example, do their individual responses to providing benefits for asylum seekers form part of a coherent general stance towards including or excluding strangers, or do the arrangements for asylum seekers, the benefit entitlement conditions, and the immigration policies strike different notes, suggesting that countries are not all of a piece when composing these various policies?

The exploration of questions such as these might best be conducted by some of the methodologies described in chapter 3 which move beyond that of 'mapping'. Regression analysis, for example, might identify and relate a range of independent variables to the stances taken by the individual countries: case studies can provide a means of unpicking the strands which make up the texture of the stance. The mapping process is more modest and has more limited objectives. However, as we show below, it establishes, in the study on which the chapter is based, that all the EU member countries operate mechanisms for excluding migrants from social security benefits but that these vary in detail. It gives a picture of the prevalence of exclusions written into legislation, and leads, in the section on 'Conceptual Issues', to a discussion of their compatibility with the concepts of non-discrimination, need, and the social transaction, which are central to social policy.

Context

Overview of migration trends

The discussion of migrants' disentitlements should be put in the context of trends in population movements but this requires a volume, let alone a chapter, on its own. The major source for trends in migration and the characteristics of migrants is the Continuous Reporting System on Migration (SOPEMI) (see for example SOPEMI, 1995). As is so often the case in trying to base comparisons on statistics, the figures, although formally equivalent, may overestimate or underestimate as a result of country-specific factors. For example, figures for migrants based on 'non-nationals' will not include people who have been naturalized, and this can lead to an underestimate in countries where naturalization is comparatively easily achieved. There are also difficulties in estimating the number of migrants by countries of origin since these statistics are based on returns from the individual receiving countries which vary in the precision with which they group migrant populations.

In this overview we merely note some important points which have a bearing on issues relating to migrants who move to the member states of the EU. The first is that although the majority of asylum seekers flee to nearby countries, which are often, like their own, among the poorest countries in the world, it is nevertheless estimated that growing numbers of migrants are destined for OECD countries (Spencer, 1994). In Europe, immigration increased in the late 1980s despite the restrictive immigration policies put in place in the 1970s. The political turmoil in Yugoslavia and the major changes in Eastern Europe were contributory factors but there was also renewed growth in the numbers of people moving to Europe from the traditional labour migration countries (Findlay, 1996). Second, among European countries Germany received the highest number of asylum applications in the period 1990–95, and Portugal the lowest (Refugee Council, 1997c). Italy, Spain and Portugal which had previously been countries of emigration have also become countries of destination (Kupiszewski, 1996; Findlay, 1996).

Barriers to benefit

Despite the persistence and growth of population movements across the world, migrants – who wish to settle, work, reunite with their families in a 'new' country, or are refugees or asylum seekers – are often barred from entitlement to cash benefits normally provided in their country of arrival. They may be required to leave the new country if they claim benefits, or certain groups of migrants may be made ineligible for benefits, or it may be impossible for them to fulfil nationality or residence requirements in the social security entitlement conditions. Residence conditions may stipulate that people must be long-term residents to qualify for benefit; or that there must be a period of residence prior to qualification; or that entitlement is conditional on proof of 'habitual residence'.

Migrants may be prevented from claiming, or are made ineligible, solely and explicitly by their migration status. Asylum seekers have the least secure migrant status: they are not nationals or residents, and their continued presence in the new country is conditional on a successful claim for refugee status. Refugees are generally afforded a status similar to that of long-term residents, and for social security purposes are often treated as if they were nationals of the country to which they have fled. Most – ten – of the EU member states also provide a form of temporary or humanitarian status which 'does not equate with refugee status' but which does allow the person to stay in the country (Refugee Council, 1997c, para. 5.3.1).

Some migrants' status hinges on their holding and retaining a work permit which may lapse, immediately, or within a given period, should they become unemployed, even when this is involuntary. Since they have entered the country on the understanding that they will be working, they are *ipso facto* not entitled to unemployment benefit, and sometimes disqualified from other benefits.

Dependants who subsequently join settled workers, in the course of family reunification, may be given permits which allow them to stay in the country only on the condition that they do not ever, or for a period, have recourse to public funds.

Mitigating arrangements

Restrictive social security entitlement conditions are less likely to exclude migrants if the country which they have left is willing to export its own benefits, i.e. the 'first' country's benefit becomes portable. However, these arrangements usually apply only to contributory benefits to which the migrating person already has some claim in the first country. The non-contributory, often means-tested, benefits, which are most likely to provide some form of safety net, are not usually portable so that the migrant has to be reliant on those of the receiving country. There are also the problems caused by inequality between countries: the country which the migrant is leaving may not have benefits to export, or the benefit may be too meagre to exist on, especially where the destination is a developed country. (For details of exporting arrangements see Bolderson and Gains, 1993.)

Many of the barriers to entitlement are overcome if the country of destination has an international social security agreement with the country of departure, under which (broadly speaking, since agreements differ considerably) each makes exporting arrangements and/ or gives access to the other's benefits. There are over 400 bilateral agreements worldwide but, as Roberts, (1998) shows, their cover varies and the poorer countries of the world from which many migrants come, tend not to be included. One reason is that bilateral international agreements are supposedly based on reciprocity, which assumes an even flow of people between the two countries and comparable social security systems. However, it is also noticeable that reciprocity may be sacrificed if there are foreign or economic policy reasons for making these treaties. In summary, the incidence of the agreements is patchy; some agreements are only partial, some countries have very few, and some – especially developing countries – may have none.

The best known agreement is the multi-lateral agreement covering EU countries. The EU Regulation (1408/71), which applies only to nationals of the EU countries, co-ordinates the social security systems of the member states in order not to impair the free movement of EU nationals between them. It provides for equal treatment in entitlement to benefit between EU nationals and nationals of the country to which they have moved, for benefit portability from one EU country to another and for the aggregation of contributions and periods of residence where entitlement and benefits amounts hinge on these. Regulation 1612/68 includes migrants in the social assistance schemes of the country to which they have moved, by disallowing discrimination against them.

The EU Regulations therefore, although not fully adequate, make arrangements which enable intra-EU migrants who are EU nationals to access benefits, either from their country of departure or in their country of destination. They do not cover nationals of non-member states (with the exception of family members or survivors of a worker who is, or was, a member state national), and are not concerned with asylum seekers. They have created preferential treatment for EU nationals who migrate within the EU, and Gough and Baldwin-Edwards (1990), who first drew attention to the problem, noted that this was a direct and undesirable consequence of the establishment of a European bloc.

Migrants who are not covered by bilateral or multilateral agreements have to rely on the willingness of their country of destination to include them in its social security measures and on any portable entitlements already accrued in their own country which that country, under its domestic policies, is willing to export. In the ensuing discussions we leave aside the issues of benefit portability and exportability which have been covered elsewhere (see Bolderson and Gains, 1993) and turn to the conditions attached to social security benefits, to residence and work permits, and to restrictions put on asylum seekers, in the 15 member countries of the EU.

Mapping the Barriers

The data on which this chapter is based, obtained from documents, questionnaires and interviews, are taken from Roberts (1998) and show in what ways the migrants who come from outside the EU are excluded, by legal rules, from benefits in the 15 member states of the EU.

To show this, material was first obtained, about the details of the entitlement rules for each social security benefit, in each country, to ascertain which benefits, in which countries, stipulate that a person has to be a national of that country, or permanently settled there, or has to have some other status related to residence.

Nationality and residence conditions built into social security provisions will operate more restrictively if at the same time immigration rules which determine the migrant's status make it difficult to fulfil these conditions. Migrants are accorded different statuses depending on their reasons for coming to the new country, and/or on the length of time they have stayed or will be permitted to stay there. The benefit entitlement rules may stipulate that a person must have achieved a given residence status.

The route to settlement is a long one in some countries, involving a process of obtaining successive permits for further, possibly longer, periods of residence. In other countries the process may be shorter, with long-term residence status following on a shorter initial period. Similarly, naturalization may become possible only after a ten or more year stay in the country, or comparatively quickly, after two to three years. Moreover, in some countries, e.g. Ireland, and to a lesser extent France, a person may be included as a national if he or she was born within the territory of the country, while in others nationality hinges on descent. In the latter case, e.g. Germany, second-generation immigrants may not be nationals, whereas those who live outside the territory, but are descendants of nationals, are (see Fulbrook, 1996; Silverman, 1996).

To get some impression of the extent to which migrants in each of the 15 countries have rights to benefits, data about the settlement process and migrants' statuses were obtained for each country and put side by side with those about benefit disentitlement.

Social security rules

Seven of the countries (Austria, Belgium, Denmark, France, Greece, Italy, and Portugal), attach nationality conditions, or preferential treatment of nationals, to some non-contributory benefits which are generally means tested. However, these benefits do not all carry the same importance in the countries' social security systems. For example, in France five means-tested benefits stipulate that a person must be a national to claim them but they are mainly special, supplementary allowances. In contrast, in Belgium the main basic social assistance benefit (the *minimex*) is reserved for nationals.

Thirteen of the 15 countries attach some kind of residence condition to benefits (i.e. long-term, prior or habitual residence). Most notably, France, Luxembourg and Spain require long periods of residence, or the holding of a long-term residence permit for some means-tested allowances. Luxembourg, for example, requires a person to have been resident in the country for ten of the last 20 years.

Refugees are usually treated as if they were nationals but not always as if they have been resident. In Belgium, Denmark, France, Ireland, Luxembourg and Greece there are some requirements of prior residence in the country before benefit can be claimed, varying from two to five years, and they also apply to refugees.

Asylum settlement rules

Our data, supplemented by recent material from the Danish Refugee Council (Liebaut and Hughes, 1997) shows that in each of the 15 countries restrictions are placed on asylum seekers' access to benefits and/or to employment. The restrictions may mean that there is limited access to benefits (Denmark) or that pocket money only, or some other special minimum and/or discretionary allowance is paid (Luxembourg, The Netherlands). Limitations take the following forms: benefits are only available for an initial short period (Italy, Spain); they are only available after a given period of stay in the country (Germany, with the exception of minor discretionary benefits); only certain categories of asylum seekers can claim benefits (Austria, Belgium, Portugal, United Kingdom); benefits are paid to asylum seekers but at lower rates than normal in the country in which they seek asylum (Finland, France, UK); there are no benefits available for asylum seekers (Greece).

There is a wide diversity of arrangements under these headings. For example, the asylum seekers from whom benefits have been withdrawn in the UK are those who, not having applied for asylum at the port of entry, are later 'in-country' applicants. In February 1997 in-country applicants made up 43 per cent of the total (Refugee Council, 1997a, para 1.21). In Portugal the non-entitled category form 96 per cent of total applications (Liebaut and Hughes, 1997, figures for 1995).

Benefit arrangements may be accompanied by, or substituted by, a variety of other social provisions ranging from the highly institutional (e.g. obligatory stays at reception centres, as in Germany and the Netherlands) to *laissez-faire*, or *ad hoc* statutory arrangements (as in Austria and in the United Kingdom), or, very rarely, more structured, specialized, needs-related provision as in France (in relation to the Chilean programme in 1974, see Joly, 1996) and possibly in the Netherlands, where the initial period in reception centres is followed up with other statutorily provided residence centres and services (Liebaut and Hughes, 1997).

None of the countries allows asylum seekers full access to the labour market. Eight do not permit it at all, and seven only in restricted circumstances, e.g. at a second stage of the asylum determination process; after a given period of stay in the country; in some regions of the country and only if no indigenous workers are available.

Rules governing naturalization and settlement

Naturalization takes a long time to acquire in Austria, Germany, Italy, Luxembourg, Portugal and Spain (at least ten years). In France and Ireland it can be acquired in under five years; in Belgium, Finland, The Netherlands, Sweden and the UK it takes five years; and in Denmark and Greece seven and eight years respectively.

Permanent residence status can be obtained easily in Finland (after two years); in France (following three one-year permits); in the UK (after four years); and in The Netherlands (after five years). These periods tend to be shorter in family reunion cases. Settlement takes longer in Germany (eight years) and in Greece, Italy, Luxembourg, Portugal and Spain there is no status of 'permanent' residence. Instead, 'long-term' residence is granted in these countries, but only after successive permit renewals, involving various qualifying periods.

Rules for short-term workers and spouses

Nearly all the countries attach conditions to migrants who have entered the country with a short-stay work permit, and nearly all to family members who join migrants already present in the country.

Spouses are entitled to benefit, and do not jeopardize their stay by claiming, in Italy, Spain and Sweden (but this policy is being reviewed in Sweden). Elsewhere, spouses who claim benefits (generally means-tested social assistance and related benefits) within given periods of arrival are likely to lose their right to stay in the country (even though there is no disentitlement condition attached to benefit itself).

The details of the arrangements for migrants who have short-stay work permits vary greatly, depending on the length of the period for which the permit is held, the duration of 'dependency' on the benefit, and the type of benefit. For example, in Sweden, unemployment benefit is not payable for migrants who hold short-stay work permits, but this only applies if that permit is for less than a year. In Denmark, a claim for benefit can jeopardize a short-term worker's continued stay but only if the claim continues for over a year and if the permit is for less than three years.

By contrast, in Portugal, even a worker who has a 20-year residence permit has no right to benefits in the event of becoming unemployed and also loses the right to stay. France, Italy and Spain do not disentitle short-term workers from benefits and do not withdraw their permits if they claim.

Making Comparisons

A rough-and-ready comparison, based on whether countries have exclusionary rulings under each of the headings above, presents a mixed picture.

Three countries (Austria, Greece and Spain) feature exclusions under all the rules. Their benefit systems could be said to be comparatively closed to migrants. As we have seen, international bilateral agreements may mitigate the effects of some of the exclusionary rules. Austria has 17 agreements with countries outside the EU, Greece has 13, and Spain has 11. We do not have data for Austria and Greece to tell us whether these agreements are with countries from which the majority of their immigrant populations originated. However, Spain has agreements with the four main countries which are the sources of its immigrant population.

Italy, Luxembourg and Portugal present two sets of potential difficulties for migrants: they have long settlement processes and some restrictive entitlement conditions. However, these countries do not appear to be among the most restrictive in relation to benefits for asylum seekers. In the case of Italy and Portugal, a contributing factor may be that asylum seekers' settlement policies are less developed (i.e. geared to restrictive measures), because they were traditionally countries of emigration to which few asylum applications were made. Luxembourg has a very high rate of intra-Community migration but very few asylum applications (Poulain, 1996, p. 58).

Ireland appears to have comparatively open social security, settlement and asylum-related rulings but does make some disallowances in relation to spouses and short-term workers. It too has traditionally been a country of emigration but differs from the Mediterranean countries in that it remains so.

Finland, The Netherlands and Sweden (which has been one of the main destination countries for Eastern European asylum seekers) come closest to Ireland. The other countries show various mixes of openness and closure in their social security and settlement rulings.

Three countries (Belgium, France and Germany) are of particular interest because they have settlement rulings which point in a different direction from those of the social security rules. Thus, Belgium and France feature comparatively more nationality conditions in their social security rulings than most of the other countries, but these are countered by the comparatively easy acquisition of nationality either through birth or through naturalization (should people wish it). The opposite operates in Germany, where there are no nationality or prior-residence conditions governing social security but where the settlement/naturalization process is difficult and/or long drawn out, and where nationality depends on descent.

In Belgium and France the settlement rules may, therefore, have some countervailing effect on the operation of the social security rules. Another, but different kind of countervailing influence lies in the form of alternative or supplementary adjacent provisions. Thus, access to benefit for asylum seekers may be restricted, but comparatively satisfactory arrangements for accommodation or other services may be made. These do not affect the operation of the benefit entitlement conditions, although they may mitigate their effects. They are not therefore used as indicators here, but it would be necessary to use them if the dependent variable were to broaden from 'barriers to benefit entitlement', which has been the subject of the study described, to include their impact. However, one problem in a comparative study is that the broader the dependent variable, the more numerous and diverse the indicators, making them harder to identify.

Conceptual Issues

Our findings show that all 15 member states restrict the rights to benefits of asylum seekers and those entering the country with short-term work permits. Just under half of the countries attach nationality conditions, and most attach residence conditions to some, mainly means-tested, benefits.

Seven countries have bilateral agreements with all or nearly all the countries which form the four main sources of their migrant population. The data on agreements relates to ten countries. France, Italy, The Netherlands and Spain have agreements with all four countries which form the main sources of their migrant population. Belgium, Denmark and Germany have agreements with three of the four countries from which their migrant population originates. The UK has agreements with two out of its four main source countries. It has no agreement with India, which is the major source of its immigrant population. Finland and Sweden have agreements with only one of their four main sources, although it is likely that a significant number of migrants from the countries without an agreement with Finland and Sweden are refugees, who would not be included in agreements anyway. However, while these agreements remove the restrictions relating to nationality and residence, they do not affect the provisions made for asylum seekers or spouses.

Two different forms of restriction are apparent in this overview of how the 15 countries treat migrants for the purposes of social security. In identifying them we borrow the terms 'direct discrimination' and 'indirect discrimination' discussed in the Guidance to the British Race Relations Act (Great Britain, Home Office, 1977). Direct discrimination involves treating someone less favourably than another on irrelevant grounds – that is, treating the person differently on the basis of criteria which do not require that difference (see Edwards, 1987). Indirect discrimination occurs where conditions are laid down which apply to everyone but where a particular group cannot comply with them.

Direct discrimination involves not treating people equally in the strict sense of equality: like cases are treated as though they were not alike, on irrelevant grounds. Thus, for example, the needs of asylum seekers are seen as not being the same as those of others. Indirect discrimination involves treating some people inequitably: dissimilar cases are treated as though they were alike. For example, the different circumstances of migrants, who as newcomers may not be able to fulfil residence conditions, are not taken into account. Clearly there are many philosophical and legal problems about what constitutes 'likeness' and therefore whether the distinctions made or not made between people can be justified by reference to some principle.

In relation to migrants what are the 'justifications' for treating some people as not alike and therefore excluding them; or for treating others as entirely alike, when their circumstances oblige them to be different, and therefore not including them?

Direct discrimination against asylum seekers

It might be justifiable to treat asylum seekers differently from others, on the grounds that they have special needs, for accommodation, medical care, legal advice, language tuition or counselling. This would constitute discrimination in their favour, on relevant grounds. However, as we have seen, they are generally provided with inferior provisions, and are negatively discriminated against. This may be 'justified' on the grounds that they are outsiders who are not yet accepted as members of the society to which they are seeking entry.

A difficulty in countering this is that an idea of membership is implicit in all social policies. People have rights and obligations by dint of their interdependence, and although there is no calculus of reciprocity, there is a notion of give and take in a social transaction, from which people gain or lose on the basis of swings and roundabouts. The social transaction is protected against 'free-riders' who try to gain without fulfilling the obligations of membership, by compelling people to exercise it through paying their share of contributions, taxes, etc.

In the past, discussions about social policy have centred, predominantly, around the nature of these rights and obligations. Increasingly, however, there are issues about the political and territorial boundaries within which they apply. It is no longer taken for granted that these are the boundaries of the nation state.

A number of questions have been raised about the role of the nation state in conferring 'membership'. One is about size and composition. Heater (1990), for example, points out that membership or, as he refers to it, citizenship, can be associated 'with any geographical unit from a small town to the whole globe itself' (quoted in Meehan, 1993, p. 54). Another question is about scope, since the state may be viewed as an administrative and fiscal convenience only. Thus 'national boundaries merely allocate special duties' in the same sense in which it is advantageous for tasks to be sub-divided and assigned to particular people (Goodin, 1988, p. 681). A third issue is about the nature and the limits of the state's legitimacy which, on one view, stems from, and is solely delineated by, international law (Baldwin, 1992).

The common thread in these arguments is that they do not presuppose consanguinity between nation, state, territory, and 'membership' which confers social rights. Instead, the state (merely) has fiscal, security and administrative functions concerned with matters relating to an internationally validated territory and the people who at any one time live within it.

Questions which challenge the size and composition of membership, and the scope and functions of the nation state, can be used to support views that the right to welfare does not reside in membership of a community but in the individual, or that if it does reside in 'membership' the concept needs stretching. It might even be envisaged that it could be stretched to its limits, leading to global provisions.

There are problems with these approaches. Intrinsic rights must apply everywhere, but it is obvious that not all countries can provide similar social rights, such as a certain number of weeks holidays for workers, or guaranteed income standards at a certain level. In the absence of major redistribution between the richer and poorer countries, the specification of intrinsic rights of substance is likely to be minimal: such rights are 'thin' rights (Soper, 1993). They can only be made 'thicker', i.e. provide substantive benefits of value, when they are relative to the society in which they are conferred.

There are (at least) two approaches to the difficulties presented by relativism in a discussion of social rights. One is to deny the moral significance of political boundaries and look to the possibility of global institutions, thus potentially marrying the idea of universal human rights with the furthest possible extensions of the concept of membership (the second approach outlined above). O'Neill (1992) has discussed globalization using the example of air traffic control. However, as she points out, there are dangers of the centralization of resources and power. Moreover, the analogy between air traffic control and welfare only holds if it is recognized that it is unsafe for all to exclude some people from benefit. Common danger, rather than communality, is the driving force here. (The analogy would only work were the withholding of benefits from migrants perceived as a threat to world peace.) A further difference is that airlines can charge the cost of globalism to their customers, who choose to fly with them, whereas governments find it electorally hard to levy more compulsory taxes. Moreover, any pro rata contribution to global provisions (for example, related to usage of airports) would not work in needs-related, non market-led provisions and would penalize poorer countries.

The second is to find a universal principle that can accommodate the fact that the world is divided into states and that there is inequality between them. Gewirth's (1982) concern with the precondition for moral agency and action may be helpful. His definition of human right as 'the right of every human being to the necessary conditions of human action' (p. 3, cited by Parry, 1991), implies that people must have the means to act. This gives rise to unspecified rights defined relative to the place of physical presence. Thus it can provide for a standard of social security in keeping with the established norms of the society in which a person may live.

Whether or not the basis of welfare resides in membership of a group, nation, country, etc., or in the intrinsic rights of individuals to exercise their capacities, it seems inevitable that its substance is contingent on the polity within which it is framed and operated. The polity boundary may be drawn at national, sub-national or, in some cases, supra-national government.

The boundaries become frontiers to be crossed in the case of asylum seekers and until they are crossed there is no equitable access to the benefits and services of the country of application. It seems that asylum seekers are deliberately regarded as 'non-members' of that country: the whole process of determining asylum-seekers' rights to refugee status challenges the claim to membership. Moreover, they are barely protected by the extension of the idea of human rights to include social rights. For example, although it has recently been argued successfully in the British courts (Court of Appeal, 1997) that asylum seekers must not be allowed to be destitute, this conferment on them of an essential human right amounts to only the thinnest social right. It has meant that some responsibility for asylum seekers, previously denied, has been acknowledged, but the ensuing arrangements have provided only the most residual of services, still depriving those who do not make application for asylum on arrival (i.e. 'at port') of entitlements to cash benefits.

Asylum seekers hope for refugee status but, as we have seen, are subject to many more restrictions than refugees. For refugees, but not specifically for asylum seekers, the principle of non-discrimination has been accepted and enforced by the international community in the Geneva Convention (1951 and subsequent extension). The right to non-discrimination is a right of form which can lead to rights of substance, but which cannot be reduced in the way in which the right to welfare can.

There are no separate international conventions which deal with non-discrimination in relation to asylum seekers, the assumption being perhaps that they are subsumed in the category of refugees and treated equally, at least until their case has been heard and decided. While this assumption may have held – post Holocaust, post defections from the USSR, and post international collaborative efforts following guilt over the Vietnam War – it has not done so since the

1980s. According to Robinson (1996), 'collaboration has been re-placed by complacent xenophobia and self-interest' (p. 72). He sug-gests that this followed on the arrival of spontaneous, rather than 'quota' asylum seekers from the Third World, who were viewed differently from 'the overwhelmingly white and European and often Christian and skilled' refugees of the earlier period (p. 70).

Thus the principle of non-discrimination has not, it appears, been extended to asylum seekers. If it were so extended, and given that membership is not open to asylum seekers, it would ensure a right which has universal application, with the potential for giving access to the most/best, and not only the least/worst social provisions.

It should be noted that the non-discrimination principle offers quite a different approach to that of harmonizing asylum policy across the EU which is currently being proposed and includes a plan to establish 'minimum standards on the reception of asylum seekers in member states' (Refugee Council, 1997b, p. 3). The Commission of the European Communities (EC) has consistently attempted to make 'enlightened if decreasingly expansive' (Papademetriou, 1996, p. 107) recommendations about equal social and economic rights for third-country nationals, but they have been resisted by member states. Instead, member states have converged to put in place more restrictive policies 'through lowest common denominator inter-governmental processes' (Papademetriou, 1996, p. 110). The danger in attempting to harmonize is that a downward-levelling process is encouraged which has to accommodate to the least-adequate provi-sion made in some countries unless the resources of, and external pressures on, the individual countries are equalized.

The above illustrates again that it is difficult to universalize with-out minimalizing, that is, it is difficult to extend the space across which benefit cover is given while retaining substance, that is, the value of the benefits. We would argue that there is less conflict between space and form than there is between space and substance. The right to non-discrimination is a procedural right of form which can be extended to be universal, even though the substantive right to specific benefits is relative.

Direct discrimination against non-nationals

In the discussion so far we have taken the treatment of asylum seekers as an example of direct discrimination. We turn now to the treatment of migrants who are disentitled from benefits in the coun-tries of their destination, because the social security entitlement rules stipulate nationality or residence.

The nationality criterion is another example of the use of direct discrimination, in this case against a whole group (foreigners) rather than, as in the case of asylum seekers, a sub-group.

The social policy paradigm described earlier, which involves a notion of give and take in a social transaction, cannot justify discrimination against non-nationals, since there is no reason why only nationals should join in the social transaction or the 'common tax and public service systems', which is the hallmark of communitarian solidarity according to Coughlan (1992, p. 112). Moreover, if there are supposedly common 'meanings, interests, values, sentiments, loyalties, affection and collective pride' (Parekh, 1994, p. 94) which define collectivity within a state it does not follow that these can be experienced by nationals only or that they constitute a qualification for the receipt of benefit. These are not, therefore, relevant principles which justify discrimination on the basis of a person being a national: benefits might just as well be reserved for blue-eyed people or any other category on equally irrelevant grounds. (This leaves open the question of whether a nationality condition is relevant for other purposes, e.g. in determining who should have a vote, which involves making decisions about the polity's future.)

Indirect discrimination against non-residents

The residence condition is an example of indirect discrimination: it is not direct discrimination because it applies to both migrants and nationals, since nationals who leave their country may find that they too are disqualified if they cannot fulfil the residence condition on their return. Migrants are none the less indirectly discriminated against, since the disqualification will affect them disproportionately.

The requirement of residence is supported by a particular view of membership, i.e. one which posits that it has to be earned over time. The residence requirements are, at first sight, less at odds with the social policy paradigm; presumably the argument is that the give and take of the shared social transaction has to be established over time, and the right to benefit has to be thus earned.

Residence criteria are not, however, applied to other areas of activity, where mere presence is sufficient. Anyone present in a country is involved in that country's infrastructure, for example, in the use of public utilities, such as street lighting; subsidized transport, museums, etc; the payment of various forms of tax, e.g. VAT.

The distinction between claims to social security benefits and these activities seems to hinge around the perception and the structure of social benefits, and of cash benefits in particular, which are not .

viewed as part of the infrastructure because they are divisible, i.e. allocated to individuals. Payments to strangers, and their opportunity costs, can be calculated as separate items of public expenditure. Because of their divisibility they can be granted or withheld relatively easily.

The divisibility of social benefits does allow for discrimination, but it is discrimination based on the relevant principle of need (see Bolderson and Mabbett, 1991) and not the irrelevant principle of residence. Residence as a prerequisite for membership is no more relevant when applied to cash benefits than it would be if it were applied to other services which are part of a society's infrastructure. Such services are also based on social transactions, but a person's presence sufficiently counts as membership.

The proposition that residence is not a necessary condition of membership is supported from a different direction by Walzer (1983). A leading philosopher of communitarianism, he nevertheless sees no contradiction between the notion that rights are conferred through membership and the notion of full rights for all who are present in a country. However, we have shown earlier that the view which sees social rights as emanating from membership inevitably keeps asylum seekers out, unless membership becomes a global concept. Walzer's acceptance into the fold of those 'present' does not therefore lower the barriers for asylum seekers whose presence is disputed. As discussed above, the further principle of non-discrimination has to be applied where membership is disputed.

The proposal that presence is a sufficient condition of entitlement is not far fetched or unrealistic: our research showed that nationality and residence conditions were not universal in countries studied. Presence is already an important concept in conferring benefit entitlement.

In practice a specific requirement of presence can complicate matters when people are absent from a country temporarily, or when they have claims which they wish to make on their 'old', or previous, country from abroad, or when they go abroad. These are issues of portability and exportability of benefits, and a detailed discussion of them becomes too technical for this chapter. Briefly, the problem of exportability is likely to affect mainly contributory benefits. Where these are seen as individually accrued, through earnings-related payments from wages, they are viewed either as individual property which constitutes a right to possession or as conferring membership of a fund belonging to workers which transcends national boundaries (see Bolderson and Gains, 1993).

The distinction between contributory benefits and others is often not as clear cut as stated above, and in some countries periods of labour-force attachment or residence are used to determine entitlement and pension amounts in lieu of contributions. Nevertheless, for convenience, it would be possible to retain the portability and exportability of benefits such as pensions, which most countries already do, without undermining the concept of presence as defining membership for most other benefits.

A second problem about adopting presence as the sign of membership is the belief that if benefit entitlement is extended to all who are present in a country, greater pressure may be exercised to keep people out. The door can be slammed either by rejecting applications or, it is thought, by making conditions of settlement so onerous that they will deter people from seeking asylum. In our study we found some examples of inverse relationships between open, general-entitlement conditions and the benefit restrictions placed on asylum seekers. Germany and the Netherlands had virtually no restrictive social security rules involving nationality or residence but had seemingly onerous asylum settlement conditions; France and Portugal exercised nationality and residence rules but seemingly fewer restrictions on asylum seekers' rights. However, the claim that there is a relationship between 'soft' social security rules and 'tough' immigration rules, or vice versa, would need to be backed by evidence about a much wider range of internal and external factors which might affect the policy trajectories in each case.

Conclusion

The enquiry began with a concern about the disentitlement of migrants from social security benefits. It established what kind of social security and settlement rules existed which debarred non-EU national migrants from entitlement in each of the EU's 15 member states of the Union. As noted in the Introduction, we see the study as constituting a process of 'mapping' which forms an essential dimension, but only one of many, of cross-national and comparative work.

With a few exceptions, there was little consistency, within the countries, in the extent to which disentitlement rules were written into social security legislation, and into immigration or asylum settlement rules. Differences were noted between countries, which gave a broad-brush indication of the extent to which their social security systems were open or closed to outsiders, but no detailed ranking was undertaken. The broad comparisons were not used to evaluate one country's openness against another. One problem with ranking is that the inconsistencies between the indicators of openness leads to an evening out of the scores, unless they are weighted (e.g unless more importance is attached to certain kinds of social security rules, or immigration rules are considered more important than social security rules, or vice versa, etc.). Moreover, the explanatory power of league tables is limited: in this exercise, for example, the indicators chosen were insufficient to give an understanding of different countries' stances towards outsiders. Further, ranking does not in itself contribute to understanding the reasons for countries' different configurations.

Thus, the study is neither evaluative nor does it attempt to explain common factors or develop models (see chapter 3). However, mapping, as undertaken here, highlights and locates similarities and differences in social security and settlement arrangements between the countries. In this way, a part of the hinterland to other researchers' explorations of how countries respond to strangers and their cultural perceptions of identity and nationhood may be staked out. Mapping requires a comparative methodology which sorts phenomena that are alike from those that are not, and the study therefore has a clearly comparative dimension.

However, the work has also led to an analysis of the discriminatory aspects of different legislative provisions. It established empirically that there are numerous disentitlements and disqualifications which exclude groups of migrants from benefits. It examined the nature of these entitlements and linked their characteristics to wider concepts of discrimination; to the social transaction which forms the social policy paradigm; and to communitarian- and rights-based philosophies. It led to a consideration of possible alternatives to the present disentitlement rules and examined the case for re-establishing asylum seekers' rights to non-discrimination and for abolishing the nationality and residence conditions written into social security entitlements. In these respects it is more typical of a policy-orientated, cross-national study which is concerned with the discovery and subsequent analysis of a wider range of issues than would be apparent from a single country study.

Further reading

Although much has been written about immigration into Western Europe very little has been written about migrants' social security. Brubacker, W. (1989) contains a chapter part of which looks at migrants' social security in the US, Canada, UK, France, West Germany and Sweden. The remainder of the book consists of comparisons of different aspects of citizenship and social membership in the six countries. Hammer (1985) presents in part I a chapter on immigration policies and provision for immigrants relating to Sweden, The Netherlands, the UK, Switzerland and West Germany. Part II presents a comparative analysis of the countries' policies. Layton-Henry, Z. (1990) compares political, civil and industrial rights of migrants in Belgium, France, West Germany, The Netherlands, Sweden, Switzerland and the UK.

12

Accumulated Disadvantage? Welfare State Provision and the Incomes of Older Women and Men in Britain, France and Germany

Katherine Rake

Introduction

This chapter attempts to explain a paradox. The rules which govern the provision of income in old age in Britain, France and Germany rarely distinguish between the sex of present or future recipients. If distinctions are made (for example, in the form of a lower retirement age) they appear to favour women. When we look at the actual incomes of older women and men, however, we see that inequality between women and men is a feature of each of the countries under study, with women everywhere fairing worse on average than their male counterparts. This situation may come as no great surprise to social policy scholars (see, e.g., Ginn and Arber, 1993; Groves, 1991; Hutton and Whiteford, 1994; Walker, 1992) and is doubtless old news for the older population themselves. Nevertheless, it points to an important lesson for those of us conducting comparative analysis of social policy: a thorough understanding of the impact of policy comes not from an abstract study of the rules governing the delivery of transfers and services, but from a detailed examination of policies in the context within which they operate.

The paradox outlined above presents an interesting case for comparative research. On the one hand, we have enormous cross-national diversity in the details of provision for old age. Taking pensions as an example, there are differences between the countries in every detail of provision: the structure of financing, management and delivery are different, as are the many, often highly complex, rules which govern eligibility and entitlement. On the other hand, we have the similarities already alluded to: formal equality of the rules which govern provision co-existing with inequality in outcomes. How do the very different national policies each translate into inequality of outcomes? What is it in the rules themselves in combination with the context in which they operate which ensures women's poorer outcomes in all three countries?

Comparing Policies and Outcomes: the Challenges of Comparative Research

As with all social research, an important part of comparative analysis is the identification of the dependent variable (the outcome or change) and independent variables (the cause of that outcome or change). The dependent variable chosen here is the distribution of income among older women and men. This choice may be contested: as well as transferring cash benefits an important part of welfare state activity is the provision of services (health care, housing, etc.) and some analysts have preferred a broader measure of outcomes which attempts to capture both aspects of state activity. Whiteford and Kennedy (1995), for example, impute a cash value of services received by individuals and groups and add this to a standard measure of income. Whilst the importance of service provision as a part of welfare state activity is beyond dispute, such an approach is problematic. The transfer of services is a transfer of a fundamentally different nature than the transfer of cash benefits (whilst I may trade income for whatever goods or services I choose, I cannot trade my hip replacement operation), and this raises important methodological questions about whether the imputed value of services can simply be added to income. Further, there is no consensus about the value of services, and indeed the cost of a service may be a poor indicator of its value. This is of consequence as any results are likely to be highly sensitive to the exact value assigned to services. Because of these difficulties, the dependent variable employed here is a simple measure of income, which is used in the knowledge that it does not capture the entirety of welfare state activity, and is an often imperfect measure of the standard of living.

The choice and operationalization of the independent variable also pose interesting challenges: whilst our focus is on the effect of social policies on the distribution of income, there are a large number of other variables which affect this distribution. At a macro level, social policies operate alongside several other institutions: employers provide for the pensions of their workers and private financial markets hold investments and pension funds from which the older population may draw an income. Policy also encounters different arrangements at the micro level: labour market and savings decisions vary across individuals and may fall into national patterns; families redistribute income amongst themselves and may completely distort the distribution made by a particular policy (Curtis, 1986). A further layer of complexity is added when we recognize that just as micro- and macro-level arrangements determine the demand for and conditions in which social policy functions, social policy creates and shapes the social reality in which it operates. To put it another way, our independent variables are themselves interrelated. At the macro level, policy, and lack of policy, impacts on the mix of welfare providers. To take an example, the combination of basic and complementary pension in France ensures a high replacement rate across the earnings spectrum, which explains, at least in part, the small private pension sector. In Britain, by contrast, the main state pension offers a low replacement rate for most earners and this, alongside tax breaks on contributions to private pensions, has aided the development of the private pension sector. At the micro level, labour market decisions, such as the decision about the appropriate retirement age, will be shaped by prevailing social policy, whilst other policies may enable or hinder the labour market participation of parents and other carers. In short, the interrelationship of social policy and the broader social context means that no clear boundaries can be drawn around the effects of social policy.

What are the implications of this for comparative studies of social policy? Comparative studies have to cope with variation at the level of dependent variable (the distribution of income is different in each country), and at the level of the independent variables (not only do policies differ, so does the context in which they operate). It is obviously not possible for comparative researchers to hold any of the independent variables constant and this eliminates the option of making and testing simple hypotheses. We must instead deal directly with this diversity by undertaking a detailed examination of these countries through national case studies, which allow us to develop some idea of how the links between policy and outcome operate in each country. This chapter offers such a set of case studies, and uses them to examine how income in old age is affected by the way in which policy incorporates the different experiences of women and men in the labour market and the family. Such an analysis allows us to move beyond a consideration of the treatment of the average or typical individual to examine how differences in women's and men's outcomes are structured.

Our focus on incomes in old age adds a further complication to our analysis: the functioning of pension systems means that at age 65 we may still be able to hear the echoes of decisions taken at age 18 as well as the influence of policies long since reformed. To understand the accumulation of entitlements to a pension, we frequently need data on a whole life-course. This presents a number of difficulties. First, the availability of longitudinal data is limited; cross-sectional data remain the most commonly gathered data. Second, even if we have longitudinal data, pension entitlements can only be assessed for the cohorts who are in, or close to, retirement (currently, the cohorts born no later than the 1930s). This may present problems if the characteristics of this cohort differs from subsequent cohorts. For example, changes in women's labour force participation mean that the pattern of lifetime participation of younger cohorts will differ from that of the present cohorts of retirees. However, given that these younger cohorts have yet to complete their working lives, any conclusion about differences will be based, at least partially, on speculation. The best that we can do in these circumstances is to look at a combination of longitudinal and cross-sectional data to assess how cohorts differ, and how these difference will impact on rates of lifetime participation in the labour market.

This study suffers from a problem which plagues much comparative research – it is trying to do two things at the same time. The chapter attempts to account for differences and similarities within the same country (intra-national variation) as well as accounting for differences and similarities across countries (international variation). A temptation, in these circumstances, is to cut through this complexity by telling a story either of difference or similarity. In essence, the process of typologizing involves such a simplification: any typology stresses the similarities among types whilst differences within types, and indeed within the same country, are played down. This weakness, alongside the limited use a typology has when looking at only three countries, explains why no typologies are employed here. In the current study, I have attempted to look at differences and similarities at the level of policy, but in terms of outcomes I have tended to emphasize the differences between women and men in each country at the expense of looking at the differences between women as a group and men as a group. Whilst divisions of class and ethnicity are doubtless important determinants of the incomes of the older population (although they are probably more important to men than women) a separate study would be needed to do them justice.

Paying the Price: British, French and German Provision for Old Age and Women's and Men's Income in Old Age

Despite often-lauded developments of the late twentieth century, such as equal opportunities legislation or increased female labour market participation, there remains a considerable cost to being female (Joshi, 1990, 1992). The cost arises from:

1   women's continuing responsibility for the majority of caring labour which operates as a constraint on their participation in the labour market;
2   lower returns to women's participation in the labour market (i.e. lower female wages).

Whilst the cost varies considerably between countries (see below), it is present in each, and has a particular effect on older women because differences between women's and men's experience at any one point can accumulate into greater differences over time. For example, after a career break a woman returns to a low-paid, low-status job which carries a higher-than-average risk of unemployment. Subsequently she experiences several spells of unemployment interspersed with low-paid work which means she experiences limited growth in earnings over her lifetime. In this instance a seemingly minor and temporally bounded difference, the career break, accumulates over time with other differences, the sum of which has a significant effect on lifetime earnings. As we will see, for many women responsibility for caring labour has both short-term consequences (for example, lost income during the period spent caring) and consequences for lifetime earnings. Social policies may compensate for these differences, lessening the cost born by women in old age. If, however, this compensation is incomplete or non-existent, policies are responsible for the translation of this accumulated difference into lower incomes and disadvantage in old age.

In the three countries under consideration the principal form of income transfer in old age is the pension system. As with most pensions, eligibility to the British, French and German pension is conditional on labour-market participation – entitlement to a final pension is earned, not granted. In the process of drawing boundaries around how pension entitlements can be earned, certain forms of work are validated over others. For example, in each of the pension systems under consideration credits are given for caring labour, but those claiming the credits can do so for a limited period of time only. The notion that caring is an exceptional diversion from the 'normal' life course of full labour-market participation is thus reinforced and those who care too much or for too long will pay a long-term forfeit in the form of severely depleted entitlements in old age. Further, in each of the pension systems final income depends, at least partially, upon lifetime earnings. The stronger the link with lifetime earnings the larger the penalty women will pay. These pension policies therefore offer a good example of the operation of what Pateman (1988) has termed the employment-centred welfare state (p. 237) which, as many others have noted before me, caters more completely to men than to women. (It is worth noting that whilst pension systems centred on employment are, internationally, the most common form of pension systems, there are alternative models. The Danish non-contributory national old age pension, for example, grants entitlement on the basis of citizenship. Where entitlement is granted on the basis of characteristics other than labour-market participation, as in Denmark, the establishment of a hierarchy of work value, in which caring work is always the loser, may be avoided.)

The basic principles of provision for the older population present an obvious tension: provision for old age is modelled on a pattern of labour-market participation more typical of men whilst old age itself is largely feminized (of the over 65s, 60 per cent in Britain and France, and 64 per cent in Germany are women (Eurostat, 1997)). A large number of the older population have employment records which bear the mark of trying to combine employment and caring duties including long gaps in their labour-market records, spells of part-time work, low earnings and low labour-market mobility and as a result are partially or fully excluded from the main pension system. In analysing the costs borne by older women, this partial or full exclusion from the pension system counts as the first cost. This cost is measured by looking at the direct rights women have to a pension, i.e. the entitlements they have earned in their own right. Partial/full exclusion of women from the main route to income in old age (pensions) means that many women rely on marriage as an alternative route to income. A woman's status as wife/widow frequently earns her entitlements which are derived from her husband's contributions. There is a cost to reliance on derived rights: entitlements are rarely equivalent in money terms to those that can be earned through direct rights; some derived rights benefits may be paid to the husband leaving the wife dependent on her partner's benevolence to pass the benefit on; benefits may be taken away when status changes (for instance, following divorce or remarriage). Following on from both the above, the third cost women may bear is a greater risk of reliance on a minimum income provision, or social assistance. Here the cost

Table 12.1   *Average monthly pension income (FF) of the over-65s by source, France, 1993*

	Direct rights	Derived rights	Additional rights	Total pension income
Women	3,217	828	285	4,331
Men	7,462	31	467	7,960
All	5,094	476	366	5,936

Source: Dangerfield (1994) table 2

takes the form of a low income combined with the stigma associated with means-tested benefits.

How large are the costs borne by women in old age? Below we analyse the distribution of individual income which gives a measure of independent access to resources and therefore of the level of costs borne by all women.

Looking first at the over 65s in France (table 12.1) income has been divided into three sources: direct rights (entitlement earned by the pensioner themselves), derived rights (widow(er)'s pension) and additional rights (table 12.1). Additional rights consist of a 10 per cent child-rearing addition (*bonification pour enfants*) paid to those who have reared three or more children, and a dependant spouse's benefit (*la majoration pour conjoint à charge*) paid, in the vast majority of cases, to husbands whose wives have limited/no direct pension rights (I have categorized this as an additional rather than a derived right as it is paid to the spouse of the dependant and not to the dependant herself).

Women receive, on average, a total pension income worth on just over half (54 per cent) men's average pension income, with women's direct rights to a pension worth only 43 per cent of men's. For French women, derived rights contribute nearly 20 per cent to their total income, compared to a contribution of less than 1 per cent to men's total income. The distribution of additional rights shows a pro-male bias although, given women's lower incomes, these additional rights contribute more to women's income (19 per cent of total income on average) than they do to men's (6 per cent). This bias towards men is explained by the payment of the dependant's addition to husbands, rather than the dependent wife herself, and by the structure of the child-rearing addition which, because it is given as a percentage of pension income, favours men who receive an average payment of

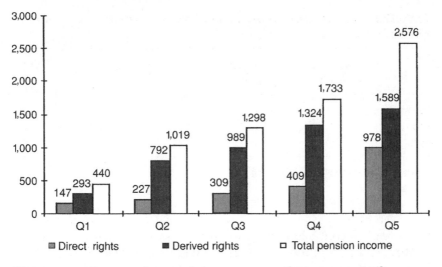

Figure 12.1 *Sources of women's income across the income quintiles –*
Germany
Source: Allmendinger et al. (1993) fig 8.4

almost twice as much as women (Dangerfield, 1994, table 3). This
creates a rather perverse distribution as the benefit of rearing children goes to those who have borne the least cost. Receipt of the
means-tested minimum pension is generally low in France reflecting
comprehensive provision within the main pension. The poorer position of women is, nevertheless, reflected here with 11 per cent of
women receiving this support in 1993 compared to 7.8 per cent of
men (Dangerfield, 1994, table 4).

For Germany, data for the old *Länder* only is presented here
(analysis of data on outcomes from the new *Länder*, and its connection to the very different life courses of East German women and
men, whilst fascinating, is beyond the scope of this present chapter).
Scheiwe (1994) conducts a breakdown of pension income by sex and
class and estimates that in 1993 women's pension income was 39.3 per
cent that of men's for blue-collar workers, and 48 per cent for white-
collar workers (p. 142), showing an even more exaggerated gap
between women and men's income than in France. Allmendinger et
al. (1993) present data for the cohort born around 1920 which allows
us to examine women's income from direct and derived rights across
the income quintiles (see figure 12.1).

What is striking about the position of German women, rich and
poor, is the dominance of derived rights over direct rights as a source

Table 12.2 *Retired women's and men's average (mean) net weekly income by source – Great Britain, 1988–1989*

	State retirement pension	Occupational pension	Other state benefits	Other income	Total
Women	23.08	7.64	6.26	13.11	50.09
Men	24.12	40.93	21.15	21.96	108.16

Source: OPCS, 1992, p. 128, table 7.17

of women's income. Direct rights to a pension account for no more than 25 per cent of total income in the middle quintiles (Q2–Q4), and little more than one-third of total income in the poorest (Q1) and richest (Q5) quintile. This situation contrasts strongly with the figures available for France, where, although derived rights are an important source of income, they do not outweigh the importance of own entitlements, at least for the average woman. Figures on the third cost to women, the level of reliance on social assistance within Germany, are difficult to come by although their omission may not be all that important given that receipt of social assistance for the older population has been falling since the 1970s (Hauser, 1995 cited in Clasen, 1997a, p. 63).

Turning lastly to Britain, table 12.2 shows the income of retired women and men in Britain in 1988/9. From the table it appears that the state pension is relatively equitably distributed between women and men. What the table cannot tell us is the amount of state pension that women earn through direct rights, because no distinction was made in the source data between direct and derived rights. For this we can look at administrative figures which show that in 1996 only 40 per cent of women claimed a pension on the basis of their own entitlements, the remainder relying on entitlements derived from their husbands (Department of Social Security, 1997, table B1.01). The paucity of women's direct rights to an occupational pension is evidenced in the table, with men receiving more than five times the income from an occupational pension than women. For couples the means-tested minimum, income support, and other state benefits are paid, in the vast majority of cases, to men hence their larger average income from state benefits. Nevertheless, older female claimants of income support outnumber male claimants by two to one – in 1996,

1.2 million female claimants aged 60 and over compared to 561,000 male claimants in the same age group (Department of Social Security, 1997, tables A2.11 and A2.13) – reflecting the very high level of reliance on income support among single, divorced and widowed women. These differences between women and men's income sum up to an average total income for women worth 46 per cent of men's average income, a slightly lower proportion than in France, and at similar levels to white collar workers in Germany.

In all three countries there is a considerable cost to being an older woman. The cost takes the form of lower overall incomes in old age and, intimately connected to this, a higher reliance on entitlements derived from one's spouse. Whilst women's incomes are on average below or barely reach half of men's incomes in all three countries, there is some variation in the pattern across countries, notably the much heavier reliance among older German women on derived entitlements. An explanation of this disadvantage is to be found in the policy treatment of differences in the relationship of women and men to two institutions: the labour market and the family. It is these relationships which we now explore.

Accumulating Disadvantage: the Mismatch of Requirements and Realities

The pattern of women and men's labour-market participation is different on a great number of counts, and worthy of a chapter in its own right. We examine a limited field here: how far do the requirements set out by the pension system take into account the realities of women and men's participation? What are the penalties paid if requirements are not met?

Employment rates for women and men vary considerably across the life course, and life-course patterns themselves differ cross-nationally (for example, higher rates of early retirement in France and Germany result in lower levels of labour-market participation for all over 50s). In all age groups, women's participation is lower than men's although the relative size of the differential varies according to the particular point we choose in the life course. If we consider all women, being employed remains a minority experience in each of the three countries: the employment rate of all women over 15 in 1995 stood at 48.8 per cent for British, 41.4 per cent for French and 43.1 per cent for German women. By contrast, the majority of men are in employment, with the gap between men's and women's rate of employment at its lowest in Britain (15 per cent), closely followed by France (16 per cent) with Germany experiencing the largest gap (21

Table 12.3   *Career breaks in Britain, France and Germany*

Women aged 22–60 years who have held a regular job at least once and for over one year

%	Britain	France	Germany
Experiencing at least one interruption	60	37	45
Of whom, experiencing interruption of 5 or more years	58	51	55
Having ceased labour-market activity following marriage and children	20	16	38

Source: Kempeneers and Lelièvre, 1991, tables 23, 26

per cent) (Eurostat, 1996, table 006). As we would expect, labour-market participation for women aged 25–49 is higher in all countries, standing at 70 per cent in Britain, 68 per cent in France and 67 per cent in Germany, but the size of the gap between women and men's participation rates remains.

Not surprisingly, women and men's employment rates differ most markedly when there are young children to be cared for. For women, these rates vary considerably across countries, suggesting that social policy provision has a significant effect on the ability of mothers to remain in the labour market. Of all countries, employment rates of women with young children are lowest in Germany (in 1988, 38 per cent of women with a child under ten were in employment), followed by Britain (46 per cent), with the highest rates in France (56 per cent). As a contrast, men with young children appear to have consistently high rates of employment and differ little in their employment patterns from their childless counterparts, or from fathers in other countries. The percentage of men with a child under ten in employment in 1988 stood at 88 per cent for Britain, 93 per cent for France and 94 per cent for Germany (Moss, 1990, table 1; see also Kempeneers and Lelièvre, 1991; Hantrais, 1994).

Whilst it is evident that women in all three countries are more likely to experience discontinuous employment, we know surprisingly little about the time that women spend out of the labour market. The cross-national data which do exist suggest interesting patterns of both similarity and difference across countries. Table 12.3 presents information on working age women who have some labour market experience and who have experienced a career break (defined as having ceased paid employment for a year or more). Whilst the percentage of women experiencing a career break differs considerably between countries, from a high of 60 per cent in Britain to just over one-third of women in France, of those who do take a break the majority in all three countries remain out of the labour market for more than five years. Further, a significant minority of women, including over one-third of German women, report that they have ceased employment completely because of marriage and children (of course, given the age range of the sample, some of these women may, in fact, resume work at a later date).

These measures capture differences at one point in time, which in turn filter into life-course differences in the total number of years spent in the labour market. Such differences are key where the pension system places a requirement that claimants have spent a certain number of years in the labour force before they can get their pension (Scheiwe, 1994). These time requirements may be:

- a minimum period of employment which must be satisfied by everyone claiming a pension; and/or
- a requirement that the individual be employed for a stated number of years in order to be entitled to a full pension.

Using longitudinal data for existing cohorts of retirees we can get some estimate of the time spent in the labour force over the lifetime and the match or mismatch between this and the time requirements set by the pension (table 12.4).

Table 12.4 gives us a measure of the gap between women's and men's average labour-market participation, and the amount that the average woman would have to increase her labour-market participation in order to match the lifetime participation of men. How do these figures match with the requirements of the pension system? For Britain, a full basic pension is granted to men after 44 years of contributions and to women after 39 years of contributions, a difference which will be eradicated by the year 2020 following the 1995 Pension Act. There is no minimum time requirement attached to the state earnings-related pension (SERPS), the additional British state pension – however, pension benefits are calculated by averaging earnings over the working life, which is assumed to last for 49 years so that those with short working lives bear a cost in the form of lower benefits. In France, the main pension system (*Régime Générale*) requires a minimum period of membership of four months although full entitlement can only be claimed after 37.5 years of membership, a

Table 12.4 *Women's and men's average lifetime participation in the labour market, Britain, France and Germany*

	Britain[a]		France[b]	Germany[c]
	Average years in full- or part-time work	Average years in part-time work	Average contributory years	Average years in full- or part-time work
Women	27	7.5	29	22
Men	47	0.6	42	38
Increase in years of participation needed for women's participation to match men's (%)	74	n/a	43	73

Notes: [a]Authors' analysis of 1924–29 cohort, Retirement and Retirement Plans Survey; [b]1926 cohort, Dangerfield, 1994, table 6 and p. 13; [c]1920 cohort, Allmendinger et al., 1993, p. 196

limit which is to be increased to 40 years following the 1994 reforms. French women's labour-market participation, which is the highest of all three countries, would still need to be increased by one-third in order to match the latest requirements for full entitlement. For the complementary pension (from the *Régimes Complementaires*), no minimum contribution period is required. A price is still paid for reduced participation as entitlements in old age are related directly to the number of pension points purchased over the working life. A minimum of five contributory years is needed to make a claim on the German social insurance pension (*Gesetzliche Rentenversicherung*); however, the formula for the final pension weights the number of contributory years so that the total time spent in the labour force plays a large part in determining pension income.

An interesting commonality emerges here: in each country the time requirements are matched by the labour-market experience of the average male pensioner, whilst the labour-market participation of the average female pensioner falls far short of the requirements. Attempts to compensate for these differences through credits for years spent out of the labour market are made in each of the three countries. Do these credits mean that this difference is not translated into disadvantage in old age?

Looking first at Germany, the 1992 Pension Reform Act instituted credits for time spent looking after children. For each child, a maximum of three years credit may be claimed at the rate of approximately 75 per cent of average earnings (rising to 100 per cent by the year 2000); the credits are estimated to be worth an extra 30DM per month (1996 value) for each year spent in child rearing (Clasen, 1997a, p. 63). Credits are also granted to those caring for the frail, and these are offered without time limit. The mismatch between the amount of time credited and the reality of time spent out of the labour market caring for children is evident; for the present cohort of retirees the three years credit compares to a gap between women's and men's participation of 16 years. Even among younger cohorts, the credits do little for the 38 per cent of German women who withdraw completely from the labour market, and offer only partial coverage for the further 25 per cent who spend more than five years looking after children full time. In France, two years of credit are given to mothers who have cared for a child for at least nine years before its sixteenth birthday. The system ensures that women spend more years undertaking caring work without credits (seven years) than with credits (two years). As in Germany, the two years does not close the gap of 12.5 years between women and men's participation for existing cohorts of retirees, and whilst the high levels of participation of French mothers may be closing this gap, table 12.3 shows that there are still a number of women – (most likely to be mothers of larger families (Hantrais, 1993, 1994)) who spend long periods out of the labour force. Further, the child-rearing addition is paid to the main pensioner (see above), which does little to compensate women directly for their time spent caring. Britain, for her part, offers home responsibility protection (HRP) which is credited to those out of the labour market and in receipt of child benefit and may be claimed up to the child's sixteenth birthday; HRP can also be claimed by those caring for the sick or disabled. For each year in receipt of HRP credits, the number of years of contribution needed to claim a full basic pension is reduced by a year, although even with HRP a minimum of 20 years contributions is needed in order to claim a basic pension. Of all credits HRP is the most generous in terms of years although, like all other credits, HRP only has value in so far as it gives entitlement to other benefits. HRP gives access to the basic pension, worth so little in Britain as to fall below the levels of means-tested social assistance benefits, and adds years but not earnings to the individual's SERPS account. Given that those who have spent time out of the labour market frequently have low earnings and therefore low entitlements to SERPS benefits, the actual value of HRP may again be limited.

Although credits offer important compensation for time spent undertaking caring work, in the present policy and labour market context such compensation is partial and the crediting system therefore remains a flawed instrument for addressing gender inequality. The weakness of the crediting system stems from different sources in different countries. First, as longitudinal and cross-sectional data on labour-force participation suggests, the amount of time credited in the French and German system falls far short of the time that women actually spend undertaking caring labour. Second, the ability of women to combine caring and paid work is constrained by the way in which the credits function. In each system, women are offered a stark choice between either caring full time and being eligible for the credit, or entering paid employment. Such policies implicitly assume that the cost of care falls only on those completely absent from the labour market. Policy does not recognize the cost borne by those who take jobs with which they can combine caring labour (e.g. local, flexible and/or part-time jobs), jobs which frequently carry a cost in terms of lower earnings. By offering an either/or option, such credits offer an incentive to full-time care which may reinforce traditional sexual division of labour and will have long-term consequences for the earnings of the carer. (A future exception to this rule will arise in the German system, following the 1999 reform which will allow credits to be added on to any earnings up to a statutory ceiling of almost twice average earnings.) Third, the credit system in Britain (SERPS) and France adds years, but not earnings, to the account of the individual, which, because of the link made between pensions and lifetime earnings, leaves those who take a career break in a poorer position in old age than those who have had an uninterrupted career. In Germany missed earnings are added in, however the level of credit currently stands at 75 per cent of average earnings, suggesting that the carer is contributing a quarter less than the average wage labourer. Fourth, if the credit system has been introduced only recently and has not been applied retrospectively, then it does nothing to help the situation of those nearest retirement who may need such help even more than their younger counterparts.

Even for those women in the labour market, the high risk of low pay which women face means that the pension problem is not necessarily solved. Low pay is problematic for the individual at a particular point in time *and* for income in old age. Low pay may completely debar the individual from the pension system and/or reduce pension

Table 12.5 *Women and men in the National Insurance scheme, Great Britain*

	Women			Men		
	Employees	Self-employed	All[b]	Employees	Self-employed	All[b]
Percentage paying NI contributions[a]	91	44	86	100	67	92
Bases (1,000s) paying NI[a]	9,603	358	9,961	11,635	1,701	13,336
Total[c]	10,600	806	11,601	11,660	2,545	14,429

Notes: [a] Payments of Class 1 and Class 2 National Insurance contributions in the tax year ending April 1995. *Source*: Department of Social Security, 1997, pp. 297–8
[b] In addition to employees and self-employed, these figures include those on government training programmes and unpaid family workers
[c] Numbers in employment in the first quarter of 1995. *Source*: Office of National Statistics, 1996

entitlements where pension benefits are linked to lifetime earnings. In Britain, membership of the National Insurance (NI) scheme is open only to those who earn above the lower earnings limit. NI contributions may not be made at all because of low earnings, or because intermittent spells of employment mean the contributions over a year are not sufficient to gain a full NI credit, so that the individual loses all claim on NI benefits, including pension entitlements. We can get some idea of the numbers of working women and men excluded from NI by comparing the numbers of NI contributors with the number of women and men in the workforce (see table 12.5).

As table 12.5 shows, membership of National Insurance has a gendered pattern across sectors of employment: 14 per cent of all women workers are excluded from NI with less than half of self-employed women counting as members. Of the estimated 2.7 million individuals in the labour market and not paying NI contributions, 60 per cent (or 1.64 million) are women. As exclusion from NI affects a disproportionate number of women, especially part-time and self-employed women, we can safely predict that the difference between women and men in the number of years of NI contributions made over the life course will be even larger than the disparity in years in employment shown in table 12.4.

In Germany also, limits are placed on membership of the part of the social insurance which counts for pension and unemployment benefit. The pension/unemployment part of social insurance does not cover those who work for fewer than 15 hours per week or who earn less than 610DM per month (1997 figure for old *Länder*), among whom we find a large number of part-time workers. Official figures of the numbers excluded are difficult to come by, but Klammer (1997) estimates that in 1992 the numbers of West Germans whose principal job did not entitle them to social insurance amounted to 2.6 million, of whom 70.5 per cent (or 1.87 million) were women (table 1). The similarity in the numbers of women excluded from the social insurance systems in Britain and Germany is striking. The threshold on participation operating in the German and British systems may be particularly punitive because of comparatively high rates of part-time employment for women (and particularly mothers): in 1995, the percentage of all working women who worked part-time was 45 per cent in Britain and 34 per cent in Germany (European Commission, 1997a). France, by contrast, has no lower earnings limit on contributions to social insurance and the lowest rate of part-time employment; 29 per cent of working women worked part-time in France (European Commission, 1997a).

Even where pay is sufficient to gain access to the pension system, a link is made in all of the pension systems between earnings and pension income, so that a further penalty to low pay is levied in later life. Dex and Sewell (1995) estimate the female/male full-time earnings ratio as highest in France at 0.795, followed by Germany at 0.73 and lastly Britain with the poorest record of 0.68. Recent OECD studies of earnings and earnings mobility reveal important gender differences in the incidence of low pay even among full-time workers (if all workers were taken into account the gender differential would be even greater because of the higher risk of low pay among part-time workers). Further, the studies show that women are more likely to experience long spells of low pay, which has particular consequences where pensions are based on lifetime earnings.

As table 12.6 shows, at least 30 per cent of women in all three countries had some experience of low pay over a five-year period. There is a particularly high incidence and continuity in low pay among German and British women, contrasting strongly with the position of men in those countries. Of all three countries, the situation in France appears to be the least bad for women, although even here the risk for women of being continuously low paid is more than three times greater than the risk for men.

Table 12.6 *Low pay in Britain, France and Germany*

Incidence of low pay among continuously employed full-time workers

	Britain			France			Germany		
	% low paid[a]	Ever low paid[b]	Always low paid[b]	% low paid[a]	Ever low paid[c]	Always low paid[c]	% low paid[d]	Ever low paid[b]	Always low paid[b]
Women	31.2	35.8	12.3	17.4	30.1	6.5	25.4	41.1	9.3
Men	12.8	10.7	1.8	10.6	17.6	2.0	7.6	13.0	0.6

Notes: [a] Earnings below two-thirds of median earnings, 1995 figures; [b] Earnings in bottom quintile of earnings, 1986–91; [c] Earnings in bottom quintile of earnings, 1984–89; [d] Earnings below two-thirds of median earnings, 1994 figures
Source: OECD, 1996b, table 3.2; OECD, 1997, table 2.4

The pension system may, nevertheless, compensate for low earnings by loosening the link between past earning and pension entitlements through an internal redistribution within the pension system. At one extreme, even in a contributory system, earnings can bear no relation to the level of pension benefit – the British basic pension operates along these lines as it pays out a flat-rate benefit regardless of earnings. However, in the pension systems in France and Germany and in the British additional pension SERPS, a link between benefits and previous earnings is established. The link between earnings and pensions may be tempered using a number of mechanisms.

- Placing a ceiling on those earnings which count towards a final pension levels down the pensions of top earners.
- A minimum pension levels up the pensions of low earners.
- Using average earnings rather than final earnings as a base to calculate pensions favours those who have limited earnings growth in their lifetime (among whom manual workers and women are over-represented).
- Using earnings over a short period of time rather than the whole life course as a base to calculate pensions 'forgives' periods spent out of the labour market and/or periods of low earnings.

There is enormous variation between Britain, France and Germany in the use of these mechanisms, with the mechanisms themselves having been particularly vulnerable to reform in the past ten years.

In all three countries, the push behind recent reforms to maintain the economic viability of the pension systems has meant a limitation on redistributive elements. There is little doubt that these reforms will affect a great number of women, particularly the low paid, although the impact will take a number of years to filter through the system.

The German pension system operates the fewest redistributive mechanisms and therefore remains closest to pure insurance or actuarial principles (Clasen, 1997a; Leibfried and Ostner, 1991). Since the 1992 Pension Reform Act there has been no internal minimum operating within the pension scheme; as a consequence redistribution towards, and protection of, low earners within the pension system is severely limited. There is a ceiling on contributions to and benefits from the pension system, set at 1.8 times average earnings and affecting the pension benefits of those at the very top of the earnings distribution. The pension is calculated on the basis of lifetime earnings weighted by the number of years spent in the labour market – this calculation offers little 'forgiveness' for years of absence beyond the credited years and/or for periods of low earnings.

Redistribution in the main French pension is assured both by a ceiling on pension income, and a minimum pension which offers some compensation for years of low earnings. Eligibility to the minimum pension is dependent on making 37.5 years of contributions (a requirement which will eventually rise to 40 years of contributions). As we have seen, even with relatively high labour-force participation this time requirement excludes many women; those failing to meet the eligibility criteria will be obliged to claim the social assistance minimum which pays the same amount as the minimum pension, but carries the additional stigma of means testing. The earnings base from which the main French pension is calculated has recently been extended from the best ten to the best 25 years of earnings. This change is likely to reduce women's entitlements, although it still leaves French women in a better position than German women or British women in SERPS, where lifetime's earnings are taken as the base. The French complementary pension operates on quite different principles and is highly earnings related, offering high pensions to *cadres* (employees in a management or supervisory position) (Palier, 1997, p. 86), among whom we count few women (see below).

In Britain, the flat-rate basic pension is undoubtedly the most redistributive of the pensions under examination, although its very low value limits its impact on the overall shape of the distribution. SERPS benefits are calculated on earnings between the NI upper and lower earnings limit and, whilst these limits operate to exclude some individuals totally (see above), SERPS benefits flatten the top end of the earnings distribution. Reforms to SERPS in 1986 changed the earnings base used to calculate the pension from the best 20 years of earnings to lifetime earnings, which, as in France, is likely to deflate women's entitlements considerably.

Closely connected to the issue of pay is that of occupational segregation by sex. Such segregation has an independent effect on women's access to pensions where different parts of the pension system cater to different occupational groups with certain privileged groups, such as civil servants, having their privilege protected and mirrored within the pension system. In France, occupation plays an important role in the overall structure of the pension system, with separately managed, special schemes operating for civil servants and other public employees, as well as different complementary pensions offered to cadres and non-cadres. The privileged cadres scheme bears the mark of sex segregation in the labour market: of all members of the cadres scheme in 1996 only 27.7 per cent were women; of retirees 19 per cent were women who drew a pension worth, on average, 37 per cent of the equivalent pension for men (AGIRC, 1996). The occupational pension sector is an important source of income in old age in the Britain. The availability of any occupational provision and the quality of that provision varies considerably from firm to firm. In 1994, of all full-time members of pension schemes, 37 per cent were women, with occupational pension coverage of all women employees standing at 38 per cent compared to 56 per cent for male workers (OPCS, 1996, table 8.2). These figures reflect the much greater likelihood of women finding themselves in sectors of the labour market where there is no provision, in part-time employment which has frequently been excluded from coverage, and/or in employment for too limited a period of time to qualify to become a member of the occupational scheme (the EU directive on atypical work, agreed in June 1997, should change this situation as it obliges employers to include part-time employees in their occupational pension schemes). Additional occupational coverage is provided in Germany by some employers although the contribution of these schemes to the total income of the older population is less important than in either France or Britain. Patterns of occupational segregation would suggest that, as in France and Britain, women are less likely to be covered by the schemes, although any thorough analysis of these schemes is limited by lack of consolidated data.

In sum, the mismatch between the requirement of pension systems and the realities of women's and men's labour-force participation has a number of sources, present in different measure in the different countries. First, all pension systems attach a time requirement to claims, which is modelled on a length of career more typical of men than women. Further, whilst labour-market participation of women may be changing, career breaks remain a feature of the life course for a large number of women, with the time-delimited credits offered in the French and German system failing to compensate for the actual time spent out of the labour market. Second, women's lower earnings put them at a greater risk of being debarred from any entitlement to an insurance-based pension in Germany and Britain, and in all three countries final pensions are lower because of the link between earnings and benefits. Third, occupational segregation means that women are more likely to be debarred from privileged schemes, or high-quality additional pensions. Whilst the degree of this mismatch varies between countries and may well be lessened over time, the evidence presented here suggests that the gender differentials, so strongly present in the current cohort of retirees, are unlikely to disappear overnight.

The Family: Sustaining Dependence

It should be clear by now that the conditions laid down for receipt of a pension are rarely met fully by women. The dependence of others on women for caring labour creates, in turn, the dependence of women on the income of others (Land, 1989; Lister, 1990, 1992). This dependence is sustained through the working life and, as the figures given above ('Paying the Price . . .') confirm, the dependence is carried into old age. Social policies interact with familial dependence on two levels: first, policies may themselves create or help to reinforce familial dependency; second, once dependence has arisen, policies may compensate for this dependence whilst the dependant relationship continues and/or when it breaks down following widowhood or divorce.

The assumption of familial dependence is present in all three countries when entitlements to social assistance benefits are calculated. Social policy reinforces this dependency by casting the family as the provider of first resort; in all three countries claims on support may only be made if *family* income falls below the level set by the family means test. In some cases the family must even support relatives who are adult members of separate households (in France and Germany familial support should, in principle, extend from grandparents to grand children and vice versa regardless of whether individuals are in different households; in practice, the requirement to support is rarely enforced across households, not least because of the practical difficulties involved). Family means testing establishes a principle of subsidiarity between families and the state, with claims to benefits only possible where family support is non-existent or has been exhausted (Leibfried and Ostner, 1991; Ostner, 1993; Chamberlayne, 1994). The assumption within such policies is that if family support is available it will, in fact, be given. Studies of the way families actually operate have brought into question the validity of such a model of benign family functioning (see, for example, Vogler and Pahl, 1994). Money is frequently concentrated in the hands of male family members; although altruistic heads of household doubtless exist there is no guarantee that money will be distributed to those family members in need, and little redress on their part if it is not. By looking at familial rather than individual needs and resources, the family means test effectively hides the needs of the individual within families which means that any neglect of individual needs goes unheeded by policy.

Where social assistance benefits are granted, they are frequently paid to the head of household who is, in the vast majority of cases, assumed to be the husband/oldest male (the one exception to this is the French means-tested minimum pension which whilst family means tested is paid directly to the eligible individual). The administration of social assistance benefits thus mimics the distribution of other forms of income by concentrating family income in the hands of male family members. The administration of social assistance and its creation of dependency within families stands in direct contrast to the administration of pensions. Pensions are paid directly to the individual regardless of family means and, as a consequence, pensions offer independence from familial support and freedom from interference from the state in the form of means testing.

Having created and/or reinforced familial dependency, social policies may also provide for relationships of dependence once these have arisen. In Britain and France, dependant's benefits are payable whilst the breadwinning spouse is alive, and in all three countries provision is made for widows (and in France and Germany for widowers) to compensate for the relationship of dependency that has broken down following the death of the spouse.

The means of delivering dependants' benefits makes for a revealing comparison. In France the means-tested dependant's addition is paid along with the pension and therefore into the wallet of the pensioner rather than the purse of the dependant. This operates to counter the cost of having a dependant, rather than offering income, and independence, to the dependant herself. In Britain, a dependant's pension is paid to a couple in which one individual has full entitlement to a basic pension, but the other has no or low direct entitlement. In this instance the dependant's pension is paid directly to the dependant, which would allow for some relief of the dependency if it were not for the fact that the level of the benefit itself is so low (in 1997 this was £37.35 per week compared to the already meagre full basic pension of £62.45). Further, the dependant's pension replaces any entitlements that the individual has to a retirement pension in their own right, so that individuals with up to 21 years of contributions (the number of years of contribution needed to gain a pension in one's own right of the same value as the dependant's pension) lose the value of their contributions.

There is variation in the form of provision for widows and widowers (whom I will refer to as survivors) in the three countries which has an important impact on survivors' incomes. In both France and Germany rights derived through one's spouse are partial, in contrast to Britain, where there is a mix of full rights (for the basic pension) and partial rights (for SERPS). Survivors in France are entitled to 52 per cent of the main pension and 60 per cent of the complementary pension; in Germany the entitlement stands at 60 per cent of the spouse's pension entitlement; in Britain survivors are granted the full basic pension and 50 per cent of the husband's SERPS entitlement. In each country the total 'rewards to marriage' are restricted to a percentage of labour-market entitlement, reflecting again that full entitlement can only be earned via the labour market.

In the same way as husbands, social policies may place strictures on access to survivors' benefits. In the German social insurance pension and the British basic pension, the survivor may claim *either* a survivor's pension *or* a pension from their own contributions. By not allowing the survivor to hold a survivor's pension in addition to their own pension, the survivor's pension is effectively means tested against the pension from own contributions. The majority of survivors are female and, as we have seen, women frequently have poor records of social insurance contributions which means that women's entitlements as widows are often greater than their own, direct rights to a pension. As a consequence, the majority of widows claim their rights as a wife and, in so doing, sacrifice any independent claims they could make as workers. The assumption that widows are dependants is also seen in the withdrawal of the widow's pension following remarriage in Germany and Britain: once the widow has entered into a new relationship of dependency with her new husband, the state no longer has duties to maintain her. By contrast, France allows for survivors' rights to be held in addition to own pension, and for rights to be maintained following remarriage. This policy formulation gives rights to survivors as independent individuals, regardless of their marital status or their own history of labour-market involvement.

In all three countries policy has dealt quite thoroughly, although maybe not adequately, with the breakdown of dependent relationships following widowhood. Rise in divorce rates and the increasing numbers of lone parents present important new challenges for policy. Are social policies dealing with the increasing number of relationships which break down before old age? What of the growing numbers of women who find themselves carrying the cost of caring without recourse to economic support from a husband? The conceptualization of pensions as common property in a marriage has informed the law in Germany where pension splitting on divorce was institutionalized following the 1992 reforms, and provides the intellectual force behind proposed changes in divorce law in Britain (such a debate has yet to occur in France, as far as I am aware). Even where provision is made the valuation of, as yet unclaimed, pension rights remains problematic. Settlements made at any one point in time may not take into account the full cost of having provided care within the family. For example, if a career break means lost earning and lower lifetime earnings mobility, then any provision which compensated for this would take into account lifetime income. The difficulty of calculating and winning such awards means that many women divorcees who, subsequent to their divorce, fail to qualify for derived rights pensions will not have this loss fully compensated for by the divorce settlement (for a fuller treatment, see Joshi and Davies, 1991).

For lone parents, among whom there are, of course many divorcees, the pension problem is a very difficult one to solve. Whilst the status of lone parenthood may not be one that lone parents carry with them throughout the life course, any experience of lone parenthood is likely to affect lifetime income and pension entitlements. As we have seen, there are two principal routes to pension income: marriage and the labour market. For lone parents, and indeed for cohabiting couples who are frequently excluded from provision for survivors, marriage as a route to pension income is not an option. As the majority of lone parents are women, the rewards to the labour market are constrained as they are for all women with lone parents particularly affected by policies which allow for the combination of caring and labour market work. Where provision of child care is thin on the ground, as it is in Germany and Britain, lone parents will find that the employment route to pension income is also blocked. In such circumstances the danger is that lone parents become caught in a lifetime of dependence on social assistance, a high cost indeed for the provision of caring labour. (For a comparative analysis of the treatment of lone parents in social policy see Hobson, 1994.)

Conclusion

Our case studies have helped us to understand a number of things about the apparent paradox of the co-existence of the formal equality of rules governing income provision in old age and the actual inequality of women's and men's outcomes. Although there are many important differences between the systems of income provision for the older population, an overriding similarity emerges: entitlement in each system is gained principally through the labour market. An alternative, although much less lucrative, route to entitlement is through marriage: survivor's and dependants' benefits may be derived through the contributions of one's spouse, although claiming derived rights may involve the sacrifice of one's own earned entitlements.

Given the primacy of the labour market, the case studies demonstrate that when formal equality of rules meets unequal conditions in the labour market, the inevitable result is inequality of outcomes. By fleshing out the rules with an understanding of the realities of women's and men's labour-market participation we were further able to see how many different aspects of the rules worked to replicate or even worsen the disadvantages experienced by women in the labour market. Policies or mechanisms which attempt to soften labour-market disadvantage exist in all three countries. To understand the effectiveness of these mechanisms we need, again, to understand prevailing labour-market and family conditions, as even the most radical or forward-thinking of mechanisms would flounder in highly unequal conditions. The comparison reveals that the experience of old age is, and for the foreseeable future is likely to remain, very different for women and men, reflecting upon the differences that women and men experience during their life courses and on the way in which these differences are accumulated and translated into disadvantage in old age.

Further reading

A number of other comparative studies of women and income in old age have been conducted. Döring et al. (1993), Walker et al. (1993) and Whiteford and Kennedy (1995) look at a wide range of European countries, with the Walker et al. (1993) volume considering broader social conditions alongside income. Two- and three-country comparisons can be found in Ginn and Arber (1992), who take the three very different cases of Britain, Denmark and Germany; Hutton and Whiteford (1994), who look at Britain, France and Germany; and

Maltby (1994), who contrasts East and West Europe in a study of British and Hungarian pension systems.

Several authors have found Britain, France and Germany to be interesting exemplars of the incorporation of gender into the welfare state at the level of policy making and outcomes. For contemporary studies, readers may want to refer to Chamberlayne, (1993, 1994), Hantrais, (1993, 1994), Jenson (1986), Lewis (1993) and Ostner (1993), whilst Pedersen (1993) looks at gender and British and French social policies from a historical perspective. Daly (1994), Langan and Ostner (1991) and Lewis (1992) consider the analysis of gender in a comparative European context and the appropriateness of existing tools of comparative analysis, especially typologies, when gender is the focus of study. Ostner and Lewis (1995) look at the importance of gender to social policies at the level of the European Union.

Studies which have looked at the effect of different national social policies on the distribution of income include Atkinson et al. (1995a); Mitchell (1991); and Smeeding et al. (1990). Each of these studies uses the comparative income database, the Luxembourg Income Study, as the basis of their analysis.

Acknowledgements

My thanks to Sarah Cheesbrough for her efficient and meticulous research assistance. I am very grateful to Arnauld d'Yvoire of the Observatoire des Retraites and Mary Daly of the University of Göttingen for providing information on the French and German system; this information was supplemented by Jochen Clasen who also provided useful comments on an earlier draft of this chapter. All errors and omissions remain entirely my own.

Bibliography

Aarnio, O. 1996: Labour market policies in the Nordic countries – some aggregate-level empirical evidence. In E. Wadensjö (ed.), *The Nordic Labour Markets in the 1990s* (part I). Amsterdam: Elsevier Science B.V.

Aaron, H. 1967: Social Security: International Comparisons. In O. Eckstein (ed.), *Studies in the Economics of Income Maintenance*. Washington DC: Brookings.

Abel, C. and Lewis, C. M. 1993: *Welfare, Poverty and Development in Latin America*. Basingstoke: Macmillan.

Abel-Smith, B., Figueras, J., Holland, W., McKee, M. and Mossialos, E. 1995: *Choices in Health Policy. An agenda for the European Union*. Aldershot: Dartmouth.

Abel-Smith, B. and Mossialos, E. 1994: Cost containment and health care reform: a study of the European Union. *Health Policy*, 28, 89–132.

Abrahamson, P. 1992: Welfare pluralism: towards a new consensus for a European social policy. In L. Hantrais et al. (eds), *The Mixed Economy of Welfare*. Loughborough: European Research Centre, Loughborough University.

Adnett, N. 1996: *European Labour Markets. Analysis and Policy*. London: Longman.

AGIRC 1996: *Renseignment Statistique sur l'Évolution du Régime de 1987 à 1996*. Paris: AGIRC.

Alber, J. 1981: Government responses to the challenge of unemployment: the development of unemployment insurance in Europe. In P. Flora and A. Heidenheimer (eds), *The Development of Welfare States in Europe and America*. New Brunswick: Transaction Inc.

—— 1995: A framework for the comparative study of social services. *Journal of European Social Policy*, 5 (2), 131–49.

Alber, J., Esping-Andersen, G. and Rainwater, L. 1987: Studying the welfare state: issues and queries. In M. Dierkes, H. N. Weiler and A. B. Antal (eds), *Comparative policy research. Learning from experience*. Aldershot: WZB Berlin/Gower.

Alcock, P. 1996: *Social Policy in Britain. Themes and issues.* Basingstoke: Macmillan.

Alcock, P., Erskine, A. and May, M. (eds) 1998: *The Student's Companion to Social Policy.* Oxford: Blackwell, SPA.

Allardt, E. 1990: Challenges for comparative social research. *Acta Sociologica*, 33 (3), 183–93.

Allmendinger, J., Brückner, H. and Brückner, E. 1993: The production of gender disparities over the life course and their effects in old age – results from the West German Life History Study. In A. Atkinson and M. Rein (eds), *Age, Work and Social Security.* London: Macmillan.

Altenstetter, C. and Haywood, S. C. (eds) 1991: *Comparative Health Policy and the New Right. From rhetoric to reality.* Basingstoke: Macmillan.

Ambrose, P. 1991: The housing provision chain as a comparative analytical framework. *Scandinavian Housing and Planning Research*, 8 (2), 91–104.

Ambrose, P. and Barlow, J. 1987: Housing provision and housebuilding in Western Europe. In W. van Vliet (ed.), *Housing Markets and Politics Under Conditions of Fiscal Austerity.* Westport: Greenwood Press.

Amenta, E. 1993: The state of the art in welfare state research on social spending efforts in capitalist democracies since 1960. *American Journal of Sociology*, 99 (3), 750–63.

Anderson, J. J. 1995: Structural funds and the social dimension of EU policy: springboard or stumbling block? In S. Leibfried and P. Pierson (eds), *European Social Policy: Betweeen Fragmentation and Integration.* Washington DC: Brookings Institution, 123–58.

Anderson, M., Bechofer, F. and Gershuny, J. (eds) 1994: *The Social and Political Economy of the Household.* Oxford: Oxford University Press.

Anttonen, A. and Sipilä, J. 1996: European social care services: is it possible to identify models? *Journal of European Social Policy*, 6 (2), 87–100.

Archer, M. S. 1990: Theory, culture and post-industrial society. In M. Featherstone (ed.), *Global Culture. Nationalism, globalization and modernity.* London: Sage.

Arve-Parès, B. (ed.) 1995: *Building Family Welfare. Report from a Nordic Seminar on Families, Gender and Welfare Policy.* Stockholm: The Network of Nordic Focal Points for the International Year of the Family.

Atkinson, A. B. 1990: Introduction. In T.M. Smeeding, M. O'Higgins and L. Rainwater (eds) *Poverty, Inequality and Income Distribution in a Comparative Perspective.* London: Harvester Wheatsheaf.

—— 1993: *On Targeting Social Security: Theory and Western Experience with Family Benefits.* Welfare State Programme Discussion Paper WST/99, London: London School of Economics/STICERD.

—— 1995: Comparing poverty rates internationally: recent studies in OECD countries. In *Incomes and the Welfare State.* Cambridge: Cambridge University Press.

Atkinson, A. B. and Micklewright, J. 1991: Unemployment compensation and labour market transitions: a critical review. *Journal of Economic Literature*, 29, 1679–727.

Atkinson, A. B. and Mogensen, G. V. (eds) 1993: *Welfare and Work Incentives: a North European perspective.* Oxford: Clarendon Press.

Atkinson, A. B., Rainwater, L. and Smeeding, T. 1994: *Income Distribution in OECD Countries: the Evidence from the Luxembourg Income Study (LIS).* Luxembourg: LIS.

—— 1995a: *Income Distribution in OECD Countries*. Paris: OECD.
—— 1995b: Income distribution in European countries. In A. B. Atkinson, *Incomes and the Welfare State*. Cambridge: Cambridge University Press.
Attias-Donfut, C. (ed.) 1995: *Les solidarités entre générations: vieillesse, familles, État*. Paris: Nathan.
Balchin, P. 1996: *Housing Policy in Europe*. London: Routledge.
Baldock, J. 1997: Social care in old age: more than a funding problem. *Social Policy and Administration*, 31 (1), 73–89.
Baldock, J. and Evers, A. 1992: Innovations and care of the elderly: the cutting-edge of change for social welfare systems. Examples from Sweden, the Netherlands and the United Kingdom. *Ageing and Society*, 12, 289–312.
Baldwin, P. 1990: *The Politics of Social Solidarity. Class Bases in the European Welfare State, 1875–1975*. Cambridge: Cambridge University Press.
—— 1996: Can we define a European welfare state model? In B. Greve (ed.), *Comparative Welfare Systems: The Scandinavian Model in a Period of Change*. Basingstoke: Macmillan, 29–44.
Baldwin, T. 1992: The territorial state. In G. Hyman and R. Harrison (eds), *Jurisprudence: Cambridge Essays*. Cambridge: Cambridge University Press.
Ball, M., Harloe, M. and Martens, M. 1988: *Housing and Social Change in Europe and the USA*. London: Routledge.
Bane, M. J. and Ellwood, D. 1994: *Welfare Realities. From Rhetoric to Reform*. Cambridge: Harvard University Press.
Bane, M. J. and Jargowsky, P. A. 1988: The links between government policy and family structure: what matters and what doesn't. In A. Cherlin (ed.), *The Changing American Family and Public Policy*. Washington DC: Urban Institute Press.
Barbier, J-C. 1995: Public policies with a family dimension in the European Union: an analytical framework for comparison and evaluation. *Cross-National Research Papers*, 4 (3), 15–32.
Bardone, L. and deGryse, E. 1994: *Poverty and social protection in the European Union*. Paper for the ISSA International Research Meeting Social Security: 'A Time for Redefinition', Vienna, 9–11 November 1994.
Barlow, J. and Duncan, S. 1988: The use and abuse of tenure. *Housing Studies*, 3 (4), 29–31.
—— 1994: *Success and Failure in Housing Provision: European Systems Compared*. Oxford: Pergamon.
Barnett, I., Groth, A. and Ungson, C. 1985: East-West housing policies. In A. Groth and L. Wade (eds), *Public Policy Across Nations*. Greenwich: JAI Press.
Barrientos, A. 1997: The changing face of pensions in Latin America. *Social Policy & Administration*, 31 (4), 336–53.
Beck, W., van der Maesen, L. and Walker A. (eds) 1997: *The Social Quality of Europe*. The Hague: Kluwer Law International.
Bell, D. 1962: *The End of Ideology*. New York: Free Press of Glencoe.
Bennett, C. 1991: Review article: what is policy convergence and what causes it? *British Journal of Political Science*, 21, 215–33.
Beveridge, W. H. 1942: *Report on Social Insurance and Allied Services*. London: HMSO, Cmnd. 6404.
—— 1944: *Full Employment in a Free Society*. London: Allen and Unwin.

Blair, T. 1996: *New Britain: My vision of a young country*. London: Fourth Estate.

Blendon, R. J., Leitman, R., Morrison, I. and Donelan, K. 1990: Satisfaction with health care systems in ten nations. *Health Affairs*, 9 (2), 186–92.

Blondel, J. 1969: *Comparative Government*. London: Macmillan.

Bolderson, H. 1988: Comparing social policies: some problems of method and the case for social security benefits in Australia, Britain and the USA. *Journal of Social Policy*, 17 (3), 267–88.

Bolderson, H. and Gains, F. 1993: *Crossing National Frontiers*. Department of Social Security Research Report No. 23. London: Her Majesty's Stationery Office.

Bolderson, H. and Mabbett D. 1991: *Social Policy and Social Security in Australia, Britain and the USA*. Aldershot: Avebury, Gower.

—— 1995: Mongrels or thoroughbreds: a cross-national look at social security systems. *European Journal of Political Research*, 28, 119–39.

—— 1997: *Delivering Social Security: A Cross-National Study*. Department of Social Security Research Report No. 59. London: The Stationery Office.

Bonoli, G. 1997: Classifying welfare states: a two-dimension approach. *Journal of Social Policy*, 26 (3), 351–72.

Bosco, A. 1997: Unemployment benefit systems. In A. Bosco and M. Hutseband (eds), *Social Protection in Europe. Facing up to changes and challenges*. Brussels: European Trade Union Institute.

Bradshaw, J. and Chen, J-R. 1997: Poverty in the UK. A comparison with nineteen other countries. *Benefits*, 18, 13–17.

Bradshaw, J., Ditch, J., Holmes, H. and Whiteford, P. 1993a: *Support for Children: A Comparison of Arrangements in Fifteen Countries*, Department of Social Security Research Report, No. 21. London: HMSO.

—— 1993b: A comparative study of child support in fifteen countries. In *Journal of European Social Policy*, 3 (4): 255–71.

Bradshaw, J., Kennedy, S., Kilkey, M., Hutton, S., Corden, A., Eardley, T., Holmes, H. and Neale, J. 1996: *Policy and the Employment of Lone Parents in 20 Countries*. York: Social Policy Research Unit/European Observatory on National Family Policies.

Brannen, J. and O'Brien, M. (eds) 1996: *Children in Families*. Brighton: Falmer Press.

Brubacker, W. (ed.) 1989: *Citizenship in Europe and North America*. New York: University Press of America.

Bryson, A. and Jacobs, J. 1992: *Policing the Workshy*. Aldershot: Avebury.

Burns, L. and Grebler, L. 1977: *The Housing of Nations: Analysis and Policy in a Comparative Framework*. London: Macmillan.

Bussemaker, J., Van Drenth, A. and Knijn, T. 1997: Lone mothers in the Netherlands. In J. Lewis (ed.), *Lone Mothers and Welfare Regimes: Shifting Policy Logics*. London: Jessica Kingsley.

Calmfors, L. 1994: Active labour market policy and unemployment – a framework for the analysis of crucial design features. In *OECD Economic Studies*, 22, 7–48. Paris: OECD.

Carlson, A. L. 1987: Family realities. *The Public Interest*, 89 (Fall): 32–5.

Carter J. 1998: Postmodernity and welfare: when worlds collide. *Social Policy and Administration*, Vol. 32 (forthcoming).

Casey, B. 1996: Exit options from the labour force. In G. Schmid, J. O'Reilly and K. Schömann (eds), *International handbook of labour market policy and evaluation.* Cheltenham: Edward Elgar.

Castles, F. (ed.) 1982: *The Impact of Parties: Politics and Policies in Democratic Capitalist States.* London: Sage.

—— 1993: *Families of Nations: Patterns of Public Policy in Western Democracies.* Aldershot: Dartmouth.

—— 1994: On religion and public policy: does Catholicism make a difference? *European Journal of Political Research*, 23, 19–40.

Castles, F. and McKinlay, R. 1979: Public welfare provision, Scandinavia, and the sheer futility of the sociological approach to politics. *British Journal of Political Science* 9, pp. 157–71.

Castles, F. and Mitchell, D. 1991: *Three worlds of welfare capitalism or four?* Australian National University Discussion Paper 21, Canberra: ANU.

—— 1992: Identifying welfare state regimes: the links between politics, instruments and outcomes. *Governance*, 5 (1), 1–26.

—— 1993: Worlds of welfare and families of nations. In F. Castles (ed.), *Families of Nations: Patterns of Public Policy in Western Democracies.* Aldershot: Dartmouth, 93–128.

Chamberlayne, P. 1993: Women and the state: changes in roles and rights in France, West Germany, Italy and Britain, 1970–1990. In J. Lewis (ed.), *Women and Social Policies in Europe.* Aldershot: Edward Elgar.

—— 1994: Women and social policy. In J. Clasen and R. Freeman (eds), *Social Policy in Germany.* London: Harvester Wheatsheaf.

Chamberlayne, P. and King A. 1996: Biographical approaches in comparative work: the 'Cultures of Care' project. In L. Hantrais and S. Mangen (eds), *Cross-national Research Methods in the Social Sciences.* London: Pinter.

Clasen, J. 1992: Unemployment insurance in two countries – a comparative analysis of Great Britain and West Germany in the 1980s. *Journal of European Social Policy*, 2 (4), 279–300.

—— 1994: *Paying the Jobless. A comparison of unemployment benefit policies in Great Britain and Germany.* Aldershot: Avebury.

—— 1997a: Social insurance in Germany – dismantling or reconstruction? In J. Clasen (ed.), *Social Insurance in Europe.* Bristol: Policy Press.

—— (ed.) 1997b: *Social Insurance in Europe.* Bristol: Policy Press.

Clasen, J. and Freeman, R. (eds) 1994: *Social Policy in Germany.* Hemel Hempstead: Harvester Wheatsheaf.

Clasen, J., Gould, A. and Vincent, J. 1998: *Voices Within and Without: Responses to long-term unemployment in Germany, Sweden and Britain.* Bristol: Policy Press.

Cochrane, A. and Clarke, J. 1993: *Comparing Welfare States: Britain in International Context.* London: Sage.

Cockett, M. and Tripp, J. 1994: *The Exeter Family Study.* Exeter: University of Exeter Press.

Cohen, M. and Hanagan, M. 1995: Politics, industrialisation and citizenship: unemployment policy in England, France and the United States, 1890–1950. *International Review of Social History*, 40, supplement, 91–129.

Comité des Sages 1996: *For A Europe of Civic and Social Rights.* Brussels: European Commission, Directorate-V.

Commaille, J. 1994: *L'esprit sociologique des lois.* Paris: PUF.

Commaille, J. and Singly, F. de (eds) 1997: *The European Family. The Family Question in the European Community*. Dordrecht: Kluwer.

Cmnd. 5629 1974: *Report of the Committee on One-Parent Families*. London: HMSO.

Compston, H. (ed.) 1997: *The New Politics of Unemployment. Radical policy initiatives in Western Europe*. Routledge, London.

Cooper, A. 1992: Some methodological and epistemological considerations in cross-national comparative research. Paper given to doctoral seminar, Faculty of Educational Studies, University of Paris, Nanterre.

Cooper, A., Freund, V., Grevot, A., Hetherington, R. and Pitts, J. 1992: *The Social Work Role in Child Protection: An Anglo-French Comparison. The Report of a Pilot Study*. London: West London Institute.

Cooper, A., Hetherington R., Baistow K., Pitts J. and Spriggs A. 1995: *Positive Child Protection: A View from Abroad*. Lyme Regis: Russell House.

Coughlan, A. 1992: The limits of solidarity: social policy national and international. Paper presented at the Social Policy Research Unit's International Conference on Social Security 50 Years After Beveridge. York: University of York, September.

Court of Appeal 1997: R v. London Borough of Hammersmith and Others ex-parte M and Others: Destitute Asylum Seekers. CA *Times Law Report*, 19 February 1997.

Culyer, A. J. 1990: Cost containment in Europe. In *Health Care Systems in Transition. The search for efficiency*. Paris: OECD.

Curtis, R. F. 1986: Household and family in theory on inequality. *American Sociological Review*, 51 (April), 168–83.

Cutright, P. 1965: Political structure, economic development, national security programs. *American Journal of Sociology*, 19 (5), 537–50

Daalder, H. (ed) 1997: *Comparative European Politics. The story of a profession*. London: Pinter/Cassell.

Daly, M. 1994: Comparing welfare states: towards a gender friendly approach. In D. Sainsbury (ed.), *Gendering Welfare States*. London: Sage.

—— 1996: *The Gender Dimension of Welfare. The British and German Welfare States Compared*. Unpublished PhD. thesis, European University Institute, Florence.

Dangerfield, O. 1994: Les retraites en 1993: des situations très différentes selon les parcours professionels. *Solidarité Santé* 4, 9–21.

Davies, B. 1992: *Care Management, Equity and Efficiency: the International Experience*. Canterbury: PSSRU, University of Kent at Canterbury.

Dawson, P. E. 1979: *Family Benefits and Income Redistribution in France and the UK, 1891–1971*. Unpublished PhD. thesis, York University.

Deacon, A. 1998: Employment. In P. Alcock, A. Erskine and M. May (eds), *The Student's Companion to Social Policy*. Oxford: Blackwell, SPA.

Deacon, B. 1993: Developments in East European social policy. In C. Jones (ed.), *New Perspectives on the Welfare State in Europe*. London: Routledge, 177–97.

Deacon, B., Hulse, M. and Stubbs, P. 1997: *Global Social Policy: International Organisations and the Future of Welfare*. London: Sage.

Del Re 1995: Social and family policies in Italy: comparisons with France. *Cross-National Research Papers*, 4 (3), 68–79.

Dench, G. 1994: *The Frog, the Prince and the Problem of Men*. London: Neanderthal Books.

Dennis, N. and Erdos, G. 1992: *Families without Fatherhood*. London: IEA.

Department of Social Security 1997: *Social Security Statistics*. London: HMSO.

Desrosières, A. 1996: Statistical traditions: an obstacle to international comparisons. In L. Hantrais and S. Mangen (eds), *Cross-National Research Methods in the Social Sciences*. London: Pinter.

Dex, S. and Sewell, R. 1995: Equal Opportunities Policies and Women's Labour Market Status in Industrial Countries. In J. Humphries and J. Rubery (eds), *The Economics of Equal Opportunities*. Manchester: Equal Opportunities Commission.

Dickens, P., Duncan, S., Goodwin, M. and Gray, F. 1985: *Housing, States and Localities*. London: Methuen.

Disney, R., Bellmann, L., Carruth, A. et al. 1992: *Helping the Unemployed. Active Labour Market Policies in Britain and Germany*. London: Anglo-German Foundation.

Ditch J. S. 1996: Comparing discretionary payments within social assistance. In A. M. Guillemard, J. Lewis, S. Ringen and R. Salais (eds), *Comparing Social Welfare Systems in Europe*. Vol. 1, Oxford Conference, MIRE: Paris, 337–67.

Ditch, J., Barnes, H., Bradshaw, J., Commaille, J. and Eardley, T. 1995: *European Observatory on National Family Policies: A Synthesis of National Family Policies 1994*. York: Social Policy Research Unit.

Ditch, J. S., Bradshaw, J. and Barnes, H. 1997a: *Synthesis of National Family Policies*. York: Commission of the European Communities.

Ditch, J. S., Bradshaw, J., Clasen, J., Huby, M. and Moodie, M. 1997b: *Comparative Social Assistance: Localisation and Discretion*. Aldershot: SPRU and Avebury.

Ditch, J. S. and Oldfield, N. 1998: Social assistance: recent trends and themes. Report to Department of Social Security (also forthcoming in *Journal of European Social Policy*).

Ditch, J. S., Oldfield, N., Astin, M. 1998: *The Social Assistance Database*. University of York (available from the ESRC Survey Archive).

Döhler, M. 1991: Policy networks, opportunity structures and neo-Conservative reform strategies in health policy. In B. Marin and R. Mayntz (eds), *Policy Networks: empirical evidence and theoretical considerations*. Frankfurt: Campus.

Doling, J. 1997: *Comparative Housing Policy: Government and Housing in Advanced Industrialized Countries*. Basingstoke: Macmillan.

—— 1998: Housing policies and the Little Tigers: how do they compare with Western Countries? *Housing Studies* (forthcoming).

Donnison, D. 1967: *The Government of Housing*. Harmondsworth: Penguin.

Donnison, D. and Ungerson, C. 1982: *Housing Policy*. Harmondsworth: Penguin.

Döring, D., Hauser, R., Rolf, G. and Tibitanzl, F. 1993: Old age security for women in the twelve EC countries. *Journal of European Social Policy* 4 (1), 1–18.

Doty, P. 1988: Long-term care in international perspective. *Health Care Financing Review* annual supplement, 145–55.

Duclaud-Williams, R. 1978: *The Politics of Housing in Britain and France.* London: Heinemann.

Dumon, W. (ed.) 1994: *Changing Family Policies in the Member States of the European Union.* Brussels: Commission of the European Communities: DGV and European Observatory on National Family Policies.

Duncan, S. and Edwards, R. 1997: *Single Mothers in an International Context: Mothers or Workers?* London: UCL Press.

Dyson, K. 1980: *The State Tradition in Western Europe.* Oxford: Oxford University Press.

Eardley, T. 1996: Lessons from a study of OECD social assistance schemes in the OECD countries. In L. Hantrais and S. Mangen (eds), *Cross-National Research Methods in the Social Sciences.* London: Pinter.

Eardley, T., Bradshaw, J., Ditch, J., Gough, I. and Whiteford, P. 1996a: *Social Assistance Schemes in OECD Countries.* Vol. 1, Synthesis Report No. 46. DSS Research Report. London: HMSO.

—— 1996b: *Social Assistance Schemes in OECD Countries.* Vol. 2: Country Reports. DSS Research Report No. 47. London: HMSO.

Eckstein, H. 1960: *Pressure Group Politics. The Case of the British Medical Association.* London: George Allen and Unwin.

Eckstein, H. and Apter, D. E. (eds) 1963: *Comparative Politics.* New York: The Free Press.

Edwards, J. 1987: *Positive Discrimination, Social Justice and Social Policy: Moral Scrutiny of a Policy Practice.* London: Tavistock Publications.

Edwards, R. and Duncan, S. 1995: Rational economic man or women in social context? In E. B. Silva (ed.), *Good Enough Mothering.* London: Routledge.

Ekert-Jaffé, O. 1986: Effets et limites des aides financières aux familles: une expérience et un modèle. *Population*, 41 (2), 327–48.

Ellwood, D. T. and Bane, M. J. 1985: The impact of AFDC on family structure and living arrangements. In R. G. Ehrenberg (ed.), *Research in Labour Economics*, 7. Greenwich Conn.: JAI Press.

Elola, J. 1996: Health care system reforms in western European countries: the relevance of health care organization. *International Journal of Health Services*, 26 (2), 239–51.

Emms, P. 1990: *Social Housing: A European Dilemma?* Bristol: School for Advanced Urban Studies, University of Bristol.

Engbersen, G., Schuyt, K., Timmer, J. and van Waarden, F. 1993: *Cultures of Unemployment. A comparative look at long-term unemployment and urban poverty.* Boulder: Westview Press.

Esping-Andersen, G. 1987: The comparison of policy regimes: an introduction. In M. Rein, G. Esping-Andersen and L. Rainwater (eds), *Stagnation and Renewal in Social Policy: The Rise and Fall of Policy Regimes.* New York and London: Armonk.

—— 1990: *The Three Worlds of Welfare Capitalism.* Oxford: Polity Press and Blackwell.

—— 1993: The comparative macro-sociology of welfare states. In L. Moreno (ed.), *Social Change and Welfare Development.* Madrid: Consejo Superior de Inverstigaciones Científicas.

—— (ed.) 1996a: *Welfare States in Transition. National Adaptations in Global Economies.* London: Sage.

—— 1996b: Welfare states without work: the impasse of labour shedding and familialism in continental European social policy. In G. Esping-Andersen (ed.), *Welfare States in Transition. National Adaptations in Global Economies*. London: Sage.

European Commission 1993: *Social Protection in Europe*. Luxembourg: Office for Official Publications of the European Communities.

——1994a: *European Social Policy. A Way Forward for the Union*. Luxembourg: Office for Official Publications of the European Communities, COM(94) 333 of 27 July 1994.

——1994b: The European Union and the family. *Social Europe*, 1 (94). Luxembourg: Office for Official Publications of the European Communities.

——1994c: *Growth, Competitiveness, Employment: The Challenges and Way forward into the 21st Century*. White Paper. Luxembourg: European Commission.

——1995a: *Employment in Europe 1995*. Luxembourg: Office of Official Publications of the European Communities.

——1995b: *The Demographic Situation in the European Union. 1994 Report*. Luxembourg: Office for Official Publications of the European Communities, COM (94) 595.

——1995c: *Social Protection in Europe*. Luxembourg: Office of Official Publications for the European Community.

——1996: *Employment in Europe 1996*. Luxembourg: Office of Official Publications of the European Communities.

——1997a: *Employment in Europe 1997*. Luxembourg: Office of Official Publications of the European Communities.

——1997b: *Labour Market Studies*. (Individual publications for each member state.) Luxembourg: Office of Official Publications of the European Communities.

Eurostat 1995: Households and families in the European Economic Area. *Statistics in Focus. Population and Social Conditions*, 5.

——1996: *Labour Force Survey Results – 1995*. Luxembourg: Statistical Office of the European Communities.

——1997: *Demographic Statistics*. Luxembourg: Statistical Office of the European Communities.

Evans, M. 1996a: *Means-testing the unemployed in Britain, France and Germany*. Discussion Paper 117, Welfare State Programme, STICERD, London School of Economics and Political Science.

——1996b: *Families on the dole in Britain, France and Germany*. Discussion Paper 118, Welfare State Programme, STICERD, London School of Economics and Political Science.

Evans, P. B., Reuschemeyer, D. and Skocpol, T. (eds) 1985: *Bringing the State Back In*. Cambridge: Cambridge University Press.

Evans, R. G. 1987: Hang together, or hang separately: the viability of a universal health care system in an aging society. *Canadian Public Policy*, 8 (2), 165–80.

Evers, A. 1993: The welfare mix approach. Understanding the pluralism of welfare systems. In A. Evers and I. Svetlik (eds), *Balancing Pluralism: New Welfare Mixes in Care for the Elderly*. Aldershot: Avebury.

——1994: Payments for care: a small but significant part of a wider debate. In A. Evers, M. Pijl and C. Ungerson (eds), *Payments for Care: a Comparative Overview*. Aldershot: Avebury.

Evers, A. and Wintersberger, H. (eds) 1990: *Shifts in the Welfare Mix. Their Impact on Work, Social Services and Welfare Policies*. Frankfurt/New York: Campus/Westview.

Evers, A. and Svetlik, I. (eds) 1991: *New Welfare Mixes in Care for the Elderly* (vols 1–3). Vienna: European Centre for Social Welfare Policy and Research.

——1993: *Balancing Pluralism: New Welfare Mixes in Care for the Elderly*. Aldershot: Avebury.

Evers, A., Pijl, M. and Ungerson, C. (eds) 1994: *Payments for Care: a Comparative Overview*. Aldershot: Avebury.

Fawcett, H. and Papadopoulos, T. 1997: Adequacy of support for the unemployed in the EU. *West European Politics*, 20 (3), 1–30.

Fay, R. G. 1996: Enhancing the effectiveness of active labour market policies: evidence from programme evaluations in OECD countries. *Labour Market and Social Policy, Occasional Papers*, No. 18, Paris: OECD.

Ferge, Z. 1997a: The changed welfare paradigm; the individualisation of the social. *Social Policy and Administration*, 31 (1), 20–44.

——1997b: A Central European perspective on the social quality of Europe. In W. Beck, L. van der Maesen and A. Walker (eds), *The Social Quality of Europe*. The Hague: Kluwer Law International, 165–81.

Ferrera, M. 1993: *EC Citizens and Social Protection. Main results from a Eurobarometer survey*. Brussels: Commission of the European Communities.

——1995: The rise and fall of democratic universalism. Health care reform in Italy, 1978–1994. *Journal of Health Politics, Policy and Law*, 20 (3), 275–302.

——1996: The 'southern model' of welfare in social Europe. *Journal of European Social Policy*, 6 (1), 17–37.

Field, M. 1989: Introduction. In M. Field (ed.), *Success and Crisis in National Health Systems: a comparative approach*. New York: Routledge.

Findlay, A. 1996: Extra-union migration: the South-North perspective. In P. Rees, J. Stillwell, A. Convey and M. Kupiszewski (eds), *Population Migration in the European Union*. Chichester: Wiley.

Fitzpatrick, T. 1996: Postmodernism, welfare and radical politics. *Journal of Social Policy*, 25 (3), 303–20.

Fletcher, R. 1972: *The Making of Sociology: A Study of Sociological Theory, Vols 1 and 2*. London: Nelson's University Paperbacks.

Flora, P. and Heidenheimer, A. (eds) 1981: *The Development of Welfare States in Europe and America*. New Brunswick: Transaction Inc.

Forrest, R. and Murie, A. 1988: *Selling the Welfare State*. London: Routledge.

France, G. 1996: Constrained governance and the evolution of the Italian National Health Service since 1980. Paper presented to workshop *Beyond the Health Care State. New dimensions in health politics in Europe*. 24th ECPR Joint Sessions of Workshops, Oslo, 29 March–3 April.

Freeman, R. 1996: The users of health care in Europe. Paper presented to workshop *Beyond the Health Care State. New dimensions in health politics in Europe*. 24th ECPR Joint Sessions of Workshops, Oslo, 29 March–3 April.

Friedman, M. and Friedman, R. 1980: *Free to Choose*. Harmondsworth: Penguin.

Fry, J. 1991: Comparative analysis of approaches to the provision and financing of health care. In W. W. Holland, R. Detels and G. Knox (eds), *Oxford Textbook of Public Health*, 2nd edn. Oxford: Oxford UP.

Fulbrook, M. 1996: Germany for the Germans? Citizenship and nationality in a divided nation. In D. Cesarani and M. Fulbrook (eds), *Citizenship, Nationality and Migration in Europe*. London: Routledge.

Gallie, D. and Alm, S. 1997: *Unemployment, gender and attitudes to work in the European Union*. Paper presented to the European Sociological Association conference, University of Essex.

Garfinkel, I. and McLanahan, S. 1986: *Single Mothers and their Children*. Washington DC: Urban Institute.

Garland, D. 1991: *Punishment and Modern Society. A study in social theory*. Oxford: Oxford University Press.

Garpenby, P. 1995: Health care reform in Sweden in the 1990s: local pluralism versus national coordination. *Journal of Health Politics, Policy and Law*, 20 (3), 695–717.

Gauthier, A. H. 1991: Family policies in comparative perspective. Discussion Paper no. 5. Oxford: Nuffield College, Centre for European Studies.

——1996a: The measured and unmeasured effects of welfare benefits on families: implications for Europe's demographic trends. In D. Coleman (ed.), *Europe's Population in the 1990s*. Oxford: Oxford University Press.

——1996b: *The State and the Family: A Comparative Analysis of Family Policies in Industrialized Countries*. Oxford: Clarendon Press.

George, V. and Taylor-Gooby, P. (eds) 1996: *European Welfare Policy. Squaring the circle*. London: Macmillan.

Gerdtham, U.-G., Søgaard, J., Andersson, F. and Jönsson, B. 1992: An econometric analysis of health care expenditure: a cross-section study of the OECD countries. *Journal of Health Economics*, 11, 63–84.

Gewirth, A. 1982: *Human Rights: Essays on Justification and Applications*. Chicago: University of Chicago Press.

Giarchi, G. 1996: *Caring for Older Europeans: Comparative Studies in 29 Countries*. Aldershot: Arena.

Gilder, G. 1981: *Wealth and Poverty*. New York: Basic Books.

——1987: The collapse of the American family. *The Public Interest*, 89 (Fall), 20–5.

Ginn, J. and Arber, S. 1992: Towards women's independence: pension systems in three contrasting European welfare states. *Journal of European Social Policy* 2 (4), 255–77.

——1993: Pension penalties: the gendered division of occupational welfare. *Work, Employment and Society*, 7 (1), 47–70.

Ginsburg, N. 1992: *Divisions of Welfare: a Critical Introduction to Comparative Social Policy*. London: Sage.

Glendinning, C. and McLaughlin, E. 1993: *Paying for Care: Lessons from Europe*. London: HMSO.

Glennerster, H. 1997: *Paying for Welfare: Towards 2000*. (3rd edn.) Hemel Hempstead: Harvester Wheatsheaf.

Goodin, R. 1988: What is so special about our fellow countrymen? *Ethics* 98 (July), pp. 663–86.

Goodman, R. and Peng I. 1996: The East Asian welfare states: peripatetic learning, adaptive change, and nation-building. In G. Esping-Andersen (ed.), *Welfare States in Transition: National Adaptations in Global Economies*. London: Sage.

Gough, I. 1979: *The Political Economy of the Welfare State.* Basingstoke: Macmillan.

Gough, I. and Baldwin-Edwards, M. 1990: The impact of EC membership on social security and health in the UK. In S. Mangen, L. Hantrais and M. O'Brien (eds), *The Implications of 1992 for Social Insurance.* Loughborough: Cross National Research Papers.

Gough, I., Bradshaw, J., Ditch, J., Eardley, T. and Whiteford, P. 1997: Social assistance in OECD countries. *Journal of European Social Policy,* 7 (1), pp. 17–43.

Gould, A. 1993: *Capitalist Welfare Systems. A comparison of Japan, Britain and Sweden.* Harlow: Longman.

Gray, A. 1993: International patterns of health care, 1960 to the 1990s. In C. Webster (ed.), *Caring for Health: History and diversity.* Buckingham: Open University Press.

Gray, F. 1982: Owner occupation and social relations. In S. Merrett with F. Gray (eds), *Owner Occupation in Britain.* RKP: London.

Gregg, P. and Wadsworth, J. 1996: *It takes two: employment polarisation in the OECD.* Discussion Paper no. 304, Centre for Economic Performance, London School of Economics, London.

Greve, B. 1994: The hidden welfare state, tax expenditure and social policy. A comparative overview. *Scandinavian Journal of Social Welfare,* 4, 203–11.

——(ed.) 1996: *Comparative Welfare Systems: The Scandinavian Model in a Period of Change.* Basingstoke: Macmillan.

Grignon, M. and Fagnani, J. 1996: Transferts de revenus et activité féminine en Europe. *L'espace géographique,* no. 2, 129–44.

Grimshaw, D. and Rubery, J. 1997: Workforce heterogeneity and unemployment: the need for policy reassessment in the European Union, *Journal of European Social Policy,* 7 (4), 290–315.

Groves, D. 1991: Women and financial provision in old age. In M. Maclean and D. Groves (eds), *Women's Issue in Social Policy.* London: Routledge.

Grubb, D. 1994: Direct and indirect effects of active labour market policies in OECD countries. In R. Barrell (ed.), *The UK Labour Market. Comparative aspects and institutional developments,* 183–213. Cambridge: Cambridge University Press.

Guibentief, P. and Bouget, D. 1997: *Minimum Income Policies in the European Union.* Lisbon: Uniao das Mutualidades Potuguesas.

Ha, S-K. 1987: *Housing Policy and Practice in Asia.* London: Croom Helm.

Hakim, C. 1989: Workforce restructuring, social insurance coverage and the black economy. *Journal of Social Policy* 18 (4), 471–503.

—— 1996: *Key Issues in Women's Work.* London: Athlone.

Hall, P. A. and Taylor R. C. R. 1996: Political science and the three new institutionalisms. *Political Studies,* 44 (5), 936–57.

Hallett, G. 1988: *Land and Housing Policies in Europe and the USA: A Comparative Analysis.* London: Routledge.

Hammer, T. 1985: *European Immigration Policy.* Cambridge: Cambridge University Press.

Hansen, H. 1997: *Elements of social security in six European countries.* Copenhagen: The Danish Institute of Social Research.

Hantrais, L. 1993: Women, work and welfare in France. In J. Lewis (ed.), *Women and Social Policies in Europe.* Aldershot: Edward Elgar.

—— 1994: Comparing family policy in Britain, France and Germany. *Journal of Social Policy*, 23 (2), 135–60.

—— 1995: *Social Policy in the European Union*. Houndmills/London: Macmillan.

Hantrais, L. and Letablier, M. T. 1996: *Families and Family Policy in Europe*. London: Longman.

Hantrais, L. and Mangen, S. 1996a: Method and management of cross-national social research. In L. Hantrais and S. Mangen (eds), *Cross-national Research Methods in the Social Sciences*. London/New York: Pinter.

—— (eds) 1996b: *Cross-National Research Methods in the Social Sciences*. London/New York: Pinter.

Hantrais, L., Mangen, S. and O'Brien, M. (eds) 1985: *Doing Cross-National Research*, Birmingham: Aston University.

Harloe, M. 1985: *Private Rented Housing in the United States and Europe*. Beckingham: Croom Helm.

—— 1995: *The People's Home: Social Rented Housing in Europe and America*. Oxford: Blackwell.

Harloe, M. and Martens, M. 1983: Comparative housing research. *Journal of Social Policy*, 13(2), 255–77.

Harris, J. 1977: *William Beveridge: A Biography*. Oxford: Clarendon Press.

Harrison, S., Hunter, D. J., Marnoch, G. and Pollitt, C. 1992: *Just Managing. Power and culture in the National Health Service*. Basingstoke: Macmillan.

Hauser, R. 1995: Das empirische Bild der Armut in der Bundesrepublik Deutschland. *Ein Überblick, Aus Politik und Zeitgeschichte*, 31–2, 24–34.

Headey, B. 1978: *Housing Policy in the Developed Economy*. London: Croom Helm.

Heater, D. 1990: *Citizenship: The Civic Ideal in World History, Politics and Education*. London: Longman.

Heclo, H. 1974: *Modern Social Politics in Britain and Sweden: From Relief to Income Maintenance*. New Haven: Yale University Press.

Hedman, E. 1994: *Housing in Sweden in an International Perspective*. Karlskrona: Boverket.

Heidenheimer, A., Heclo, H. and Adams, C. 1975: *Comparative Public Policy: The Politics of Social Change in Europe and America*. London: Macmillan.

—— 1990: *Comparative Public Policy. The politics of social choice in America, Europe and Japan* (3rd edn). New York: St Martin's Press.

Hetherington, R., Cooper A., Smith P. and Wilford G. 1997: *Protecting Children: Messages from Europe*. Lyme Regis: Russell House.

Higgins, J. 1981: *States of Welfare: Comparative Analysis in Social Policy*. Oxford: Blackwell and Martin Robertson.

—— 1986: Comparative social policy. *The Quarterly Journal of Social Affairs*, 2 (3), 221–42.

Hill, M. 1996: *Social Policy. A comparative analysis*. Prentice-Hall: London.

Hills, J. 1996: *New Inequalities. Changing Distribution of Income and Wealth in the UK*. Cambridge: Cambridge University Press.

Hills, J., Ditch, J. and Glennerster, H. (eds) 1994: *Beveridge and Social Security: An International Retrospective*. Oxford: Clarendon Press.

Hillyard, P. and Watson, S. 1996: Postmodern social policy: a contradiction in terms? *Journal of Social Policy*, 25 (3), 321–46.

Hinrichs, K. 1995: The impact of German health insurance reforms on redistribution and the culture of solidarity. *Journal of Health Politics, Policy and Law*, 20 (3), 653–87.

Hiscock, J. and Hojman, D.E. 1997: Social policy in a fast-growing economy: the case of Chile, *Social Policy and Administration*, 31 (4), 354–70.

HMSO 1989: *Caring for People: Community Care in the Next Decade and Beyond.* Presented to parliament by the Secretaries of State for Health, Social Security, Wales and Scotland by command of Her Majesty November 1989. Cm 849. London: HMSO.

Hobson, B. 1994: Solo mothers, social policy regimes and the logics of gender. In D. Sainsbury (ed.), *Gendering Welfare States*. London: Sage.

Höcker, H. 1994: The organisation of labour market policy delivery in the European Union. *MISEP*, 48, Winter, 26–35.

Holliday, I. 1992: *The NHS Transformed*. Manchester: Baseline Books.

Holmes, H. and Neale, J. 1996: *The Employment of Lone Parents. A Comparison of Policy in 20 Countries*. London: Family Policy Studies Centre and Joseph Rowntree Foundation.

Home Office 1977: *Racial Discrimination: a Guide to the Race Relations Act 1976*. London: Home Office.

Houben, P. 1997: Challenges in the modernisation of Dutch housing and care for the elderly. *Housing Studies*, 12 (3), 355–66.

Huber, E., Ragin, C. and Stephens, J. D. 1993: Social democracy, Christian democracy, constitutional structure and the welfare state. *American Journal of Sociology*, 99 (3), 711–49.

Hughes, D. 1996: NHS managers as rhetoricians: a case of culture management? *Sociology of Health and Illness*, 18 (3), 291–314.

Hugman, R. 1994: *Ageing and the Care of Older People in Europe*. Basingstoke: Macmillan.

Hutten, J. and Kerkstra, A. (eds.) 1996: *Home Care in Europe: a Country-Specific Guide to its Organization and Financing*. Aldershot: Arena.

Hutton, S. and Whiteford, P. 1994: Gender and retirement incomes: a comparative analysis. In S. Baldwin and J. Falkingham (eds), *Social Security and Social Change: New Challenges to the Beveridge Model*. London: Harvester Wheatsheaf.

Illsley, R. 1987: Pathways into and through services for the elderly in Europe: a research design. *Revue Epidemiologie et Santé Publique*, 35, 339–48.

Illsley, R. and Jamieson, A. 1990: Contextual and structural influences on adaptation to change. In A. Jamieson and R. Illsley (eds), *Contrasting European Policies for the Care of Older People*. Aldershot: Avebury.

ILO (International Labour Organisation) 1995: *World Employment*, Geneva: ILO.

Immergut, E. 1990: Institutions, veto points and policy results: a comparative analysis of health care. *Journal of Public Policy*, 10 (4), 341–416.

—— 1992: *Health Politics. Interests and Institutions in Western Europe*. Cambridge: Cambridge University Press.

Jackson, P. 1993: Managing the mothers: the case of Ireland. In J. Lewis (ed.), *Women and Social Policies in Europe*. Aldershot: Edward Elgar.

—— 1997: Lone mothers: the case of Ireland. In J. Lewis (ed.), *Lone Mothers and Welfare Regimes: Shifting Policy Logics*. Aldershot: Edward Elgar.

Jamieson A. 1989: A new age for older people? Policy shifts in health and social care. *Social Science and Medicine*, 29 (3), 445–54.

——(ed.) 1991: *Home Care for Older People in Europe: a Comparison of Policies and Practices*. Oxford: Oxford University Press.

Jamieson, A. and Illsley, R. (eds) 1990: *Contrasting European Policies for the Care of Older People*. Aldershot: Avebury.

Jani-Le Bris, H. 1993: *Family Care of Dependent Older People in the European Community*. Dublin: European Foundation for the Improvement of Living and Working Conditions.

Janoski, T. 1994: Direct state intervention in the labour market: the explanation of active labour market policy from 1950 to 1988 in social democratic, conservative, and liberal regimes. In T. Janoski and A. M. Hicks (eds), *The Comparative Political Economy of the Welfare State*. Cambridge: Cambridge University Press.

——1996: Explaining state intervention to prevent unemployment: the impact of institutions on active labour market policy expenditures in 18 countries. In G. Schmid, J. O'Reilly and K. Schömann (eds), *International Handbook of Labour Market Policy and Evaluation*. Cheltenham: Edward Elgar.

Janoski, T. and Hicks, A. (eds) 1994: *The Comparative Political Economy of the Welfare State*. Cambridge: Cambridge University Press.

Jeandidier, B. 1997: La spécificité des politiques familiales en Europe. *Recherches et prévisions*, 48, 27–44.

Jensen, K. and Madsen, P. K. (eds) 1993: *Measuring labour market measures*. Kolding: Danish Ministry of Labour.

Jenson, J. 1986: Gender and reproduction. Or babies and the state. *Studies in Political Economy* 20, 9–46.

Joly, D. 1996: *Haven or Hell? Asylum Policies and Refugees in Europe*. Basingstoke: Macmillan.

Jones, C. 1981: Cutting taxes in California. *Parliamentary Affairs*, XXXIX (1), 81–94.

——1985: *Patterns of Social Policy: an Introduction to Comparative Analysis*. London: Tavistock.

——1990a: *Promoting Prosperity: The Hong Kong Way of Social Policy*. Hong Kong: Chinese University Press.

——1990b: Hong Kong, Singapore, South Korea and Taiwan: economic welfare states. *Government and Opposition*, 25 (4), Autumn, 447–62.

——1993: The Pacific Challenge: Confucian Welfare States. In C. Jones (ed), *New Perspectives on the Welfare State in Europe*. London: Routledge, 198–217.

Jones Finer, C. 1997: Social Policy. In P. Dunleavy, A. Gamble, I. Holliday and G. Peele (eds), *Development in British Politics*. Basingstoke: Macmillan, 304–25.

Joseph Rowntree Foundation Inquiry 1996: *Meeting the Costs of Continuing Care*. York: Joseph Rowntree Foundation.

Joshi, H. 1990: The cash opportunity costs of childbearing: an approach to estimation using the British data. *Population Studies*, 44, 41–60.

——1992: The cost of caring. In C. Glendinning and J. Millar (eds) *Women and Poverty in Britain: the 1990s*. London: Harvester Wheatsheaf.

Joshi, H. and Davies, H. 1991: The pension consequences of divorce. *CEPR Discussion Papers*, 35. London: CEPR.

——1992: Daycare in Europe and mothers' forgone earnings. *International Labour Review*, 132 (6), 561–79.

Kaim-Caudle, P. R. 1973: *Comparative Social Policy and Social Security. A ten country study*. London: Martin Robertson.

Kamerman, S. B. and Kahn, A. J. 1978: *Family Policy: Government and Families in Fourteen Countries*. New York: Columbia University Press.

——(eds) 1982: Income transfers, work and the economic well-being of children: a comparative study. *International Social Security Review*, 3, 345–82.

——(eds) 1997: *Family Change and Family Policies in Great Britain, Canada, New Zealand and the United States*. Oxford: Clarendon Press.

Karr, W. 1997: Die konzeptionelle Untererfassung der Langzeitarbeitslosigkeit. *Mitteilungen aus der Arbeitsmarkt- und Berufsforschung*, 1, 37–46.

Kemeny, J. 1981: *The Myth of Home Ownership: Public Versus Private Choices in Housing Tenure*. London: Routledge.

——1992: *Housing and Social Theory*. London: Routledge.

——1995: *From Public Housing to the Social Market: Rental Policy Strategy in Comparative Perspective*. London: Routledge.

Kemp, P. 1990: Income-related assistance with housing costs: a cross national comparison. In D. Maclennan and R. Williams (eds), *Housing Subsidies and the Market: An International Perspective*. York: Joseph Rowntree Foundation.

Kempeneers, M. and Lelièvre, E. 1991: Employment and family within the twelve. *Eurobarometer 34*. Brussels: Eurostat.

Kerkstra A. and Hutten, J. 1996: A cross-national comparison on home care in Europe: summary of the findings. In J. Hutten and A. Kerkstra (eds), *Home Care in Europe: a Country-Specific Guide to its Organization and Financing*. Aldershot: Arena.

Kerr, C., Dunlop J., Harbison F. and Myers A. 1962: *Industrialism and Industrial Man*. London: Heinemann.

Kiernan, K. 1996: Family change: parenthood, partnership and policy. In D. Halpern, S. Wood, S. White and G. Cameron et al. (eds), *Options for Britain*. Aldershot: Dartmouth Press.

Kiernan, K., Land and Lewis, J. 1998: *Lone Mothers in Twentieth Century Britain*. Oxford: Oxford University Press.

King, D. 1987: *The New Right: Politics, Markets and Citizenship*. London: Macmillan.

——1995: *Actively Seeking Work? The politics of unemployment and welfare policy in the United States and Great Britain*. Chicago: University of Chicago Press.

King, D. and Rothstein, B. 1993: Institutional choices and labour market market policy: a British–Swedish comparison. *Comparative Political Studies*, 26, 147–77.

Klammer, U. 1997: Wieder einmal auf der Verlierer (inner) seite – Zur Arbeitsmarkt und sozialpolitischen Situation von Frauen in Zeitalter der 'Sparpakete'. *WSI Mitteilungen* 50 (1), 1–12.

Klein R. 1993: O'Goffe's tale. In C. Jones (ed.), *New Perspectives on the Welfare State in Europe*. London: Routledge, pp. 7–17.

——1995: Big bang health care reform – does it work?: the case of Britain's 1991 National Health Service reforms. *Milbank Quarterly*, 73 (3), 299–337.

Kolberg, J. E. 1991: The Gender Dimension of the Welfare State. *International Journal of Sociology* 21 (2), 119–48.

Korpi, W. 1980: Social policy and distributional conflict in the capitalist democracies. *West European Politics*, 3 (3), 296–316.
—— 1983: *The Democratic Class Struggle*. London: Routledge.
Kraan, R., Baldock, J., Davies, B., Evers, A., Johansson, L., Knapen, M., Thorslund, M. and Tunissen, C. 1991: *Care for the Elderly: Significant Innovations in Three European Countries*. Frankfurt am Main: Campus Verlag.
Kraft, K. 1994: *An evaluation of active and passive labour market policy*. Discussion Paper FS I 94–208. Berlin: Science Research Centre.
Kronauer, M. (ed.) 1993: Unemployment in Western Europe. *International Journal of Political Economy*, 3 (special issue).
Ku, Yeun-wen 1995: The development of state welfare in the Asian NICs, with special reference to Taiwan. *Social Policy and Administration*, 28 (4), 345–64.
Kupiszewski, M. 1996: Extra-union migration: the East-West perspective. In P. Rees, J. Stillwell, A. Convey and M. Kupiszewski (eds), *Population Migration in the European Union*. Chichester: Wiley.
Kvist, J. and Ploug, N. 1996: *Social Security in Northern Europe. An institutional analysis of cash benefits for the unemployed*. Working paper 1. Copenhagen: Centre for Welfare State Research, Danish National Institute of Social Research.
Kvist, J. and Sinfield, A. 1996: *Comparing tax routes to welfare in Denmark and the United Kingdom*. Copenhagen: The Danish National Institute of Social Research.
Kvist, J. and Torfing, J. 1996: *Changing welfare state models*. Working Paper 5. Copenhagen: Centre for Welfare State Research, Danish National Institute of Social Research.
Laing, W. 1993: *Financing Long-term Care: the Crucial Debate*. London: Age Concern England.
Land, H. 1989: The construction of dependency. In M. Bulmer, J. Lewis and D. Piachaud (eds), *The Goals of Social Policy*. London: Unwin Hyman.
Langan, M. and Ostner, I. 1991: Gender and welfare: towards a comparative framework. In G. Room (ed.), *Towards a European Welfare State?* Bristol: School of Advanced Urban Studies.
Layard, R., Nickel, S. and Jackman, R. 1991: *Unemployment – macroeconomic performance and the labour market*. Oxford: Oxford University Press.
Layton-Herry, Z. (ed.) 1990: *The Political Rights of Migrant Workers*. London: Sage.
Le Grand, J. 1982: *The Strategy of Equality: Redistribution and the Social Services*. London: Allen and Unwin.
Lee, S. L., Yuan, L. L. and Poh, T. K. 1993: Shelter for all: Singapore's strategy for full home ownership by the year 2000. *Habitat International*, 17 (1), 85–102.
Lefaucheur, N. 1995: French policies towards lone parents: social categories and social policies. In K. McFate, R. Lawson and W. J. Wilson (eds), *Poverty, Inequality and the Future of Social Policy*. New York: Russell Sage Foundation.
Lefaucheur, N. and Martin, C. 1993: Lone parent families in France: situation and research. In J. Hudson and B. Galaway (eds), *Single Parent*

Families: Perspectives on Research and Policy. Toronto: Thompson Educational Publishing.

——1995: *Qui doit nourrir l'enfant dont le père est 'absent'? Rapport de recherche sur les fondements des politiques familiales européennes (Angletere – France – Italie – Portugal).* Rennes: Ecole nationale de la santé publique.

Leibfried, S. 1991: *Towards a European Welfare State: on integrating poverty regimes.* Centre for Social Policy Research, Research Working Paper No 2, Bremen: University of Bremen.

——1993: Towards a European welfare state? In Jones, C. (ed.), *New Perspectives on the Welfare State in Europe.* London: Routledge, 133–56.

Leibfried, S. and Ostner, I. 1991: The particularism of West Germany welfare capitalism: The case of women's social security. In M. Adler, C. Bell, J. Clasen and A. Sinfield (eds), *The Sociology of Social Security.* Edinburgh: Edinburgh University Press.

Leibfried, S. and Pierson, P. (eds) 1995: *European Social Policy: Betweeen Fragmentation and Integration.* Washington DC: Brookings Institution.

Leigh, D. 1995: *Assisting workers displaced by structural change. An international perspective.* Michigan: W. E. Upjohn Institute for Employment Research, Kalamazoo.

Lesemann, F. and Martin, C. (eds) 1993: *Les personnes âgées: dépendance, soins et solidarités familiales. Comparaisons internationales.* Paris: La Documentation Française.

Lewis, J. 1992: Gender and the development of welfare regimes. *Journal of European Social Policy,* 2 (3), 159–73.

——1993: Women, work, family and social policies in Europe. In J. Lewis (ed.) *Women and Social Policies in Europe.* Aldershot: Edward Elgar.

——(ed.) 1997a: *Lone Mothers in European Welfare Regimes. Shifting Policy Logics.* London: Jessica Kingsley.

——1997b: Gender and welfare regimes. Further thoughts. *Social Politics,* 4 (2): 160–77.

Liebaut, F. and Hughes, J. 1997: *Legal and Social Conditions for Asylum Seekers and Refugees in Western European Countries.* Copenhagen: Danish Refugee Council.

Lister, R. 1990: Women, economic dependency and citizenship. *Journal of Social Policy* 19 (4), 445–67.

——1992: *Women's Economic Dependency and Social Security.* Manchester: Equal Opportunities Commission.

Lockhart, C. 1981: Values and policy conceptions of health policy elites in the United States, the United Kingdom and the Federal Republic of Germany. *Journal of Health Politics, Policy and Law,* 6 (1), 98–119.

Lødemel, I. and Schulte, B. 1992: Social assistance; a part of social security or the Poor Law in new disguise? Paper presented at the conference Social Security Fifty Years after Beveridge, University of York, 27–30 September 1992.

Loughlin, S. and Peters, B. G. 1997: State traditions and administrative reform. In M. Keating and J. Loughlin (eds), *The Political Economy of Regionalism.* London: Frank Cass.

Lo Vuolo, R. 1997: The retrenchment of the welfare state in Latin America: the case of Argentina. *Social Policy and Administration,* 31 (4), 390–409.

Luckhaus, L. 1994: Individualisation of social security benefits. In C. McCrudden (ed.), *Equality of Treatment between Women and Men in Social Security*. London: Butterworths.

Lundquist, L. 1986: *Housing Policy and Equality: A Comparative Study of Tenure Conversions and their Effects*. London: Croom Helm.

——1992: *Policy, Organisation and Tenure: A Comparative History of Housing in Small Welfare State*. Gothenburg: Scandinavian University Press.

Lüschen, G., Cockerham, W. C. and Kunz, G. 1987: Deutsche und amerikanische Gesundheitskultur – oder: What they say when you sneeze. *Medizin, Mensch, Gesellschaft*, 12, 59–69.

——(eds) 1989: *Health and Illness in America and Germany. Comparative sociology of health conduct and public policy*. Munich: R. Oldenbourg Verlag.

Mabbett, D. and Bolderson, H. 1998: Open and shut cases: contrasting systems of benefit delivery in five countries. *Benefits*, Issue 23, (forthcoming).

McCrone, G. and Stephens, M. 1995: *Housing Policy in Britain and Europe*. London: UCL Press.

MacFarlan, M. and Oxley, H. 1996: Social transfers: spending patterns, institutional arrangements and policy responses. *OECD Economic Studies*, 27, pp. 147–94.

McFate, K., Smeeding, T. and Rainwater, L. 1995: Markets and states: poverty trends and transfer system effectiveness in the 1980s. In K. McFate, R. Lawson and W. J. Wilson (eds), *Poverty, Inequality and the Future of Social Policy*. New York: Russell Sage Foundation.

McGuire, C. 1981: *International Housing Policies*. Lexington: Lexington Books.

McLanahan, S. and Booth, K. 1989: Mother-only families: problems, prospects, and politics. *Journal of Marriage and the Family*, 51 (August), 557–80.

McLaughlin, E. (ed.) 1992: *Understanding Unemployment*. London: Routledge.

Maltby, T. 1994: *Women and pensions in Britain and Hungary: A cross-national and comparative case study of social dependency*. Aldershot: Avebury.

Marmor, T. R., Mashaw, J. L. and Harvey, P. L. 1990: *America's Misunderstood Welfare State: Persisting Myths, Enduring Realities*. New York: Basic Books.

Marsh, L. 1943: *Report on Social Security for Canada*. Ottawa: King's Printer.

Marshall, T. H. 1950: *Citizenship and Social Class and other Essays*. Cambridge: Cambridge University Press.

——1985: *Social Policy*. 5th edn, with an introduction by A. M. Ree. London: Hutchinson.

Martin, C. 1995: Father, Mother and the Welfare State. Family and Social Transfers after Marital Breakdown. *Journal of European Social Policy*, 5 (1), 43–63.

Martin, J. P. 1996: Measures of replacement rates for the purpose of international comparisons: a note. *OECD Economic Studies*, 26, 99–116.

Math, A. 1996: Non-take-up of benefits in France. *Cross-National Research Papers*, 4 (1), 33–40.

May, M. 1998: The role of comparative study. In P. Alcock, M. May and A. Erskine (eds), *The Student's Companion to Social Policy*. Oxford: Blackwell.

Meehan, E. 1993: *Citizenship and the European Community*. London: Sage.

Meulders-Klein, M-T. 1993: The status of the father in European legislation. In Danish Ministry of Social Affairs (ed.), *Report from the Conference: Fathers in Families of Tomorrow, June 17–18, 1993*. Copenhagen: Danish Ministry of Social Affairs.

Meulders-Klein, M-T. and Théry, I. (eds) 1993: *Les recompositions familiales aujourd'hui*. Paris: Nathan.

Midgley, J. 1997: *Social Welfare in Global Context*. Thousand Oaks, California: Sage.

Millar, J. 1994: Understanding labour supply in context: households and income. In A. Bryson and S. MacKay (eds), *Is it worth working?* London: PSI, 77–92.

Millar, J. and Warman, A. 1996: *Family Obligations in Europe: The Family, the State and Social Policy*. York: Joseph Rowntree Foundation.

Millar, J. and Whiteford, P. 1993: Child support in lone-parent families in Australia and Britain. *Policy and Politics*, 21 (1), 59–72.

Ministerie van Sociale Zaken en Werkgelegenheid 1995: *Unemployment benefits and social assistance in seven European countries*. Werkdocumenten No. 53. Den Haag: Ministerie van Sociale Zaken en Werkgelegenheid.

MISEP policies (various years) European Employment Observatory, European Commission, Directorate General Unemployment, Industrial Relations and Social Affairs, Berlin: Institute for Applied Socio-Economics.

Mishra, R. 1993: Social policy in the postmodern world. In C. Jones (ed.) *New Perspectives on the Welfare State in Europe*. London: Routledge, 18–40.

MISSOC 1997: *Social Protection in the Member States of the European Union*. Situation on 1 July 1996 and evolution. Luxembourg: Office for Official Publications of the European Communities.

Mitchell, D. 1991: *Income Transfers in Ten Welfare States*. Aldershot: Avebury.

Mitton, R., Willmott P. and Willmott P. 1983: *Unemployment, Poverty and Social Security in Europe: a Comparative Study of Britain, France and Germany*. London: Bedford Square Press.

Moran, M. 1992: The health-care state in Europe: convergence or divergence. *Environment and Planning C: Government and Policy*, 10, 77–90.

—— 1994: Reshaping the health-care state. *Government and Opposition*, 29 (1): 48–63.

—— 1995: Three faces of the health care state. *Journal of Health Politics, Policy and Law*, 20 (3), 767–81.

Moran, M. and Wood, B. 1993: *States, Regulation and the Medical Profession*. Milton Keynes: Open University Press.

Morgan, P. 1995: *Farewell to the Family. Public Policy and Family Breakdown in Britain and the USA*. London: IEA.

Morris, J. 1993: *Independent Lives: Community Care and Disabled People*. Basingstoke: Macmillan.

Morris, L. 1990: *The Workings of the Household. A US–UK Comparison*. Cambridge: Polity Press.

Mosley, H. 1993: Employment protection in Europe, *MISEP policies*, 44, 21–6, European Commission.

Moss, P. 1990: Childcare in the European Communities 1985–1990. *Women of Europe Supplements* 31 (August).

Munday B. (ed.) 1993: *European Social Services*. Canterbury: European Institute of Social Services, University of Kent at Canterbury.

——1996: Introduction: definitions and comparisons in European social care. In B. Munday and P. Ely (eds), *Social Care in Europe*. Hemel Hempstead: Prentice-Hall.

Munday, B. and Ely, P. (eds) 1996: *Social Care in Europe*. Hemel Hempstead: Prentice-Hall.

Murray, C. 1984: *Losing Ground. American Social Policy, 1950–1980*. New York: Basic Books.

Neubauer, E., Dienel, C. and Lohkamp-Himminghofen, H. 1993: *Zwölf Wege der Familienpolitik in der Europäischen Gemeinschaft. Eigenständige Systeme und vergleichbare Qualitäten? Studie im Auftrag des Bundesministeriums für Familie und Senioren*, 22 (1). Stuttgart/Berlin/Köln: Verlag W. Kohlhammer.

Newson, T. 1986: *Housing Policy: An International Bibliography*. London: Mansell.

Nijkamp, P., Pacolet, J., Spinnewyn, H., Vollering, A., Wilderom, C., Winters, S. 1991: *Services for the Elderly in Europe: a Cross-national Comparative Study*. Leuven: Katholieke Universiteit.

Oakley, A. 1986: *Social Welfare and the Position of Women*. Richard Titmuss Memorial Lecture, Hebrew University of Jerusalem.

O'Connor, J. 1993: Gender, class and citizenship in the comparative analysis of welfare regimes: theoretical and methodological issues. *British Journal of Sociology*, 44 (3), 501–18.

OECD 1963: *Labour Market Policy in Sweden*. Paris: OECD.

——1981: *The Welfare State in Crisis*. Paris: OECD.

——1988: *Ageing Populations: the Social Policy Implications*. Paris: OECD.

——1991: *Evaluating labour market and social programmes. The state of a complex art*. Paris: OECD.

——1992: *Reform of Health Care: a comparative analysis of seven OECD countries*. Paris: OECD.

——1993: *Employment Outlook*, Paris: OECD.

——1994a: *The Reform of Health Systems. A review of seventeen OECD countries*. Paris: OECD.

——1994b: *Caring for Frail Elderly People: New Directions in Care*. Paris: OECD.

——1994c: *The OECD Jobs Study: Evidence and Explanations; Part 1: Labour Market trends and underlying forces of change; Part 2: The adjustment potential of the labour market*, Paris: OECD.

——1995: *Employment Outlook*, Paris: OECD.

——1996a: *Caring for Frail Elderly People: Policies in Evolution*. Paris: OECD.

——1996b: Earnings inequality, low paid employment and earnings mobility. *Employment Outlook*, July, 59–107.

——1997: Earnings mobility: taking a longer run view. *Employment Outlook*, July, 27–61.

Office of National Statistics 1996: *Labour Market Trends* 104 (12), (December).

OHE (Office of Health Economics) 1995: *Compendium of Health Statistics*, 9th edn. London: Office of Health Economics.

O'Higgins, M., Rainwater L. and Smeeding T. M. 1990: The significance of LIS for comparative social policy research. In T. M. Smeeding, M. O'Higgins and L. Rainwater (eds), *Poverty, Inequality and Income Distribution in a Comparative Perspective.* London: Harvester Wheatsheaf.

O'Neill, O. 1992: Justice and boundaries. Paper presented at Newnham College, Cambridge University, September.

OPCS 1992: *Retirement and Retirement Plans.* London: HMSO.

—— 1996: *Living in Britain, Results for the 1994 GHS.* London: HMSO.

Orloff, A. 1993: Gender and the social rights of citizenship: state policies and gender relations in comparative research. *American Sociological Review*, 58 (3), 303–28.

Ostner, I. 1993: Slow motion: women, work and the family in Germany. In J. Lewis (ed.) *Women and Social Policies in Europe.* Aldershot: Edward Elgar.

—— 1997: Lone mothers in Germany before and after unification. In J. Lewis (ed.), *Lone Mothers and Welfare Regimes: Shifting Policy Logics.* London: Jessica Kingsley.

Ostner, I. and J. Lewis 1995: Gender and the evolution of European social policies. In S. Leibfried and P. Pierson (eds), *European Social Policy.* Washington DC: The Brookings Institution.

Oxley, M. 1987: The aims and effects of increasing housing allowances in Western Europe. In W. van Vliet (ed.), *Housing Markets and Policy under Fiscal Austerity.* Westport: Greenwood.

Øyen, E. (ed.) 1990: *Comparative Methodology: theory and practice in international social research.* London: Sage.

Pacolet, J., Versieck, K. and Bouten, R. 1994: *Social Protection for Dependency in Old Age.* Leuven: Katholieke Universiteit Leuven, Hoger Instituut voor de Arbeid.

Pacolet, J., Bouten, R., Lauoje, H. and Vessieck, K. 1998: *Social Protection for Dependency in Old Age in the 15 Member States and Norway. Main results of a comparative study.* Brussels: European Comission.

Palier, B. 1997: A 'liberal' dynamic in the transformation of the French welfare system. In J. Clasen (ed.), *Social Insurance in Europe.* Bristol: Policy Press.

Pankoke, E. 1990: *Die Arbeitsfrage. Arbeitsmoral, Beschäftigungsrisiken und Wohlfahrtspolitik im Industriezeitalter.* Frankfurt: Edition Suhrkamp.

Papademetriou, D. 1996: *Coming Together or Pulling Apart? The European Union's Struggle with Immigration and Asylum.* International Migration Policy Program. Washington DC: Carnegie Endowment for International Peace.

Parekh, B. 1994: Three theories of immigration. In S. Spencer (ed.), *Strangers and Citizens.* Institute for Public Policy Research. London: Rivers Oram Press.

Parry, G. 1991: Paths to citizenship. In U. Vogel and M. Moran (eds), *The Frontiers of Citizenship.* London: Macmillan.

Parry, R. 1995: Redefining the welfare state. In E. Page and J. Hayward (eds), *Governing the New Europe.* Cambridge: Polity.

Pateman, C. 1988: Patriarchy and the welfare state. In A. Gutmann (ed.), *Democracy and the Welfare State.* Princeton: Princeton University Press.

Pedersen, P. J. and Westergård-Nielsen, N. 1993: Unemployment: a review of the evidence from panel data. *OECD Economic Studies*, 20, 66–114, Paris: OECD.

Pedersen, S. 1993: *Family, Dependence and the Origins of the Welfare State: Britain and France 1914–1945*. Cambridge: Cambridge University Press.

Pennings, F. 1990: *Benefits of doubt. A comparative study of the legal aspects of employment and unemployment schemes in Great Britain, Germany, France and the Netherlands*. Netherlands Institute for Social Law Research. Deventer: Kluwer.

Peters, T. J. and Waterman, R. H. 1982: *In Search of Excellence*. New York: Harper and Row.

Petmesidou, M. 1996: Social protection in Greece: a brief glimpse of a welfare state. *Social Policy and Administration*, 30 (4), 324–47.

Pfaff, M. 1990: Differences in health care spending across countries: statistical evidence. *Journal of Health Politics, Policy and Law*, 15 (1), 1–67.

Pfaller A., Gough, I. and Therborn, G. 1991: *Can the Welfare State Compete? A Comparative Study of Advanced Capitalist Countries*. Basingstoke: Macmillan.

Phoenix, A. 1993: The Social Construction of Teenage Motherhood: A Black and White Issue? In A. Lawson and D. L. Rhode (eds), *The Politics of Pregnancy*. New Haven: Yale University Press.

Pierson, C. 1991: *Beyond the welfare state?* Polity Press: Oxford.

—— 1995: Comparing welfare states. *West European Politics*, 18 (1), 197–203.

Pierson, P. 1994: *Dismantling the Welfare State? Reagan, Thatcher and the Politics of Retrenchment*. Cambridge: Cambridge University Press.

—— 1995: Fragmented welfare states: Federal institutions and the development of social policy. *Governance*, 8 (4), 449–78.

—— 1996: The new politics of the welfare state. *World Politics* 48 (2), 143–79.

Pijl, M. 1994: When private care goes public: an analysis of concepts and principles concerning payments for care. In A. Evers, M. Pijl and C. Ungerson, *Payments for Care: A Comparative Overview*. Aldershot: Avebury.

Pinch, S. 1997: *Worlds of Welfare: Understanding the Changing Geographies of Social Welfare*. London: Routledge.

Ploug, N. and Kvist, J. 1996: *Social Security in Europe*. The Hague: Kluwer Law International.

Pooley, C. 1992: *Housing Strategies in Europe, 1880–1930*. Leicester: Leicester University Press.

Popenoe, D. 1988: *Disturbing the Nest. Family Change and Decline in Modern Societies*. New York: Aldine de Gruyter.

Poulain, M. 1996: Migration flows between the countries of the European Union: current trends. In P. Rees, J. Stillwell, A. Convey and M. Kupiszewski (eds), *Population Migration in the European Union*. Chichester: Wiley.

Power, A. 1993: *Hovels to High Rise: Social Housing in Europe since 1850*. London: Routledge.

Pryor, F. 1968: *Public Expenditures in Communist and Capitalist Nations*. Homewood, IL: Irwin.

Przeworski, A. 1987: Methods of cross-national research 1970–1983. In M. Dierkes, H. Weiler and A. Antal (eds), *Comparative Policy Research. Learning from experience*. Aldershot: WZB Berlin/Gower.

Rainwater, L., Rein, M. and Schwartz, J. E. 1986: *Income Packaging in the Welfare State. A Comparative Study of Family Income.* Oxford: Oxford University Press.

Ramprakash, D. 1994: Poverty in the countries of the European Union: a synthesis of Eurostat's statistical research on poverty. *Journal of European Social Policy*, 4 (2), 117–28.

Ranade, W. (ed.) 1998: *Markets and Health Care. A comparative analysis.* Harlow: Longman.

Refugee Council 1997a: *Statistical Analysis.* London: The Refugee Council, March.

—— 1997b: *Update.* London: The Refugee Council, July.

—— 1997c: *Asylum Statistics 1986–1996.* Revised edn. London: The Refugee Council, November.

Rein, M. and Rainwater, L. 1981: *From Welfare State to Welfare Society.* Cambridge Mass: Harvard University Press.

—— (eds) 1986: *Public–private Interplay in Social Protection.* New York: M.E. Sharpe.

Reissert, B. 1994: Unemployment compensation and the labour market: a European perspective. In S. Mangen and L. Hantrais (eds), *Unemployment, the informal economy and entitlements to benefits*, Cross-National Research Papers, 3rd series. Loughborough University: European Research Centre.

—— 1997: How are unemployment benefit systems coping with changes occurring in the labour markets? In A. Bosco and M. Hutseband (eds), *Social Protection in Europe. Facing up to changes and challenges.* Brussels: European Trade Union Institute.

Reubens, B. C. 1970: *The hard-to-employ. European programmes.* New York: Columbia University Press.

—— 1977: *Bridges to work. International comparisons of transition services.* London: Martin Robertson.

Rhodes, M. 1996: Globalization and West European welfare states: a critical review of recent debates. *Journal of European Social Policy*, 6 (4), 305–27.

—— (ed.) 1997: *Southern European Welfare States: Between Crisis and Reform.* London: Frank Cass.

Rhodes, R. A. W. 1997: *Understanding Governance. Policy networks, governance, reflexivity and accountability.* Buckingham: Open University Press.

Richards, E. 1996: *Paying for Long-term Care.* London: Institute for Public Policy Research.

Richards, M. P. M. and Dyson, M. 1982: *Separation, Divorce and the Development of Children. A Review.* Cambridge: University of Cambridge Child Care and Development Group.

Ridley, F. F. 1996: The new public management in Europe: comparative perspectives. *Public Policy and Administration*, 11 (1), 16–29.

Ringen, S. 1987: *The Possibility of Politics: A Study in the Political Economy of the Welfare State.* Oxford: Clarendon.

Roberts, S. 1998: *Not One of Us: Social Security for Third Country Nationals in the European Union.* PhD. thesis, Brunel University.

Robinson, V. 1996: Redefining the front line: the geography of asylum seeking in the new Europe. In P. Rees, J. Stillwell, A. Convey and M. Kupiszewski (eds), *Population Migration in the European Union.* Chichester: Wiley.

Rodgers, B. 1979: *The Study of Social Policy: a comparative approach.* London: George Allen and Unwin.

Room, G. 1986: *Cross-national Innovation in Social Policy: European Perspectives on the Evaluation of Action-research.* Basingstoke: Macmillan.

Room, G. (ed.) 1995: *Beyond the Threshold: The Measurement and Analysis of Social Exclusion.* Bristol: Policy Press.

Rose, R. 1991: Is American public policy exceptional? In B.E. Schafer (ed.), *Is America Different? A New Look at American Exceptionalism.* Oxford: Oxford University Press.

Rosewitz, B. and Webber, D. 1990: *Reformversuche und Reformblockaden im deutschen Gesundheitswesen.* Frankfurt: Campus.

Ross, G. 1995: Assessing the Delors Era and Social Policy. In S. Leibfried and P. Pierson (eds), *European Social Policy: Betweeen Fragmentation and Integration.* Washington DC: Brookings Institution, 357–88.

Rounavaara, H. 1992: *Forms and Types of Housing Tenure: Towards Solving the Comparison/Translation Problem.* Paper given at European Cities: Growth and Decline, Conference, The Hague, April.

Sainsbury, D. (ed.) 1994: *Gendering Welfare States.* London: Sage.

Sainsbury, D. 1996: *Gender, Equality and Welfare States.* Cambridge: Cambridge University Press.

Saunders, P. 1990: *A Nation of Home Owners.* London: Unwin Hyman.

Scarpetta, S. 1996: Assessing the role of labour market policies and institutional settings on unemployment: a cross-country study. *OECD Economic Studies,* 26, 43–98.

Scheiwe, K. 1994: German pension insurance, gendered times and stratification. In D. Sainsbury (ed.), *Gendering Welfare States.* London: Sage.

Schieber, G. J. and Poullier, J.-P. 1990: Overview of international comparisons of health expenditures. In *Health Care Systems in Transition. The search for efficiency.* Paris: OECD.

Schmid, G. 1996: Process evaluation: policy formation and implementation. In G. Schmid, J. O'Reilly and K. Schömann (eds), *International Handbook of Labour Market Policy and Evaluation.* Cheltenham: Edward Elgar.

—— 1997: *The Dutch employment miracle? A comparison of the employment systems in the Netherlands and Germany.* MISEP, 59, 23–31.

Schmid, G. and Reissert, B. 1988: Do institutions make a difference? Financing systems of labor market policy. *Journal of Public Policy,* 8 (2), 125–49.

—— 1996: Unemployment compensation and labour market transitions. In G. Schmid, J. O'Reilly and K. Schömann (eds), *International handbook of Labour Market Policy and Evaluation.* Cheltenham: Edward Elgar.

Schmid, G., Reissert, B. and Bruche, G. 1992: *Unemployment insurance and active labour market policy. An international comparison of financing systems.* Detroit: Wayne State University Press.

Schmid, G., O'Reilly, J. and Schömann, K. (eds) 1996: *International handbook of labour market policy and evaluation.* Cheltenham: Edward Elgar.

Schmidt, S. 1989: Convergence theory, labour movements and corporatism: the case of housing. *Scandinavian Housing and Planning Research,* 6 (2), 83–101.

Schömann, K. 1995: *Active Labour Market Policy in the European Union.* Discussion paper FS I 95-201, Berlin: Social Science Research Centre.

Schömann, K. and Kruppe, T. 1996: The dynamic of employment in the European Union. *MISEP,* 55, 33–43.

Schunk, M. 1996: Constructing models of the welfare mix: care options of frail elders. In L. Hantrais and S. Mangen (eds), *Cross-National Research Methods in the Social Sciences*. London: Pinter.

Seeleib-Kaiser, M. 1995: The development of social assistance and unemployment insurance in Germany and Japan. *Social Policy and Administration*, 29 (3), 269–93.

Selman, P. and Glendinning, G. 1996: Teenage pregnancy: do social policies make a difference? In J. Brannen and M. O'Brien (eds), *Children in Families*. Brighton: Falmer Press.

Shalev, M. (ed.) 1996: *The Privatization of Social Policy? Occupational Welfare and the Welfare State in America, Scandinavia and Japan*. Basingstoke: Macmillan.

Sillince, J. 1990: *Housing Policies in Eastern Europe and the Soviet Union*. London: Routledge.

Silverman, M. 1996: The revenge of civil society: state, nation and society in France. In D. Cesarani and M. Fulbrook (eds), *Citizenship, Nationality and Migration in Europe*. London: Routledge.

Sinfield, A. 1993: Unemployment benefit – an active right for citizens. In European Institute of Social Security (ed.) EISS Yearbook 1992. *Reforms in East and Central Europe*. Leuven: Acco.

—— 1997: Blaming the benefit: the costs of the distinction between active and passive programmes. In J. Holmer and J.C. Karlsson (eds), *Work – Quo Vadis? Re-thinking the question of work*. Aldershot: Ashgate.

Skocpol, T. 1995: *Social Policy in the United States: Future Possibilities in Historical Perspective*. Princeton: Princeton University Press.

Smeeding, T., O'Higgins, M. and Rainwater, L. 1990: *Poverty, Inequality and Income Distribution in Comparative Perspective: the Luxembourg Income Study (LIS)*. Hemel Hempstead: Harvester Wheatsheaf.

SOPEMI 1995: *Trends in International Migration, Annual Report for 1994*. Paris: OECD.

Soper, K. 1993: The thick and thin of human needing. In G. Drover and P. Kerans (eds), *New Approaches to Welfare Theory*. Aldershot: Edward Elgar.

Sorrentino, C. 1993: International comparison of unemployment indicators. *Monthly Labor Review*, March, 3–24.

Soydan, H. 1996: Using the vignette method in cross-cultural comparisons. In L. Hantrais and S. Mangen (eds), *Cross-National Research Methods in the Social Sciences*. London: Pinter.

Spencer, S. 1994: Introduction. In S. Spencer (ed.), *Strangers and Citizens*. London: Institute for Public Policy Research.

Spicker, P. 1996: Normative comparisons of social security systems. In L. Hantrais and S. Mangen (eds), *Cross-national Research Methods in the Social Sciences*. London: Pinter.

Steenvoorden, M., van er Pas, F. and de Boer, N. 1993: *Family Care of the Older Elderly: Casebook of Initiatives*. Dublin: European Foundation for the Improvement of Living and Working Conditions.

Steinmo, S. 1993: *Taxation and Democracy*. New Haven and London: Yale University Press.

Steinmo, S., Thelen, K. and Longstreth, F. (eds) 1992: *Structuring Politics. Historical Institutionalism in Comparative Perspective*. Cambridge: Cambridge University Press.

Stephens, J. 1979: *The Transition from Capitalism to Socialism*. London: Macmillan.

Symes, V. 1995: *Unemployment in Europe. Problems and policies*. London: Routledge.

Takahashi M. 1997: *The Emergence of Welfare Society in Japan*. Aldershot: Avebury.

Taylor-Gooby, P. 1991: Welfare state regimes and welfare citizenship. *Journal of European Social Policy*, 1 (2), 93–105.

—— 1996: The future of health care in six European countries: the views of policy elites. *International Journal of Health Services*, 26 (2), 203–19.

Temple, W. 1941: *Citizen and Churchman*. London: Eyre and Spottiswood.

Tester, S. 1994: Implications of subsidiarity for the care of older people in Germany. *Social Policy and Administration*, 28 (3), 251–62.

—— 1996: *Community Care for Older People: a Comparative Perspective*. Basingstoke: Macmillan.

Tester, S. and Freeman, R. 1996: *Diffusion of Innovations in Policies for Care of Frail Older People*. Paper presented at British Society of Gerontology conference Liverpool, September.

Teune, H. 1990: Comparing countries: lessons learned. In E. Øyen (ed.), *Comparative Methodology: Theory and Practice in International Social Research*. London: Sage.

Therborn, G. 1993: Beyond the lonely nation-state. In F. G. Castles (ed.), *Families of Nations: patterns of public policy in Western democracies*. Aldershot: Dartmouth.

Titmuss, R. M. 1974: *Social Policy*. London: Allen & Unwin.

—— 1987a: Introduction to the 1964 Edition of *Equality* by R. H. Tawney. In B. Abel-Smith and K. Titmuss (eds), *The Philosophy of Welfare: Selected Writings of Richard M.Titmuss*. London: Allen and Unwin, 1–17.

—— 1987b: Social welfare and the art of giving. In B. Abel-Smith and K. Titmuss (eds), *The Philosophy of Welfare: Selected Writings of Richard M. Titmuss*. London: Allen and Unwin, 113–27.

Tosics, I. 1987: Privatisation in housing policy: the case of Western countries and Hungary. *International Journal of Urban and Regional Research*, 11 (1), 61–77.

Turner, B., Hegedus, J. and Tosics, I. 1992: *The Reform of Housing in Eastern Europe and the Soviet Union*. London: Routledge.

Twigg, J. 1996: Issues in informal care. In *Caring for Frail Elderly People: Policies in Evolution*. Paris: OECD.

Ungerson, C. 1994: Morals and politics in 'payments for care': an introductory note. In A. Evers, M. Pijl and C. Ungerson (eds), *Payments for Care: a Comparative Overview*. Aldershot: Avebury.

—— 1995: Gender, cash and informal care: European perspectives and dilemmas. *Journal of Social Policy*, 24 (1), 31–52.

United Nations Statistical Commission/Economic Commission for Europe Conference of European Statisticians 1987: Recommendations for the 1990 censuses of population and housing in the ECE region: regional variant of the world recommendations for the 1990 round of population and housing censuses. *Statistical Standards and Studies*, 40. New York: United Nations.

Uusitalo, H. 1985: Redistribution and equality in the welfare state. *European Sociological Review*, 1 (2), 163–76.

Valiente, C. 1995: Rejecting the past: central government and family policy in post-authoritarian Spain (1975–94). *Cross-National Research Papers*, 4 (3), 80–96.

van Doorn, M. 1997: *Navigating through uncharted waters. A comparative study of active labour market policies in the Netherlands, Sweden and Great Britain.* Werkdocumenten no. 53, The Hague: Ministerie van Sociale Zaken en Werkgelegenheid.

van Kersbergen, K. 1995: *Social Capitalism: A study of Christian democracy and the welfare state.* London: Routledge.

van Oorschot, W. 1995: *Realizing Rights.* Aldershot: Avebury.

van Solinge, H. and Wood, J. 1997: *Sample Surveys as a Potential Data Source for the Study of Non-Standard Household Forms and New Living Arrangements: An Inventory of Data Sources on European Households and Families.* The Hague: NIDI.

van Vliet, W. 1990: *International Handbook of Housing Policies and Practices.* New York: Greenwood Press.

van Vliet, W. and van Weesep, J. 1990: *Government and Housing: Developments in Seven Countries.* Vol. 36, Urban Affairs Annual Reviews. Newbury Park: Sage.

Veit-Wilson, J. 1998: *Setting Adequacy Standards: How governments define minimum incomes.* Bristol: Policy Press.

Vincent, J. 1996: Who's afraid of an ageing population? Nationalism, the free market, and the construction of old age as an issue. *Critical Social Policy*, 16, 3–26.

Vogler, C. and J. Pahl 1994: Money, power and inequality within marriage. *The Sociological Review* 42 (2), 263–88.

Wagstaff, A., van Doorslaer, E. et al. 1992: Equity in the finance of health care: some international comparisons. *Journal of Health Economics*, 11, 361–87.

Walker, A. 1992: The poor relation: poverty among old women. In C. Glendinning and J. Millar (eds), *Women and Poverty in Britain: the 1990s.* London: Harvester Wheatsheaf.

Walker, A. and Maltby, T. 1997: *Ageing Europe.* Buckingham: Open University Press.

Walker, A., Guillemard, A-M. and Alber, J. 1993: *Older People in Europe: Social and Economic Policies – the 1993 Report of the European Observatory.* Brussels: Commission of the EC.

Wall, A. (ed.) 1996: *Health Care Systems in Liberal Democracies.* London: Routledge.

Wallerstein, J. S. and Kelly, J. B. 1980: *Surviving the Breakup: How Children and Parents Cope with Divorce.* New York: Basic Books.

Walzer, M. 1983: *Spheres of Justice.* Oxford: Blackwell.

Warman, A. and Millar, J. 1996: Researching family obligations: some reflections on methodology. *Cross-National Research Papers*, 4 (1), 23–31.

Webber, D. 1988: Krankheit, Geld und Politik: zur Geschichte der Gesundheitsreformen in Deutschland. *Leviathan*, 16 (2), 156–203.

——1989: Zur Geschichte der Gesundheitsreformen in Deutschland – II Norbert Blüms Gesundheitsreformen und die Lobby. *Leviathan*, 17 (2), 262–300.

Weber, A. 1990: Ordnungspolitische Aspekte europäischer Gesundheitssysteme. *Medizin, Mensch, Gesellschaft*, 15 (2), 76–86.

Weir, M., Orloff, A. S. and Skocpol, T. 1988: *The politics of social policy in the United States*. Princeton: Princeton University Press.

Whiteford, P. and Kennedy, S. 1995: *Incomes and Living Standards of Older People: A Comparative Analysis*. London: HMSO.

Wilensky, H. L. 1975: *The Welfare State and Equality: Structural and Ideological Roots of Public Expenditure*. Berkeley: University of California Press.

——1990: Common problems, divergent policies: an 18-nation study of family policy. *Public Affairs Report*, Institute of Governmental Studies, 31 (3), 1–3.

Wilensky, H. L., Luebbert, G. M., Reed-Hahn S. and Jamieson A. M. 1985: *Comparative Social Policy*. Berkeley: Institute of International Studies, University of California.

Wilkinson, R. G. 1996: *Unhealthy Society*. Routledge: London.

Willemsen, T., Frinking, G. and Vogels, R. 1995: *Work and Family in Europe: The Role of Policies*. Tilburg: Tilburg University Press.

Wilsford, D. 1989: Tactical advantages versus administrative heterogeneity: the strengths and limits of the French state. In J. Caporaso (ed.), *The Elusive State. International and comparative perspectives*. Newbury Park: Sage.

——1994: Path dependency, or why history makes it difficult but not impossible to reform health care systems in a big way. *Journal of Public Policy*, 14 (3), 285–309.

——1995: States facing interests: struggles over health policy in advanced industrial democracies. *Journal of Health Politics, Policy and Law*, 20 (3), 571–613.

Wilson, G. 1997: A postmodern approach to structured dependency theory. *Journal of Social Policy*, 26 (3), 341–50.

Wynn, M. 1983: *Housing in Europe*. London: Croom Helm.

Index

Ambrose, P., 69
Alber, J., 158, 165
Anttonen, A., 150
asylum seekers, 201, 206–7, 211–14
Atkinson, A. B., 52
Australia
  housing, 65, 66
  minimum income, 121
  social assistance, 116, 123, 124,
    126–32
Austria
  family policy, 107–11
  health system, 82
  migrants' benefits, 206–8
  social assistance, 134

Baldwin, P., 35–6, 50–1, 55
Belgium
  family policy, 106–11
  migrants' social security, 206–9
  social assistance, 120, 124, 126–33
Benelux countries, 82
Beveridge, W., 19, 21
Beveridge Report, 19–21, 117
Bolderson, H., 35–56, 200–19
Bonoli, G., 46
Bradshaw, J., 37–8, 98, 118, 131,
  182

Canada
  and the Beveridge Report, 20
  housing, 65, 66
  social assistance, 118, 124, 125–32
Castles, F., 24, 38, 46
care, long-term
  concepts, 140–1, 146–8
  and comparative research, 139–40
  definition of, 136–7
  European research, 138, 145–6
  methodological issues, 144–5,
    151–5
  new data, 154–5
  ideological contexts, 148–9
  policy issues and trends, 137–9,
    140–4
  theoretical issues, 140–4, 148–51
case studies, 3, 36, 49–54, 55, 152
child support, 37, 98
children, 109, 110
Clasen, J., 1–12, 159–78
comparative social policy research, 2,
  3–4, 34–56, 96, 139–140, 142,
  156–7, 221–3
  challenges and problems, 139–45,
    172, 221–3
  description, 61–2
  early studies, 3, 59–60

evaluative studies, 36–41, 62,
166–9
operationalization of variables,
221–3
ranking of countries, 38, 44, 100,
112, 217–18
statistical data, 37–9, 52, 73, 98,
103, 144, 152–4, 172
and welfare effort, 2, 37, 49–54, 55
comparisons
evaluative, 36–41
equivalence in, 53, 54, 140–1,
146–7, 156, 173–4
large-scale, 2–3, 37, 41–4, 98, 152
meaning of, 2, 34, 61–4
conceptualization, 92, 101–11, 141,
146–8, 160–3, 169, 171–3,
209–17
conceptual frameworks, 52–3, 55, 70
convergence, 31–2, 43–4, 48, 64–6,
83, 88
cross-national research, *see*
comparative social policy
research
cultural factors and social policy, 51,
67, 91–4, 102, 112, 140

Dawson, P. E., 182
decommodification, 45, 143
Delors, J., 27
Dench, G., 187
Denmark
families, 102–3
family policy, 107–11
households, 103
and migrants' social security, 206–9
social assistance, 120, 125–34
disincentives, 169–70
Ditch, J., 114–35
diversity and social policy, 26, 29
Doling, J. 59–79
Donnison, D., 59–60, 64–5

employment patterns, 189, 229–33
Esping-Andersen, G., 4, 16, 24, 44–9,
117–18, 143, 182, 191
European Council, 120

European Observatories, 97, 101–2,
104
European Union,
family policy, 97, 98, 105, 106
housing data, 74
migration, 200–1, 214
poverty programmes, 26
social assistance, 119
social policy, 26–8

families, 101–11
administrative definitions, 108–11
dependence on, 240
policy definitions, 103–8
reconstituted, 103, 104, 106
statistical definitions, 101–3
structure of, 186
family policy, 95–113
and child care, 107
comparative studies, 96–101, 149,
182
conceptualization, 101–11
meaning of, 96, 104
and social policy, 104
and social security, 109–10
and taxation, 110–11
Ferge, Z., 29
Finland, 102, 107–11, 206–9
Flora, P., 96
France
and Beveridge, 20
employment patterns, 229–33
family policy, 106–11, 240–3
health system, 82, 84, 86
households, 103
housing, 67–68
lone motherhood, 196, 197
migrants' benefits, 205–9
older people, 224–43
pensions, 224–9
social assistance, 120, 123, 125–34
Freeman, R., 80–94

Gauthier, A., 99, 100
Germany
employment patterns, 229–33
family policy, 102, 106–11, 240–3

health system and policy, 82, 84, 85, 87
households, 103
housing, 65, 70
lone motherhood, 195
migrants' benefits, 205–9
pensions, 224–9
welfare statism, 19–20
social assistance, 116, 120, 124, 125–33
Gewirth, A., 212–13
Gilder, G., 187
globalization, 32, 48–9
Greece
families and policy, 102, 104, 106–11
housing, 64
households, 103
migrants' benefits, 206–8
social assistance, 122, 125–33

Hantrais, L., 95–113
health policy, 80–94
comparative research in, 81, 90–1
and culture, 91–4
institutions, 80, 81, 86, 88–91, 93
reforms, 82, 83, 85–8
spending, 82, 83
systems, 82, 89, 91
Harloe, M., 66
Heclo, H., 36, 50–1, 165
housing costs, 124
housing policy, comparative, 59–79
approaches to, 62–4, 78
early studies, 59–60
literature, 76–7
outcomes, 76
regimes, 61–4, 67, 74
statistical data, 73–6
and tenure, 68–73
theory, 64–8

IMF (International Monetary Fund), 121
Iceland, social assistance, 128, 130
immigration, 127, 200–19

institutions and institutionalism, 30, 50
in health policy, 80, 81, 86, 88–91, 93
in unemployment compensation, 164–5
Ireland
households, 103
families and policy, 104, 106, 111
migrants' benefits, 205–9
social assistance, 116, 123, 126, 129–33
Italy
families and policy, 102, 104, 107–11
health system, 82, 84
migrants' benefits, 206–8
social assistance, 116, 124, 125, 126–33

Janoski, T., 164
Japan, 123, 126, 128, 129, 131
Jones Finer, C., 15–33

Kaim-Caudle, P., 163
Kemeny, J., 66–7

labour market policies, 159–78
beneficiary rates, 175
change in, 164–6
definition of, 160–3
evaluative studies, 166–9
methodological issues, 171–5
replacement rates, 173, 174–5
and work disincentives, 169–71
labour market transitions, 160–1
Lewis, J., 181–99
lone motherhood, 181–99
debate, 186–8
dependency patterns, 188–91
employment, 189
structures of, 183–6
terminology, 192
and welfare regimes, 191–6
lone parents, 103, 104–5, 106, 130–1, 243

Luxembourg, 106–11, 120, 128–33, 206–8
Luxembourg Income Study, 38–40, 118

Mabbett, D., 35–56
Mediterranean countries, 107–11
methods of comparative research, 34–56, 144, 171
  case studies, 3, 48
  common factor analysis, 41–8
  description, 61–2, 163–4
  mapping, 117, 141, 200–1, 205–9, 217–18
  model families, 37, 98
  multi-dimensional strategy, 55, 77–8, 101
  and natural science, 34–5
  panel of experts, 115, 98–9, 152
  policy simulation, 100
  regression analysis, 41–4, 201
migrants and benefit restrictions, 200–19
  barriers to benefits, 202–5
  conceptual issues, 209–17
  country patterns, 208–9
  direct discrimination, 210–15
  indirect discrimination, 210, 215–17
  naturalization, 207
  short-term workers, 207–8
  trends, 201–2
minimum income, 120–21, *see also* poverty
Mishra, R., 28–9
Mitchell, D., 38, 39, 46
Murray, C., 187, 190

Netherlands, The
  families and policy, 104, 107
  housing, 66
  lone motherhood, 195
  migrants' social security benefits, 206–9
  social assistance, 116, 124–33
New Zealand
  housing, 66

  social assistance, 116, 123, 124–32
non-governmental organizations, 125, 142
Nordic countries, 82, 106–11, 124, 125, 134, *see also* Scandinavia
Norway, 124–34

older people, 138, 147
  welfare provision for, 220–43
  and pensions, 224–9
  and financial support, 240–2

pensions, 224–9
  credits, 233–4
  dependents' addition, 241–2
  derived rights, 225–9
  divorce, 243
  in France, Germany and the UK, 233–40
  labour market participation, 231–3, 234, 239
  and lone parents, 243
  and previous earnings, 236
  and redistribution, 237–9
  and social assistance, 225, 228
Pierson, P., 50
policy change, 86–7, 134–5, 164–6
policy context, 220, 221–3
Portugal
  family policy, 107–11
  health system, 82
  housing, 64
  migrants' social security, 206–8
  social assistance, 123, 124, 126, 129, 131
Post Fordism, 66
poverty, 38, 52, 119

Rake, K., 220–46
redistribution, 105, 237–9
redistribution paradigm, 38–40
regime theory, 23–6, 44–9, 64, 143, 149–50, 157, 182
Reissert, B., 166, 171
residualism, 47
Roberts, S., 200–19

Scandinavia, 82, 118, 185, 189, 196–7, *see also* Nordic countries
Schmid, G., 165–6, 171
Schömann, K., 168
Singapore, 70
Sipilä, J., 150
social assistance, 114–35
   conditionality, 125–8, 130–1
   definition of, 115–16
   and discretion, 125, 134
   eligibility, 125–8
   expenditure, 122–4
   history, 116–21
   income tests, 131–2
   level of, 128–30
   operating principles, 124–5
   and pensions, 225, 228
   policy development, 134–5
   policy objectives, 121–2
   typologies, 132–5
social expenditure, 21–2, 37, 41–4, 83–5, 137, 138–9
social insurance, 39, 46–7, 119, 120, 161
   Bismarckian, 117
   and health policy, 84–5, 89, 93
   National Insurance in UK, 21, 117, 235
   and pensions, 224–9, 234–7, 241–2
   USA, 117
social protection, 110, 120, 122
social rights, 212–13
social security, 36, 39, 46–7, 51, 108–10, 117, 119, 204
   and migrants, 200–19
   and pensions, 224–9
Spain
   housing, 64
   social assistance, 124, 125–9
stratification, 45
subsidiarity, 148, 240
Sweden
   family, 103, 107
   health policy, 82, 84, 86
   housing policy, 65, 66, 68
   housing research, 60, 62
   migrants' social security, 207–9

social assistance, 123, 126–34
Switzerland, 65, 66, 86, 124–34

Tester, S., 136–58
Titmuss, R., 23–4, 26, 46, 117
Turkey, 116, 124, 125–33

unemployment benefits, 159–78, 169–71, *see also* labour market policy
United Kingdom
   employment patterns, 229–33
   families and policy, 104, 106, 107, 240–3
   health system and policy, 82, 84, 87
   housing, 65, 68, 70
   lone motherhood, 183–96
   older people, 224–43
   pensions, 224–9
   social assistance, 116, 120, 124, 125–33
   welfare statism, 18–25
United States of America
   health policy, 84
   housing, 65, 66, 68
   lone motherhood, 183–96
   social assistance, 116, 120, 128–32
universalism, 20, 47

Walzer, M., 216
welfare effort, 2, 4, 37, 40, 41–4
welfare mix, 148–9, 102, 112
welfare pluralism, 148, 151
welfare regimes and typologies, 44–9, 186, 223
   family policy, 98, 112
   housing, 64–5, 67
   lone motherhood, 191–6
   social assistance, 132–5
   social care, 143, 150, 157
   theory, 23–6, 44–9, 64, 143, 149–50, 157
   unemployment compensation, 166
welfare states and welfare statism, 15–33, 41–4
   in Asia Pacific, 30
   in Britain, 18–25, 220–43

crisis, 23
definition, 15–18, 31
development, 2, 15–33, 41–4
economic performance, 22–5
Europe, 25–8
in France, 220–43
in Germany, 19–20
and older people, 224–46
research, 2, 15–33

typologies, 4, 18, 23–6, 31, 44–9,
　52, 117–18, 166
South America, 30
southern Europe, 30
welfare society, 40
welfare systems, 36–7
Wilensky, H.L., 41, 43, 76
work test, 130
World Bank, 121